P9-DER-257

# Too Rich

# TOO RICH

## The Family Secrets of Doris Duke

Pony Duke
and
Jason Thomas

HarperCollinsPublishers

HarperCollins books may be purchased for educational, business, or sales promotional use. For information please write: Special Markets Department, HarperCollins Publishers, Inc., 10 East 53rd Street, New York, NY 10022.

FIRST EDITION

*Designed by Caitlin Daniels*

*Photo insert researched, edited, and designed by Vincent Virga*

---

Library of Congress Cataloging-in-Publication Data

Duke, Pony, 1937–
Too rich : the family secrets of Doris Duke / Pony Duke and Jason Thomas. — 1st ed.
p. cm.
Includes index.
ISBN 0-06-017218-5
1. Duke, Doris, 1912–1993. 2. United States—Biography.
3. Celebrities—United States—Biography. I. Thomas, Jason, 1943– .
II. Title.
CT275.D8769D85 1996
973.9'092—dc20
[B] 95-42526

---

96 97 98 99 00 ❖/RRD 10 9 8 7 6 5 4 3 2 1

This book is dedicated to Doris Duke, who should have believed the person who told her "never trust anyone."

# CONTENTS

*Photographs follow page 144.*

# PREFACE

I never loved my godmother, Doris Duke. I doubt if anyone, other than her father, Buck Duke, ever really loved her. For most of her life, she never trusted anyone, so it was difficult for anyone to become close enough to this complex woman to love or be loved by her.

When I look back on my childhood and teenage years, I was actually far closer to my cousin Franklin Delano Roosevelt, who while President of the United States still took time every week to talk with me. My relationship to FDR was exactly the same as it was to Doris (for she was also a cousin), except he was related on my mother's side. When I was a child, he was our neighbor in Dutchess County, New York, and I spent a lot of time with him. I loved Franklin.

But I did like Doris. She wanted to be loved. She tried to find real affection from so many people but found mostly fortune hunters and opportunists. When a person failed to meet Doris Duke's standards, whether it be in business or the bedroom, he or she was exiled.

Doris Duke gave no second chances to the people who became a part of her life. She would accept a new person into her inner circle and could be very generous, as long as she was given the opportunity to offer before being asked.

She was generous with me.

Doris was not fond of small children, thus she remained a towering, imperial presence in the memories of my childhood. At our family gatherings, especially the traditional Thanksgiving dinners (command performances for every member of the family on the orders of my grandmother Cordelia Biddle Robertson), none of the Duke and Biddle children would ever consider climbing into the well-dressed lap of cousin Doris or even shyly taking her hand as we walked into the large dining room where servants and turkey and champagne awaited.

Today I wonder whether Doris might have liked an outpouring of sincere affection from one of us children. But she was so tall and her soft whisper-rasp voice was somehow menacing to a tyke like me.

Since her childhood, Doris had been taught to remain aloof from everyone. She had been dubbed by the press to be the richest little girl in the world and, as a woman, her escapades were followed by hordes of fortune hunters and reporters. During the moneyless years of the Great Depression, the public was fascinated with the very rich and Doris was the very richest. She experienced the same kind of notoriety in the twenties, thirties, forties, and fifties as Madonna, Princess Di, and Jackie Onassis attracted in later decades. Doris told me she despised the publicity. In truth, I think she enjoyed it and became proficient in manipulating the gossip columnists.

When her father died, Doris was twelve years of age. Educated in isolation from her peers, today she would be branded a school dropout. Her mother, Aunt Nanaline, was a self-centered personality who did not encourage group activities or peer associations.

Doris grew up alone and isolated.

Doris could be very self-absorbed, but I now realize that she did try to make a very select group of people's lives happier. People called her cheap, but she simply opted to spend her money the way she wanted.

"Everybody seems to know exactly what I should do with my

cash, which is always give it to them," Doris told me once at the end of a night of jazz, dancing, and champagne.

Whatever one might think of her spending habits, her ability to safeguard, conserve, and increase her wealth was impressive. At her death, she was worth many times over what she received as her inheritance. She was shrewd, tough, and persistent in the management of her money and someday her great wealth will be put to the service of humanity through her foundation. And, as far as I am concerned, the sooner this happens the better.

As I look back, I realize that she tried to remain a part of my life by taking her godmother responsibilities most seriously. She showed her austere affection in her usual way, through fabulous and thoughtful presents. Like the sapphire cuff links!

On my twenty-first birthday, a perfectly wrapped package arrived from my godmother. Inside was a pair of sapphire cuff links, each a flawless, fifteen-carat stone set in several ounces of gold. Today the value of those cuff links would be enough to purchase a fine house or pay the tuition and board for a student to graduate from Duke University. But then, those cuff links were not my favorite gift. I preferred the new Dodge convertible and the rifle that were gifts from my father. I was careless with the cuff links and quickly lost them at some party where clothes and cuff links were often abandoned before dawn or the end of the champagne.

Yes, I was a kid who always had everything; there was a guardian angel looking after me at that time of my life: Doris Duke. I do not know whether I was too callow to appreciate her efforts. No, that isn't true. I did appreciate what Doris did on my behalf. It was just that every member of the family had learned that Doris hated to have people kissing-up to her; too many people did. She preferred helping someone anonymously if possible, and was most uncomfortable as the recipient of gushing gratitude. So I never thanked her adequately.

When I married my first wife, I received a monstrously heavy solid sterling loving cup that stood almost four feet in height. This was so typical of Doris Duke, who did not come to the wedding but delighted in imagining the comments her relatives would make about the enormous trophy. She never attended any of the family weddings because her presence attracted the press and transformed the wedding into a Doris Duke photo opportunity. She did not want to take the spotlight away from the bride and groom. Not until years later did I realize that the cup was a priceless 1890 art masterpiece from the Jockey Club in Hong Kong. It was very precious to Doris, as it was one of the first pieces of art she had collected on her first honeymoon trip around the world. It was one of the foundation pieces of the massive collection of precious things that was to become the eclectic Doris Duke art repository. That trophy had been one of the earliest of an endless procession of beautiful things her instinctive eye had selected. It meant a lot to her.

My first initiation into the legendary Doris Duke playgirl lifestyle came in 1960 when my handsome, high-spirited, and wonderful uncle Nick Biddle decided he wanted a ten-day debacle in Paris following the death of his mother, Mary Duke Biddle, my great-aunt and Doris's first cousin. He asked me to come along for the ride. I was at an age where the high life was most attractive, an attitude I maintained for the next ten years.

Doris was at her apartment in Paris and was between men at the time, so she was eager to show the nightlife to the handsome Nick and her godson.

The party only lasted for two days.

We started at the Monsignor Club for dinner and Crystal champagne (Doris's favorite) and progressed to the seedy Club Venus where Doris danced with Nick, myself, and anyone else who wanted to dance. Later we went to an all-night jazz joint run by American Negroes (they were not blacks then) where Doris seemed to know everyone and even played the piano as a backup for some of the musicians.

We danced and sang all night.

But when the dancing was over, Doris wanted to talk. She looked far away and talked into the morning. It was as if she wanted to purge herself of every memory that was eating into her soul. She told us secrets, secrets she said she had never told anyone. For a few hours we were a family, her family.

I felt sorry for her.

She wanted someone to love her. She had had lovers. She had come close to being happy. It was apparent as the night continued that she was taking stock of her life.

Without sleep, we went to lunch the following day at the Ritz Hotel, followed by a repeat of the previous night. Doris was never tired. This was the life that she was bred to live. She was meant to dance until dawn.

Again at dawn she wanted to talk. I was just out of college and had begun to live my life, yet what she told me was both revealing and shocking.

For a few brief days in Paris, the guarded and secretive Doris Duke had lowered her rigid wall of privacy and shared the secrets of her life. I do not know why she did this. We never again spoke of the events of those days in Paris. But after Paris, I always thought of my godmother in a different way . . . a way the reporters and the public never saw.

And I started to really like her.

Two weeks later, I reluctantly returned to work doing what ambitious and well-connected young men from rich and powerful families did: I became a stockbroker at the brokerage house of Hardy and Company, a small but very profitable Wall Street firm.

It was 1960 and I earned less than one hundred dollars a week as a struggling young broker. Then financial lightning struck from the Park Avenue penthouse of Doris Duke. Without telling me, she moved a large portion of her equity account to Hardy and Company. I was sick one afternoon and had gone home to my apartment on East Seventy-seventh Street, a flat that could only be described as "humble," when the phone rang.

The senior trader's voice was trembling on the phone.

"You are getting business like we have never seen at this firm." His voice quivered with the kind of power-greed that is unique to Wall Street. "It's Doris Duke!"

My salary instantly climbed to two thousand dollars weekly, which in 1960 was a very large amount of money. Within two weeks, I was made a partner in the firm.

Every week, orders for millions of dollars' worth of stocks

were placed through me. Within the next year, Doris bought tens of millions of dollars in stocks and I made a huge amount of money. She was purposely (I learned later) doing this to build my reputation and career. Since this was my first job, I thought this was the way business was supposed to be. You get a job. You become an immediate success. You make a lot of money. If I had been content to go to my office each day and build my future fortune on the basis of the piles of commissions that my godmother's account was generating, I would have been a millionaire in two years and a multimillionaire by the age of thirty.

But I was offered what I thought was a better job.

Jules Stein, the entertainment mogul, had asked me to be his assistant at Universal Pictures and M.C.A., the powerful entertainment organization. To me, the movie business was a lot more exciting than Wall Street.

So I quit.

The day I left Hardy and Company, the seemingly endless stream of orders that had come daily from Doris Duke ceased. She was the company's largest single account. Needless to say, I was greatly missed at Hardy and Company.

Doris launched my career in typical Doris Duke subterfuge. She knew how to use money and power to build my career to a pinnacle of unbelievable success in only a few weeks.

Then I threw it away.

There was never any criticism from Doris. Not a hint of reproach was evident. She had done what she had done in secrecy, and even if everyone understood, she herself never revealed these efforts. She might have been angry. She might have been hurt. However, she would never permit me or my father or any member of the family to know.

Yet she never made any effort to help me again.

I know that many people, including most of the family, considered Doris to be a spoiled, arrogant, self-absorbed, eternal child, but I wonder if that was entirely true.

I know she could care.

It became evident as this book took shape that Doris Duke was a woman who carefully controlled and managed her life as well as the people she permitted to become part of that life. It should be noted here that, while the memories of Doris Duke are from my own (and other family members') recollections, this book was in reality written by my friend Jason Thomas. It was as a result of his questioning and insight that I finally began to understand Doris's reasons for so many of her actions.

I now know she was capable of accomplishing anything for any person who overcame the wall that surrounded her heart. Some thirty years later, I look back at the efforts she made to be a part of my life and I wish I had treated her better. But I didn't want her to think I was after her money. I didn't want her to believe I was like all the others.

So I cut her out of my life.

Before she might cut me out of hers.

And for that, I am sorry.

Pony Duke
Trout Creek Ranch
Montana

# 1

# THE BILLION-DOLLAR WILL

In the early morning hours of October 28, 1993, shortly after the immensely wealthy and sometimes eccentric Doris Duke died—or was murdered—in the bedroom of her Beverly Hills mansion (one of five residences), telephones started ringing all over the world.

The members of the rich and powerful Duke family were being informed that their billionaire relative was dead at the age of eighty.

Her closest relative, Ambassador Angier Biddle Duke, a first cousin, was brushing his teeth in front of a steamy mirror in the black-tiled bathroom of his $2 million Manhattan co-op in the River House, the ultra-exclusive bastion of old WASP money, when he got the call that Doris Duke was dead.

On the phone was her butler and final friend during the last years of her flamboyant life, Bernard Lafferty, whose Irish-accented voice was quivering with emotion.

"She died early this morning at home," the butler said. "She did not suffer at the end. She was not in pain."

"When is the service?" the former ambassador to Spain and Morocco asked with the dignified correctness of one who had been trained to respond calmly at moments of births and deaths. There was no emotion in his voice, just the controlled reaction of a man trained for diplomacy. Ambassador Duke was used to handling the details of death. As chief of protocol for the Kennedy White House, he had overseen the funeral of assassinated President John Fitzgerald Kennedy. "The family will want to gather."

"No, we don't intend on having a service," the butler continued. "She didn't want a service."

"Oh?" the surprised relative, who had been one of the few people on earth Doris Duke might have considered a peer, said softly. In one way, it was a relief not to have to travel across the country to eulogize his cousin, but yet, it seemed somehow disrespectful not to do so. She was a Duke. Doris was that combination of brilliance and passion, generosity and greed, indulgence and loyalty, that had seemed to have been a part of the emotional makeup of the Duke bloodline since the days after the Civil War when their North Carolina dirt farmer grandfather, Washington Duke, had taken his last fifty cents and started the tobacco empire that would later become the American Tobacco Company.

Doris Duke was of his blood and she was gone. Her butler had said she was dead. Her deathbed had not been surrounded by sobbing family but by servants and pets. But then, few members of the Duke family would shed tears over the demise of their cousin. There had been too many emotions expended on her behalf over the previous eight decades. The family had developed a numbness to the actions of Doris Duke; a calculated lack of feeling that had slowly developed as they insulated themselves from her angers and rages and vindictiveness. He understood why he was not experiencing a wrenching sadness at the loss of his cousin, only emptiness, a void in his carefully arranged life, that had been the province and exclusive emotional territory of Doris. He felt there should be a service. It was the correct thing to do. It was protocol.

And the butler had told him there would be no service.

He had used the words, "We don't intend on having a service." We. How odd! What an unusual selection of phrasing. What kind of relationship did this Irish butler forge with cousin Doris that he would feel that the two of them were a "we"? Doris Duke was not the kind of woman who formed lasting "we" relationships. Nobody since her father, Buck Duke, had remained close enough to Doris Duke to have formed the kind of lasting relationship where decisions might have been made on a "we" basis . . . not family . . . not friends . . . not lovers . . . not husbands . . . not business associates . . . not anyone on earth. Doris Duke trusted no single person besides herself to make decisions that would influence her life. Throughout, people had come to Doris Duke. She had entertained herself with them, and she had discarded them. Doris had treasured beauty and music and animals, but not friendship. Friendship was a finite quantity that was something to be consumed instead of cherished. Ambassador Duke could think of no person on earth who could say "we" when referring to any action or event that would influence the life of cousin Doris . . . or her death.

But the butler, Bernard Lafferty, had very casually and naturally said "we" and it sounded right and unpretentious to the politically sensitive ear of the stunned relative. This was more than a house servant. This man was an influence.

The ambassador waited for Lafferty to leave the line before placing his own finger on the disconnect button. Still holding the receiver to his ear, the ambassador thought for a moment. Who needed to be called? Who would want to be told? Who cared? The eighty-year-old patriarch of the Duke family, a family that came from North Carolina farm stock at the end of the Civil War to become one of the richest families in the world, felt a strange kind of emotionless relief that his cousin was finally out of his life.

Ambassador Angier Biddle Duke and his brother, Tony Duke, were her closest relatives. Ambassador Duke's son, Pony, was Doris Duke's godson.

"Doris had always been somewhat of an embarrassment to me," Ambassador Duke later commented over a bowl of bran and steamed prunes in the restaurant of his private club. He had often been called upon by the family to do damage control when Doris

Duke made headlines either from her marriages and affairs, her strange and ever-changing assortment of controversial and often unsavory friends, her adoption of a middle-aged woman as her only daughter, and even the violent death of an associate at the gates of her summer mansion at Newport.

She died, rich and lonely, behind the thick drapes of the bedroom of her Beverly Hills estate, a house that had once belonged to another mysterious and tragic celebrity, Rudolph Valentino. For days, she had lain in a coma with tubes extending from her stomach and throat, a woman who was worth between $1.2 and $3 billion dollars, her anemic body finally starved to death. Her butler, Bernard Lafferty, slept on a cot that had been brought to the room.

Just as Doris Duke had been born in a state-of-the-art hospital that her father had ordered constructed in his new Fifth Avenue mansion, she died surrounded by the best medical apparatus available in the twentieth century, brought to her Beverly Hills bedroom.

She did not want to die in a hospital.

It was only when the low gurgle made as air was sucked through the breathing hole in her throat stopped that Lafferty knew she was dead. With the developed instincts of a career servant, Lafferty waited until it was morning in New York before notifying the other members of the powerful Duke family. It was the kind of consideration that was expected from an experienced domestic. There was no reason to awaken anyone. Nothing would be accomplished by rousing Ambassador Duke and the other members of the Duke clan from their Porthault sheets when there was nothing that anyone could do for Doris. This would be the last expected act of domestic service that Bernard Lafferty would ever perform as a butler.

He knew what was in the will.

He knew that he was no longer just the unusual barefoot and ponytailed butler to the richest member of the Duke family. Because of that will, he was in every way an equal. On this October morning, Lafferty realized, the Dukes did not yet know that he was now a member of the family—with his share of the family fortune.

But soon they would find out.

In Manhattan, Ambassador Duke still held the phone receiver to his ear while he decided who should be called first. His fingers went to the push buttons and a very private line in an old New York law firm rang on a senior partner's desk.

"Doris has died," he said. "I want to see a copy of the will."

The day that Doris Duke was born, November 22, 1912, the *New York Times* dubbed her "the richest baby in the world." And she was. Her tobacco and electric power magnate father, Buck Duke, who once controlled nearly every facet of the world tobacco industry before antitrust laws forced him to relinquish part of his empire, was one of the richest men in the world. The baby Doris was to be an only child. When Buck Duke died, Doris was twelve years of age. He bequeathed his adored and badly spoiled daughter at least $100 million in debt-free assets and the instincts to preserve and expand this fortune. Because of Doris's age, Buck's will had provided a series of bequests and trusts to protect the future of his beloved heiress.

These trusts would oversee Doris Duke for all eighty years of her life. Buck Duke was not an educated man but he was a brilliant man, and the terms of his will not only protected Doris but might ultimately settle the thousands of pages of litigation and suits that have been filed against the complex and often confusing forty-five-page last will of Doris Duke drawn only a few months before her death.

The massive estate and various foundations were placed under the control of Bernard Lafferty, giving him enormous discretionary power over the spending of one of the world's great fortunes.

A former business manager and her one-time physician have charged that Doris Duke was murdered, pointing to a final cadre of lawyers, physicians, and the butler Lafferty as among those who could be responsible.

The estranged, middle-aged adopted daughter, who always said that she cared nothing for the money, has hired lawyers to demand the whole fortune.

The trustees of Duke University, which was endowed by her

father and named to honor her grandfather Washington Duke, hope that the foundations will be used to further develop the North Carolina institution.

Tax collectors in several states are eyeing the potential $500 million of taxes that could be levied against the estate, should the will and the tax-exempt foundations that it created be overturned.

Dozens of lawyers are circling the billions like Savile Row–tailored jackals, some nipping at the edges, others digging experienced teeth into basic organs for the tastiest financial flesh, namely petitioning the courts to release hundreds of thousands of delicious dollars in fees.

"Doris would have liked this," Ambassador Duke said. "She often said that she detested the notoriety and bad publicity that came her way but I think she enjoyed the attention. If she didn't, she could have done things so very differently. She was a smart and self-centered woman."

Doris had been dead only a few hours when dozens of attorneys representing relatives, business associates, servants, and almost every person who had ever been involved with her, requested copies of the will. Within days, copies of the final will would be thumbed by carefully manicured fingers from New York City to Honolulu to Paris to Australia as hopeful beneficiaries scanned the pages for their names.

The final will, which was drawn the previous April of 1993 while Doris was a patient at the Cedars-Sinai Medical Center in Los Angeles, was much like the many wills she had capriciously ordered drawn in the past. These documents always created a number of foundations designed to perpetuate some of Doris Duke's pet projects.

But this will had a significant change from all the earlier wills.

That change concerned Bernard Lafferty.

The first twenty-two pages of the new will were little changed from previous wills. They recited the guidelines for the perpetuation of the many trusts and foundations that Doris Duke had established over her lifetime and listed dozens of individual bequests to people who had populated her life over the years (some of these people were later amazed that Doris still remembered them).

But then came page twenty-three . . . the Lafferty clauses.

There she appointed Lafferty as individual executor, giving him an immediate $5 million up front and an annual salary of $500,000, with an unlimited fund for expenses.

The appointment and firing of the members of the board of directors was left to the sole discretion of Bernard Lafferty, as was the appointment of whatever trust company or bank would be selected to oversee the mammoth estate. Lafferty also held the absolute right to remove the trust company at will.

In less than three pages of legalese, Bernard Lafferty, the butler with a propensity for inebriate forages into the wine cellars, had been transformed into Mr. Bernard Lafferty, the expensively suited executor of one of the world's largest and most eccentric estates.

Lafferty developed instant enemies.

Walker Inman II, the son of Walker Inman, Doris's usually inebriated half-brother and the badly spoiled son of Doris's mother, Nanaline Duke, from her first marriage, started legal action to change his position in the will. Walker II has gone through millions of dollars from the estate of his grandmother to get a bigger slice of the estate than the approximately $350,000 annual stipend he would have received from a $7 million trust established for his benefit. Young Walker also alleges that he should be the executor of the estate and not Lafferty. While some members of the family have reservations about the ability of Bernard Lafferty to oversee the fortune, they agree that the wild and headstrong Walker II has never exhibited even the slightest instinct for sound financial management.

In fact, the younger Inman has blown most of his own fortune.

While the bulk of the billions goes to education, children's welfare, conservation and environmental causes, and art and historical restoration foundations, there were dozens of people who would have found themselves instantly rich by bequests that Doris made to her business and personal associates.

And not all of these associations were of the human variety.

Doris Duke loved animals far more than she ever loved people. She most assuredly trusted her horses, cows, camels, deer, ducks, geese, and more than a dozen dogs, more than she ever trusted anything that walked erect. In one special request, she left a trust of one hundred thousand dollars for the benefit of a little dog that lived at Falcon's Lair, the Beverly Hills estate where she died. It was this shaggy little creature that gave Doris Duke much of the affection that made her last uncomfortable days on earth bearable.

She left her eyes to the New York Eye Bank. This was unusual because during her life, she spent millions on creams, miracle products, exotic injections of sheep placenta, and plastic surgery in an effort to make her body as perfect as it could be. It was a puzzlement that this woman who was so vain about her looks would entertain the possibility of her eyes being surgically removed from her corpse.

She left explicit instructions that she be buried at sea. "I want to be eaten by sharks," she would comment to shocked listeners, usually at a dull dinner party. "It is something I learned in Hawaii and I find it perfectly natural. It is ecologically sound and fits my personal philosophy."

She gave five hundred thousand dollars to her jazz piano instructor.

There was a two-hundred-thousand-dollar bequest to her most faithful servant of decades, the ancient John Gomez, who oversees the tropical architectural masterpiece estate she built in the days of the Great Depression on Diamond Head in Hawaii. Members of the family thought this was a measly sum to give an employee who had been loyal to Doris for his entire life. But then this bequest was reexamined and analyzed and it was decided that the ever-pragmatic Doris realized that Johnny was even older than she, and two hundred thousand dollars would be ample for the remainder of his lifetime. "She did not care for the way he had been treated by some of his relatives and she did not want to leave them rich," one friend commented.

The minister of the Black Baptist Church in Nutley, New Jersey, got $1 million for allowing Doris to sing with the spirited choir of his congregation.

Duke University and the Metropolitan Museum of Art were

each given $10 million. The university had hoped for more but the museum curators were completely surprised and delighted as Doris had shown little interest in their institution prior to her death.

The lists of individual bequests, ranging from $3 million to a few thousand dollars, continued for several pages. She ordered that her expensive memberships in the ultra-snooty Newport Country Club and the Spouting Rock Beach Association be relinquished without the clubs having to pay a refund.

She forgave debts to six people including movie producer Franco Rossellini, who had owed her a remaining one hundred and fifty-eight thousand dollars of the large amounts of cash this charming Italian conniver had enticed from the notoriously cheap Doris Duke.

Imelda Marcos was not so fortunate.

The wife of the ousted president of the Philippines was rescued by Doris from having to cool her expensively shod heels in a New York jail after the U.S. Government filed charges against her and froze her assets. Doris, who was a neighbor of the Marcoses in Hawaii, paid the $5 million bail and underwrote the additional $5 million fee paid to Wyoming-based super-lawyer Gerry Spence. Imelda went free and her assets were released but she never repaid Doris.

Doris Duke left final instructions that this money be collected from Imelda, who now says she does not have the wherewithal to repay.

But while the tone of the will was crisp and properly legalese, the tenor of the document became emotional in references to Chandi Duke Heffner, the thirty-something daughter Doris adopted in 1988 and expelled from her life in 1990.

Not only did Doris Duke disinherit Heffner from her estate, she attempted to remove her from the benefits of a trust established by her father in 1924 to provide for any relative of the Duke family so that no one would ever go hungry. Doris received two thirds of the income of the trust, which was to go to her children following her death. Then, twenty-one years after the death of the last Duke heir of Washington Duke who was living at the time of the 1924 creation of the trust, the principal funds of the trust would either be divided between Doris's children and the other heirs on record or, should Doris die without offspring, her two-thirds share would go to the Duke Endowment for the benefit of projects usually in the area of North Carolina. In the past, the trustees have accepted and permitted adopted children to be considered full-fledged participants in the trusts.

"Doris could do a lot of things to get her way," said one lawyer with close ties to the family, "but she never found a way to unadopt Chandi. Doris knew how to pull all the strings but there were no strings to be pulled. Chandi was her daughter—legally. Doris could lock the gates and ignore Chandi but contempt would not be enough to completely rid herself of the girl. It was one of the few mistakes that her fortune could not correct."

Adopted daughter Chandi could inherit $90 million someday.

Until that day, Chandi would have to survive on the $4 to $5 million annual income from this trust, which is entirely separate from Doris's fortune.

But not if Doris Duke had her way.

"I declare that, despite my 1988 adoption of Chandi Heffner (who was thirty-five years old at the time), it is my intention that she not be deemed to be my child for the purposes of disposing of trust property," an angry Doris said in the will. "I am confident that my father, who created certain trusts for my lifetime benefit, would not want Chandi Heffner to have any interest in any such trust, even if I wanted her to have an interest (which I do not)."

Chandi wants that $90 million.

And she has a good chance of getting it. While Doris Duke can disinherit her, it is questionable whether she can unadopt Chandi from the grave. Reluctantly, members of the family concede that Doris might not have the right to reinterpret the terms of her father's trust. One of the reasons that she adopted Chandi, she told people during happier times in the mother-daughter relationship, was to keep that trust from ever benefiting some of the people in North Carolina whom she blamed for starting rumors of a lesbian relationship between herself and Chandi.

"I don't want those damn petty little gossips down there to

ever get a dime," she would say to anyone who would listen as she and her new daughter sipped champagne on the terrace of her Hawaiian palace on the Pacific. "Ever!"

But nothing was forever in the gilded world of Doris Duke.

It was not possible for any person or project to remain in the enthusiastic good graces of this temperamental and demanding woman who believed that her endless checkbook could buy anything and anyone.

But in the end, she could not buy health. God knows, she tried. There were exercise programs and special foods. She traveled the world in search of exotic health treatments to eternalize and rejuvenate the body. Her mind and her body were massaged and manipulated in a quest for total well-being. She wanted eternal youth.

She was, however, eternally rich. She left warehouses filled with the treasures of the world, boxes of unset diamonds, hidden bank accounts throughout the world, and an entangled mass of foundations to continue her bidding into eternity.

She left a will signed in an unsteady childlike hand.

And a butler who has become her living ghost.

# 2
# THE START OF THE DUKE FORTUNE

The fortune that would make Doris Duke one of the richest women in the world can be traced to a single fifty-cent piece—the entire capital of forty-seven-year-old Washington Duke in 1865.

Washington Duke was a poor North Carolina red clay dirt farmer who was walking barefoot back to his small plot of land in Orange County after being mustered out of the Confederate Navy. Captured in April of 1865 during the siege of Richmond, he was sent to a Union prison. Uneducated and unpolished, Duke had been considered near white trash by the plantation-bred officers of the South. This was because, although he was a Southerner who loved his home, Duke conspicuously conflicted with most ideals that were considered Southern.

He never would own slaves and thought slavery was evil. He was a staunch Methodist in a world populated with Baptists. He believed that women should have the opportunity to be educated. He supported the Union and was proud to call himself an American at a time when his friends and neighbors were calling themselves Rebels. He was against the war but fought for his South. He was a believer in the Temperance Movement at a time when most Southerners considered brandy to be an important part of life. But worst of all, he was an enthusiastic and unrepentant Republican.

In 1865 he was restarting his life with a fifty-cent bankroll.

In the first shrewd financial dealing of his postwar career, Washington Duke convinced a Yankee soldier to exchange the fifty-cent piece for Duke's last Confederate five-dollar bill. Rebel currency had become worthless so it was a very good trade.

It was the first of many business moves that would establish Duke and later his sons, Ben and Buck, as the first really rich Southerners to emerge from the business world of the Reconstruction South.

Washington had a vision of a South where the economy was based on business and commerce instead of the plantation agriculture of the much adulated past. He had no interest in devoting himself to the favorite pastime of the Reconstruction Era Southerner—tragically lamenting all that had been lost. Duke thought that the war was a stupid mistake and recalled that "the good old days" had not been all that good for him and his family.

"If he hadn't become so rich," his son Buck would comment some fifty years later, "some of those North Carolina Democrats might have hung him."

But it was likely that the Civil War aided Washington Duke's success. Before the war, he was able to feed his small family from the income scraped from three hundred not-so-desirable acres of farmland that he had accumulated in Orange County, North Carolina. A very responsible man, he would have continued to scrape a living from that red clay for the rest of his life had the war not intervened.

Like most Southern men, Washington Duke was impoverished after the war. Unlike his broken neighbors, he saw this as an opportunity to experiment with ideas that had been forming in his mind for decades. These ideas would do much to rebuild the state of North Carolina.

The Yankees had stripped the remains of the crops on his land with the exception of some tobacco that had been stored away in 1863 when all the other crops and livestock had been sold.

Before the war, Washington Duke and his first wife, Mary,

lived with their sons, Sidney and Brodie, in what could only be described as a shack. Mary died in this tiny frame house. In December of 1852, he wed his second wife, Artelia Roney. A year later, a daughter, Mary Elizabeth, was born. Benjamin Newton Duke was born on April 27, 1855, and James Buchanan "Buck" Duke was born on December 23, 1856. The typhoid epidemic of 1858 took, first, young Sidney, and, ten days later, Artelia.

It was then that Washington decided on a plan that would provide a better life for his surviving family. A new kind of yellow leaf flue-cured tobacco had been discovered by Captain Abisha Slade in nearby Caswell County. Actually one of his slaves had accidentally overheated the tobacco when he fell asleep while tending one of the curing sheds. Washington decided to raise and cure tobacco. Together with his small sons, Ben and Buck, he beat the tobacco with wooden flails, sifted it by hand, and packed it in bags with the logo "Pro Bono Publico," a Latin term the uneducated Washington had seen on a nearby courthouse.

With this load of smoking tobacco, Washington became an itinerant salesman and went on the road to trade his treasure for whatever he could.

He earned forty dollars in gold on his first trip as a tobacco salesman, which was an amazing sum in the Reconstruction South.

This was the start of what would later become the American Tobacco Company. At first, Washington and his sons worked the fields while sister Mary sewed and filled the bags of tobacco in the small frame house until the family was preparing as much as six hundred pounds of tobacco each day.

In 1866, the family earned almost nine thousand dollars, which was an enormous amount of money. They all worked sixteen-hour days and the children's education suffered, a fact that deeply bothered Washington Duke.

In 1872 the family's income had reached an astonishing seventy-five thousand dollars.

About that time, Washington rewarded his children by arranging for their educations. Buck and Ben were first sent to sessions at an academy near Durham. Later Ben and Mary went to the

New Garden School, which would become Guilford College.

Buck returned to work.

The much older brother, Brodie, was the first member of the family to move to Durham, where he produced his own brands of plug tobacco, including the soon-to-be-famous "Duke of Durham."

At that time, Brodie was a hard worker who never drank liquor, but all that was to change later in his life.

Washington decided to move to the brash new railroad town of Durham because that seemed to be where the business was. In 1874, he sold his property and loaded his family onto a wagon and headed for the boomtown.

The Duke family built a factory on Main Street.

The aging Washington Duke traveled across the country selling his tobacco from a wagon and an ambitious Buck Duke wanted to go on the road, too. It would be poetic to be able to say that the young Buck was an immediate success but he was not. He lamented to his brother Ben that he "was not pulling my weight." All that would change.

In 1880, Brodie Duke began demonstrating signs of the drunken and wastrel life that would dominate the rest of his years. Washington decided that Brodie would never be the kind of older brother that Ben and Buck would need. This combined with the fact that the patriarch Duke was sixty years of age caused him to make a decision that both helped and hurt the future of his sons.

Earlier, George Washington Watts had purchased a one-fifth interest and had become Ben Duke's partner in running the factory and business aspects of the growing firm. Now, Washington sold his interest in W. Duke and Sons to an ambitious and highly driven man by the name of Richard Harvey Wright. The company became W. Duke, Sons and Company. Wright traveled throughout the world building the company.

Washington Duke, whose main interest had become the rebuilding of the South through education, would devote the remainder of his life to creating educational opportunities for the people of North Carolina. He always had been saddened that no matter how much he accomplished and how much money he amassed, he was an uneducated man. His efforts and much of his fortune would result in Trinity College, later to become Duke University, relocating in Durham.

Buck, at first, had no interest in his father's passion for supporting education.

He was having problems with his new partner.

Buck both appreciated the abilities and disliked the fact that outsiders had become a part of this family firm built by the roughened hands of his father, his brother, his sister, and himself.

Buck wanted to switch the firm from pouch tobacco to cigarettes, which had only recently become popular among the European chic.

It was then that he discovered the power of sex appeal in advertising. The first time the out-and-out allure of a beautiful woman was used to lure a man into buying a product was in a marketing promotion conducted by W. Duke, Sons and Company in Atlanta. At the time, a luscious and abundantly endowed French actress of the day, Madame Rhea, both shocked and enticed the capital of Georgia. She was saucy and somewhat racy, a real temptress. Madame Rhea was asked if she would consent to pose holding a package of Duke cigarettes for an advertisement in the *Atlanta Constitution* under the heading "ATLANTA'S FAVORITE." The huge posters were hung everywhere in the city. It was the first such celebrity endorsement in advertising history and was soon followed by more beautiful women holding, but not smoking, cigarettes.

In those days it was too shocking for a woman to smoke.

Madame Rhea and the dozens of beauties who would follow were merely there to encourage men to chose a Duke product.

The Dukes also carry the dubious fame of having given the world the sport of professional roller derby. In the 1880s, the company hired what was then called a "polo club on skates" and dubbed them the "Cross Cut Polo Club of Durham." They sent them across the country to "slug it out" with other roller clubs. As blood flowed and teeth flew, Duke representatives passed small packages of cigarettes to the men in the audience.

Later Buck would sponsor baseball and early basketball teams but he always considered these sports to be nothing more than an advertising promotion for his cigarettes. This was probably his costliest mistake as many of the teams of today were originally financed by Duke money.

Only to him, athletics were little more than interesting diversions designed to attract crowds where he could promote his cigarettes. If anything about the latter part of the twentieth century would surprise Buck Duke it would be that the sports empire he threw away would generate billions of dollars in revenues annually.

Still, in 1885 Buck Duke was interested only in the Bonsack machine, which could mass-produce cigarettes.

Until the creation of this machine, cigarettes were hand-rolled in a manner not unlike cigars. Buck tested one such machine in 1884, but it had its faults and frequently broke down. Other cigarette companies thought the ever-experimenting Buck Duke had finally found the idea that would ultimately ruin the company.

The year 1885 was to be one of the most difficult times for the growing Duke empire. Buck wanted to reinvest most of the profits into the Bonsack machines, while Richard Wright wanted the profits distributed among the partners. At the same time the directors of the Bonsack Company were concerned that Buck Duke, who was gaining a reputation as a ruthless businessman, would have too much influence and control over their emerging company if he were to become such a huge customer.

The concern of Wright and the Bonsack Company was well founded.

Wright examined W. Duke and Sons' original partnership agreement and noticed an unusual clause aimed at Brodie Duke. The contract included a pledge that each partner would "conduct himself in such a manner as to reflect credit upon the firm and not drink liquors to intoxication."

There was more to this clause:

Should any partner "violate any one of the obligations, covenants or stipulations for one time, except that relating to intoxication, and as to that violation of five times during any one year, such violation shall dissolve this co-partnership so far as the party making such violation is concerned."

This was known to the family as "the sober up Brodie clause," put in in an attempt to encourage him to stay away from liquor.

It did not work.

Brodie, whose inclusion in the partnership was nothing more than an act of charity on the part of his brothers, was drunk usually five days a week. Worse yet, he was a loud and obnoxious drunk who enjoyed blanketing the good Christian folk of Durham with slurred expletives as he rode about in his carriage.

Brodie loved brandy and whores.

He patronized both in public.

According to the partnership agreement, Brodie could be bought out at any time because of his antics, for a mere eight thousand dollars. Wright used this clause and others to try to dissolve the partnership. This action infuriated Buck Duke because Wright had never paid Washington Duke the twenty thousand dollars for the founder's share in the company. Washington Duke, at Buck's insistence, foreclosed on Wright's property, which had been given as security against the debt.

Buck Duke was starting to detest Richard Wright. He despised disloyalty and considered Wright's actions to be corporate treason. This would be a lesson he would impress, decades later, on his tiny daughter Doris.

"Do not tolerate disloyal people," Buck Duke would tell her as she sat on his knee. "Get rid of them. Put them out of your life where they cannot hurt you."

Wright was a formidable antagonist. He wanted the Dukes to buy his interest at an inflated price that was estimated to be as high as five hundred thousand dollars. When they refused, he threatened to sell his share to a rival company that could use the position within the Duke organization to destroy its competitor.

Duke swore that he would ruin Wright.

He finally bought Wright's interest for a mere $39,750. Wright then went into a new partnership with two members of the Bonsack Company's board of directors. Buck countered by undercutting the prices of Wright's cigarettes in every market where

Wright tried to sell. By 1887, Wright was a beaten man and offered to resign if Buck Duke would stop his attack.

Buck was not finished. He considered actions of the two members of the Bonsack board who sided with Wright to be treasonous and decided to focus his venomous sights on that company. There was much to occupy Buck's eighteen-hour days. Wright had been overseeing the company's new plants in New York City and Buck was spending more time there, at the same time he was "handling the Bonsack situation." The Dukes were the biggest users of the Bonsack cigarette machines and they had much leverage with the company. But the future of W. Duke and Sons also depended on the cigarette-rolling machines that could only be bought from and maintained by the Bonsack Company.

Duke and Sons paid a royalty to the Bonsack Company on every cigarette made. Because they were the largest customer, they had negotiated to pay the lowest royalty—a business move that gave them an edge over their competitors.

Buck Duke not only took the Bonsack Company to court but informed other companies that had negotiated set royalty agreements with the company that there had been a secret and preferential deal struck with Wright.

The Bonsack Company paid one hundred and thirty thousand dollars just to settle the Duke claim.

This was not a total victory for Buck. When former partner Richard Wright learned of the very favorable royalty that Buck had negotiated with the Bonsack Company, he again filed a lawsuit that alleged that Buck and Ben had hidden huge profits from him and that Wright's interest in the firm was worth far more than the $39,750 he had been paid. After years of lawsuits, the Dukes settled by paying Wright an additional fifty thousand dollars.

Buck Duke was not only a dangerous enemy but a man who was to become the most powerful person in the world tobacco market. Wright had made a serious mistake in being disloyal to him.

By the late 1880s, Buck had gained complete control of the Bonsack Company, as well as the two chief rival cigarette machine manufacturers. This happened at a time when most other tobacco firms were realizing that Buck Duke had been absolutely correct when he predicted that people would prefer cigarettes over plug and pipe tobaccos.

Other cigarette companies tried to buy or lease cigarette making machines and found themselves negotiating with their most ruthless competitor, Buck Duke.

Buck's favorite way to negotiate was to purchase the potential competition as quickly as possible. In the late 1880s, he bought four of his business rivals. Because he owned or controlled all the patents on cigarette-making machines, Duke could manipulate every aspect of the cigarette business, and tobacco manufacturers hated him for that. Buck could choose to keep a competitor out of the rapidly growing cigarette segment of the business and ultimately force the rival out of business or he could regulate the growth of their companies by limiting the numbers of cigarettes that they could produce.

Meanwhile the consumer public was demanding more cigarettes.

And they were losing interest in all other forms of tobacco.

In 1890, Buck formed the American Tobacco Company with an initial capitalization of $25 million, a huge amount of money at that time. The American Tobacco Company controlled more than 90 percent of the cigarette business.

"There was a lot of whining about how I conducted my business during those years," Buck Duke would say after he had become the world's tobacco czar. "These were the same people who laughed at me ten years earlier when I decided to make cigarettes. They even said that I was crazy. Yet I ended up owning their companies."

Buck Duke was devoting most of his time to the growing New York City tobacco factory and had rented a sparse room on the Lower East Side for three dollars a week. Since he arrived at his factory before his employees and stayed until the last worker was gone, there was no need for a fine residence.

Buck was a farm boy, not a city sophisticate.

He went to New York City for the exact same reasons that

Washington Duke had taken the business to Durham: because it was where people did business. The metropolis was the center of money and commerce for the nation and much of the world. But Buck's heart was in the farm he had bought in New Jersey, a place that would one day grow into the lavish twenty-two-hundred-acre Duke Farms.

Buck's social life was meager. There was little time for women. Because Buck had learned the value of what today's business dubs "market surveys" he had his salesmen compile records of varieties and amounts of cigarettes that sold in certain areas. He would spend hours poring over these facts in an effort to predict future trends in the public taste.

This is not to say that Buck did not dally with the opposite sex. He was just focused on his work.

It was known that he had taken a personal interest in several of the beautiful and always buxom women who adorned his cigarette advertisements, but his dalliances had been extremely discreet. If there was one thing that Buck Duke did not want, it was for his proper Methodist father to learn of his escapades, however limited.

Washington Duke already was concerned about the sexy advertising. Churches were preaching against the revealing advertisements of Duke-owned cigarettes while little boys were enthralled with these exotic women and their plunging cleavage.

And, like them, Buck Duke was entranced by the female breast.

While his advertising campaigns would, indeed, be considered mild when compared to the naked calendars and nude magazines that would come a few decades later, the painted faces, abundant breasts, and hints of ankles in Buck's advertising were so widely and openly circulated, the prudes of the day were outraged.

The "tobacco ladies" could be found pasted on huge billboards or on the walls of railroad stations. Smaller versions were inserted in almost every pack of cigarettes, which were still mostly a male product.

The fact that Buck was still relatively young and becoming very rich was of interest to many New York women but not to the "quality" ladies of this new and highly suspect society. He was considered a North Carolina bumpkin with his heavy Southern accent and country lifestyle.

In spite of the fact that Buck Duke had given millions of American men and boys their first look into the world of glamorous women, he was somewhat shy and almost naive in his own scanty romantic relations.

But he was starting to take stock in the potential for pleasure that his growing fortune could bring. Like many young sports of the day, he was proud of his fine team of horses and carriage, which he drove with excess speed through the city streets.

He moved to a suite in the posh Hoffman House Hotel, which was where the rich, the important, the scandalous, and very powerful people mingled. Here was the first location of the now legendary power breakfast. Here was where the fate of business and industry was decided over champagne and oysters.

It was here in the grand lobby of the Hoffman House Hotel that he met a woman who was the living and breathing image of his cigarette dream woman.

# 3

# BUCK'S WOMEN

There had been a lot of scandal centered on the first Mrs. Buck Duke. She was, most assuredly, a slut. But she was a fabulous slut, possibly the best slut money could buy in the first decade of the twentieth century.

Buck Duke had an instinctive eye for quality, even in whores.

Lillian McCredy was a beautiful woman who met all the requirements that Buck Duke wanted in a wife, some social position, enormous breasts, and the ability to participate in creative bouts of enthusiastic sex that would last for hours.

"I got my sex drive from Daddy," Doris would explain many years later. "Daddy and Uncles Ben and Brodie were all very different. Ben was religious and Brodie was a drunk. Daddy was creative and the ultimate businessman. But they all liked sex. Every member of the Duke family is oversexed. It's in the genes. The government should test our chromosomes."

Early in his career, Buck had been all business and no play. He cared nothing about creature comforts, but he always had a great interest in the female form.

But Lillian was unique.

Thus the luscious Lillian's enthusiasm for romping in naked

abandon through the rooms of the East Side townhouse where she had been Buck's kept woman for more than a decade at the turn of the century, and her talent for placing strawberries (a favorite of Buck Duke's) in unexpected cavities of her anatomy were enough to keep the randy Buck a one-mistress man.

"I once was listening outside the library door and heard Daddy say to Uncle Ben," Doris giggled, "'It is fortunate that my favorite fruit wasn't watermelon or Lillian might have done herself harm.'

"Not that there would not have been room for the watermelon," Doris added dryly. "I don't think Uncle Ben was all that amused."

Buck, who liked to travel from business venture to business venture and affair to affair in his private railroad car, would have been happy to continue his bachelorhood with Lillian as his chandelier-swinging mistress. He would have been satisfied to keep Lillian as his number-one distraction from his recurrent bouts of gout ("She does manage to keep me off my feet," he told family members), but the pious patriarch, Washington Duke, and brother Ben, whose more proper wife was making promising inroads into society, told Buck to either get rid of the redheaded tramp or marry her.

He married her.

He was forty-eight years of age when he limped down the aisle.

Lillian had earned what little social position she had the old-fashioned way. She married it. She came to New York from Camden, New Jersey, to study to be a singer. Soon she married a stockbroker named McCredy, who quickly divorced his French-novel-reading wife after she reenacted the plots of the books by bedding a trio of young males. She had a definite taste for Cubans.

Buck picked her up in a hotel lobby.

She revived his libido, and he revived her bank account. Always a generous man, he draped diamonds and emeralds and rubies on her usually naked body and spent thirty thousand dollars for a nice townhouse at 11 East Sixty-eighth Street.

Meanwhile Lillian was cheating on Buck.

While Buck was of modest height, more than ample girth, and

limped from the gout, his wallet was an aphrodisiac for Lillian. Still, she was a woman who liked some variety and the dashing and red-haired Major Frank T. Huntoon was always available. A slender and authentic old-family New York blue blood, Huntoon was older than Buck by twenty years, yet his goutless and rapier-slim body was more agile under the coverlets.

Washington Duke had ordered the marriage to end the newspaper scandal based on the escapades of the rich and rotund Buck and the beautiful and abundant Lillian.

It was a quiet wedding on November 29 of 1904. They immediately sailed to Europe aboard the *Baltic* for a winter vacation on the French and Italian Rivieras.

The weather was miserable and so was Lillian. Once she had actually snared "the big Buck," she was no longer the sweet and ever-enticing mistress. She became a complaining wife.

The following January, Washington Duke was taken ill. Buck caught the next liner home to be near his father in Durham, North Carolina, the home base of the Duke dynasty. Then the indestructible Buck was taken ill. His pesky foot was dangerously infected, the result of neglect that brought on blood poisoning. He was immediately taken to the operating room and ordered to confine himself to his bedroom for a period of six weeks.

Meanwhile his father was dying.

Washington Duke had fallen in the lobby of a Durham bank, breaking his arm. Later he fell again and broke his hip. On May 8, 1905, the staunch and generous old Methodist who had started the Duke fortune with fifty cents after leaving the Confederate Army in 1865, died at the age of eighty-five.

Both Ben and Buck were devastated. Always close, Buck the creative business genius and Ben the much more proper Methodist Republican who ran the factories (brother Brodie had already drunk and wenched himself to death), the brothers mourned together. It was at this time that they decided to make Trinity College, their father's favorite cause, into Duke University as a memorial to Washington Duke. In the beginning, Washington Duke had lured Trinity College to Durham with a donation of fifty thousand dollars (he insisted that the Southern college admit women, which the North Carolina gentility considered ridiculous but understandable since Duke was a Republican). A later gift of $2.1 million made it the richest college in the Southeast but even this endowment would seem small when compared to what Buck Duke would later donate.

The Duke brothers were preoccupied with establishing the college as a memorial to their father, which permitted Lillian the unattended freedom to cheat with her honey Huntoon.

If Washington Duke had died a few months earlier, Buck Duke would never have married the hot-to-trot-down-the-aisle Lillian McCredy.

But married he was and Lillian was transforming herself from mistress into wife and the transformation was expensive. Buck's millions afforded her the excesses of frilly clothes, jewels, carriages, and new-on-the-market luxury motorcars. He was even ready to give her a Fifth Avenue mansion, although he would have rather built a new chateau, patterned after one he saw in the rainy gloom of the French countryside during his honeymoon.

Instead, learning of Lillian's indiscretions, Duke decided that he wanted out of the marriage.

Since the ever-ready Huntoon was still available at the drop of a jodhpur, the wily Buck decided to wait for the nymphodic Lillian to screw herself out of the marriage and into the divorce courts.

"Lillian was always in heat," Doris would recount after an abundance of champagne on the terrace of Rough Point. "Of course she was long gone in every way before I was around but I would hear stories from the servants. Mother even had an occasion to remind Daddy about the slut."

The clever Buck Duke decided to wage psychological warfare on his philandering wife. She adored the city with its music and hotel lobbies and Huntoon, so Buck decided they should spend the summer on his new farm in Somerville, New Jersey.

There he intended to build a palace that would rival the epoch Biltmore that a Vanderbilt had constructed on a mountaintop near Asheville, North Carolina. It was a competition between the blue-blooded tycoon Vanderbilt and the rapidly bluing-blooded Dukes. A contest that started on the home turf of the Dukes:

North Carolina. These were the days when social position was established by the amassing of great piles of wealth, even greater power, a few good deeds, great horses, presentable wives, spoiled children, mansion "cottages" at Newport, and gaggles of French maids, English butlers, and footmen. But the ultimate symbol of success, which translated into respect and power, was a personal country palace of more than one hundred rooms and private railroad stations with parking for unlimited private Pullmans.

An average of three hundred workmen carved Duke Farms out of the New Jersey underbrush. Lakes were built and sometimes refilled and moved when Buck Duke pictured a more appealing possible vista. Some sixty thousand dollars was spent on a heated horse stable. (Buck was the one who nurtured the love of animals in Doris, who later said, "The only real love I ever had was from my father and my animals.")

While the stonemasons were building the foundations of the new Palais du Duke, Buck decided to remodel the existing house and added the usual tycoon accoutrements: a drawing room, a great hall dining room, eleven bedrooms with ample indoor baths, central heat, electricity, telephones, stock market ticker tapes, fireplaces, and hot water tanks. There was also a fountain and a life-sized statue of the late President McKinley (nasty wags at the time hinted that the statue and the fountain were part of the same display but this was just a tasteless rumor). Of course, there was the obligatory clock tower and carillon, which was the latest tycoon toy. On the other hand, the lighted half-mile racetrack was distinctly Buck Duke, although it did not last long when he opted for another lake and fountain on the site. He also built a mountain but decided it didn't look balanced in the rolling hills and flatlands of New Jersey so he had it torn down.

This temporary house was satisfactory for Buck while the real house was being sculpted on an artificial hill he had built as its setting.

This was a man's house, with dark colors, heavy oak and mahogany furniture, and massive sculptures of horses and cattle that on closer examination would prove to be extremely well-endowed bulls.

And then there were the Smith sisters.

Since the middle 1890s, Maggie Smith had been the housekeeper and cashier at the estate. She took her responsibilities in overseeing the Duke purse very very seriously. Her younger and very beautiful sister Mary was a favorite of Bucks and as one wag commented, "Maggie takes care of the Duke purse but Mary sees to the condition of Buck's family jewels."

Both sisters became rich from playing the stock market with the canny advice of Buck Duke, who traded with the same ease that he formed tobacco trusts and electric power companies.

This was the perfect environment to torture Lillian, who hated the country, couldn't stand the infernal quacking and hissing of the ducks and swans, and detested younger and prettier mistresses. There was not even enough closet room in the house. And no Huntoons in the afternoons.

Buck decided that the Smiths should eat with the newlyweds. He invited them on drives around the estate. It was made very clear that while Lillian was the queen of the New York City dukedom, the Smith girls ruled the country. Lillian could not even select a dinner menu at Duke Farms, where she dined mostly on humble pie.

She fled back to New York.

Buck ordered her back to New Jersey.

"She told Daddy to stay in New Jersey or go to hell if he could tell the difference," Doris would later smile. "I might have liked that woman. She was a lot more fun than my mother."

Knowing that Lillian was more than ready to flee right into the arms and bed of the lurking Huntoon, Buck unleashed his pack of detectives on the pair. But an abundance of sex had not damaged any of Lillian's brain cells and she knew that Duke was ready to cut his losses and run, so she developed a case of midlife chastity.

Buck conspired with his lawyers and detectives (he was one of the originators of industrial espionage and had much experience with detectives) for a plan that would convince the passionate Lillian that she would be safe in allowing her hormones to flow.

He left for London.

"Try to enjoy yourself while I am gone, my darling," he said to Lillian. "I am sure you will find something to do."

She did.

But the London trip was far briefer that Lillian had been led to believe and Buck secretly returned to New York and hid himself away in brother Ben's Fifth Avenue mansion. Armed with statements of his wife's peccadilloes with the tall Major Huntoon, as copiously recorded by her personal maids, Buck put the process servers on the violet scent of his wife.

Lillian smelled a rat. A big fat rat with a crutch who liked to smoke Cuban cigars.

She countersued, saying that Duke had jeopardized her health by making her ride in the open compartment of the touring limousine during hailstorms and hitting her with his crutch.

She said that Buck called her vile names, such as whore, wench, and bitch, usually after consuming huge amounts of brandy.

Buck responded that the names were accurate.

All this made marvelous headlines that amused all of New York with the exception of brother Ben and his wife, who were being accepted into the highest levels of society. Ben had married the former Sarah Angier, who was the daughter of a respectable North Carolina family.

And Ben and Sarah actually loved each other.

The Ben Dukes had made inroads into respectable society but this acceptance of the couple from the hills and flatlands of North Carolina into the social set was tenuous. Every time Buck and Lillian escapaded into the press, brother Ben would shudder.

Meanwhile, Lillian never stopped diddling the major. Even when the divorce and the accompanying publicity were at their peak, she would sneak away for some major sex. All of this was being efficiently recorded by her servants and the detectives who uncovered information that really riled Buck. It seemed that the major had primed Lillian for wedded bliss on the night before the wedding.

On the honeymoon, Huntoon passed notes to Lillian. They exchanged romanticisms in the personal columns of the New

York newspapers, where they referred to Buck as "the mean old Octopus" in their lovers' code. This blatant trysting resulted in a twinge of jealousy in Buck Duke, and those who knew the sometimes ruthless tycoon realized that this was a mistake.

In the end, Lillian got nothing from the divorce.

Years later, after losing the millions that she had accumulated during her time with Buck or extorted from him in later years, Lillian managed to embarrass Duke into paying an extra $3 million by saying that his next marriage to Nanaline Holt Inman was invalid because he was still legally married to his first wife when he wed the very proper Atlanta widow. Later when Lillian had been conned out of her fortune by a younger man, she again asked Buck for bucks. But Buck, whose natural instinct was to be generous, had no shred of affection left for her. She got nothing. Buck would die in a huge mahogany bed in his lavish bedroom in the New York mansion. Lillian would die shortly after in a cold room of a rundown boardinghouse with only her pet Mexican hairless dog, Pom-Pom, as a mourner.

She starved to death.

"Once wronged," Doris philosophized, "a Duke never forgets and absolutely never forgives."

Once free of Lillian, Buck Duke looked toward the Duke Farms where his home-grown, luscious Mary Smith was flourishing on the vine. The possible headlines that could be printed should the zillionaire Duke bed and wed the parlor maid sent brother Ben on a search for a "proper" wife for his brother, a woman of refinement with an education that was not limited to the Kama Sutra.

Ben—actually it was his wife, Sarah—found the beauteous widow Inman. Nanaline Holt Inman of the Macon Holts, whose first husband was a moderately successful Atlanta cotton buyer, Will Inman, came from the tattered remains of the plantation aristocracy.

Money was not as important to the impoverished nobility of the Old South as was background and breeding and who you were before the War of Northern Aggression.

This is not to say that Nanaline did not covet the buck.

While she was born to the scent of magnolias behind the white columns of her grandfather's Greek revival mansion on the best street of postwar Macon, her outwardly placid and comfortable life was financially unstable.

Her lineage was grand but her father's fortune was eroded. Then, when she was in her teens, her father disappeared at sea and her mother was forced to open the house to boarders and to sew beautiful dresses for the wives and daughters of the nouveau riche in the postwar South. Dresses that the then Nannie Lane Holt (she later adjusted her name to the more fashionable Nanaline) would never be able to afford.

She was educated at the Branham School and Wesleyan Female College and was very pretty—coached in the flirtations and charms of a Southern belle.

"Mother had learned to pretend that she actually liked men," Doris would snap years later. "She didn't like men. She didn't even like me. She loved her two-story boudoir with the dozens of individual closets so that each of her precious dresses could be properly protected. I would look at the way she caressed her furs and silks and diamonds and wish she felt the same way about me."

Those who knew Nanaline Duke well know that she never recovered from the day her mother and she were forced to leave the house in Macon because they could no longer afford its graceful grandeur. She detested seeing her home and the traditions it represented sold at auction. She swore she would never be poor again. And she wasn't.

Since her first husband had been considerate enough to die of diabetes at the age of thirty-eight, Nanaline Inman found herself a young and attractive widow with a young son, Walker Inman, and enough money to finance a genteel search for her next husband. The only hint of a scandal was the mysterious sudden death of her firstborn son just before his second birthday.

She confided to family members that she did not understand how to properly care for a small child and this inability led to the boy's death. Today the death would probably be labeled child abuse.

She first went after Ben Duke, whom she met at Lake Toxaway, a North Carolina spa resort that was a favorite of Ben and his wife. The proper and happily married Methodist instincts of the Ben Dukes prevented Nanaline from any inroads into the Duke fortune from this direction but Ben's wife realized that Nanaline would be perfect for Buck.

Nanaline was quickly introduced to Buck before he had a chance to wed the nubile maid Mary Smith. In reality, Buck would probably never have married the lush Mary of the lea when he already had grazing rights whenever he wanted.

But Ben wanted his brother married into respectability. He had suffered enough from the antics of his brother Brodie, who used to take private railroad cars filled with New York hookers back to Durham.

Ben wanted to improve the image of the family. He wanted his children to have every advantage. They had money; he wanted them to be given respect.

He exerted the influence over Buck that had previously been the sole domain of his father, Washington Duke.

Nanaline was the exact opposite of the spectacular redheaded Lillian. Nanaline was small and carefully understated in her dress. Her hands were delicate and flawless and incapable of the vulgar yet enticing motions that had so excited Buck into a second burst of youthful testosterone.

Like most well-bred Southern women, Nanaline had learned to suffer her men. She seemed not to mind that Buck's girth was expanding daily and overlooked the fact that he smoked two dozen hand-rolled Cuban cigars each day.

Cars and diamonds arrived at Nanaline's hotel suite on a frequent basis and she accepted these presents from Buck with appropriate reluctance and understatement.

In the spring of 1907, Buck bought a fabulous mansion at the corner of Fifth Avenue and East Seventy-eighth Street as a wedding gift for Nanaline. (He would later level the fantastic house to build the legendary Duke New York digs.) And on January 24, 1907, Buck and Nanaline were wed.

But Buck's mind was not entirely on the marriage. Two weeks

earlier, the government had filed antitrust actions against Buck Duke and his American Tobacco Trust. It seemed that the government investigators had learned that Buck had amassed all of the tobacco empires in the country under his control. Through industrial espionage and canny business moves, Buck controlled every great tobacco tycoon including R. J. Reynolds, who had found himself secretly owned. When the other tobacco barons, led by R. J. Reynolds, learned that they were owned by the Dukes, they secretly sicced the government on him.

After two years in court, in 1909, the American Tobacco Trust was broken. Duke, because of his close friendship with President William Howard Taft, was not sent to jail. But his empire was diminished. So he started looking for new empires to build.

He also began building the grandest mansion in New York City on the most expensive piece of real estate in the world. Buck selected Horace Trumbauer, architect to the robber barons, to construct the "Château on Seventy-eighth Street." Trumbauer had designed the enormous Whitemarsh Hall, the manse of the super-rich Stotesburys, who were the foundation of the Main Line aristocracy of Philadelphia, and Clarendon Court, the Newport mansion where, decades later, Claus von Bülow's rich wife would lapse into the fatal coma which the courts later said the elegant Claus did not cause. Later Trumbauer would design the Oxfordish main buildings of Duke University.

The Duke mansion is based on the Château Labottiere in Bordeaux. Only the Duke house is much larger and has a bigger ballroom. The house, begun in 1909, was completed in 1912 on the lot where Buck had leveled the previous $1.2 million mansion. An interesting insight was Buck Duke's selection of Julian Abele, a young black architect, to draw the plans. Buck, like his father, was a believer in equal rights for blacks and women long before this concept was politically correct.

Duke concentrated on the New York City château and halted the construction of the palace at Duke Farms. Today a series of security tunnels and a massive foundation remain on the site of what might have been the greatest house in the Western Hemisphere.

The Fifth Avenue house consists of three aboveground floors

and two sub-basements. The basements house the kitchens, pantries, servants' dining room, heating systems, and various offices for the housekeeper, butlers, and majordomos. The main floor is comprised of a main hall and grand staircase that is the size of a carved marble basketball court, the library and adjoining dining room to one side, and the music/ballroom with its musicians' balcony opening into a beautiful drawing room on the other side. The second floor includes eight huge bedrooms and six marble baths. A suite overlooking Fifth Avenue would be for Doris and her governess. This room opened to a chamber used as a buffer room between Doris's realm and Nanaline's bedroom (this room opened into a huge bath and the massive two-story dressing room with its dozens of tiny individual closets with gold engraved labels indicating the gown that was being protected behind the rows of carved mahogany doors). Buck Duke's room adjoined his wife's and overlooked the imposing East Seventy-eighth Street entrance to the house. The rest of the rooms were for guests. The third floor or servants' floor was unusual in that a certain degree of luxury carried over to the rooms for the twelve retainers who lived full-time in the house. In a period when most servants' rooms were hovels, these rooms were spacious and airy with ample baths for the gaggle of butlers and maids who lived there (the chefs stayed in the kitchen area so that they could be summoned quickly should the Dukes desire an off-hour snack, and the chauffeurs stayed near the cars in a nearby garage and stable); Buck Duke had insisted that every effort be made to make his household staff comfortable and spent considerable money toward that end.

In the spring of 1912, Nanaline Duke was pregnant. Nanaline did not really want to be pregnant. She doted on young Walker Inman and attempted to foist the whining Walker onto Buck as a potential male heir. But Buck detested the brat.

Instead he adored brother Ben's bright young son, Angier, and the brothers spent thousands of hours educating the boy to someday run the vast Duke empires that had now spread throughout the world.

Nanaline feared that much of the Duke millions would be

placed under the control of young Angier and she wanted every dime of that she could clutch. So she hit the sheets with Buck until in her early forties she found herself pregnant. Buck was overjoyed at the new potential baby Duke. And Nanaline had the heir she wanted.

Immediately after learning of the pregnancy, Buck Duke put pressure on the architects and contractors to finish the house. The first and only child that the fifty-five-year-old Buck Duke was going to father was to be born under the copper and slate roof of the $3 million "grandest house in New York."

Buck Duke's child would be born in Buck Duke's house just as he himself was born under the modest shingled roof of Washington Duke's North Carolina cabin.

# 4

# THE $100 MILLION TYKE

The smell of disinfectant wafted out of the sterilized bedroom of the Fifth Avenue house where twenty-four-hour doctors and a battalion of nurses were awaiting the arrival of the baby Duke.

"This is revolting," Nanaline moaned as the nurses again scrubbed the private surgery that Buck had filled with every piece of medical equipment that might possibly be needed. "I detest that smell and all that hammering."

The nurses and dozens of carpenters who were rushing to finish the city château chattered in the upstairs hallway behind the closed double doors where the forty-something Nanaline had been exiled to bed for several months.

Buck Duke wanted his future heir, preferably a son, to have the absolute best care that his high-priced doctors could provide. He had a near phobia about germs and kept squads of nurses and servants swabbing the marble floors with ammonia and water.

Buck had approached birthing in much the way he approached a business deal. He researched the subject, hired the finest possible people, and spent whatever was necessary to guarantee success.

He had considered every possibility.

"He knew that his wife was actually past the child-bearing years," one family member recalled. "He had secretly discussed the possibility of a difficult birth with the doctors and left orders that if they had to choose between saving the mother or saving the child, it would be the child who would survive. The child was, after all, a real Duke and Nanaline was only a Duke by marriage."

Buck was smoking a cigar in the library late on the night of November 22, 1912, when a smiling doctor came to the door and said, "You have a little girl."

"How is she?" Buck asked.

"She is fine and healthy," the doctor replied, delighted that the baby was in excellent condition, in spite of the fact that the mother was forty-three years of age, because he could submit an astronomical bill to the elated millionaire. "The mother is fine, too."

"Oh, that's good," Buck added as an afterthought. He did not wait for the elevator but bounded, a most ungraceful movement for a portly fifty-five-year-old with a bad leg, up the curving marble staircase to the suite of rooms housing the private maternity ward. A nurse placed the baby, wrapped in spotless white linen, into Buck's arms. He was so overcome with emotion that he could not talk.

So what if the babe was not a male heir. This little girl, who would be called Doris, would be more than equal to any man on earth. She was Buck Duke's only child and he would see that she was taught how to have and keep money.

It was not so terrible that Doris had not been born male.

Ben's son, Angier, was being groomed to run the empire, and, while wild in a typical Duke fashion, seemed to be the perfect combination of Buck's business brilliance and creativity and Ben's attention to details and management ability.

Young Walker Inman, age seventeen, retreated to his room, where he instructed the servants to bring him his usual cocktail every twenty minutes until he passed out. Nanaline had begun trying desperately to have a baby when Buck had told her in the sternest of business tones that, "Walker will never have a place in any Duke businesses. The boy is a spoiled sot. He will get nothing from me."

Worrying that she had produced no heir and that Ben's son was destined to take over the management of the fortune, the normally sedate and demure Nanaline had many times in the last year appeared in Buck's smoke-soaked bedroom (she had installed double beds in her room) and used her wiles to excite the libido that had been largely uninspired since the days of the sexual athletics of first wife, Lillian.

Now she had her own heir to ensure that most of Buck's estate would pass to her and the child and ultimately to Walker. As soon as she could escape from her bed, she would start lobbying for Doris.

"I am glad Doris was a girl," Nanaline said years later, "because if I had produced a son, Buck might have left the boy in a position to completely control the companies someday. This way, I thought that would never happen with Doris and I could bring Walker in sometime in the future."

Nanaline was very wrong.

She had forgotten that Buck was the son of the man who had demanded that Trinity College admit women before he would donate the money to bring the campus to Durham. All the Dukes believed in equality for women and Buck would devote hours to educating Doris in areas usually reserved only for male heirs.

Buck's fortunes had been enriched by his female-oriented advertising campaigns. His early ads filled with beautiful, famous, and exciting women recommending Lucky Strikes led to the "new and modern woman of today" not only lighting a cigarette for her man but openly smoking it herself. With this well-planned advertising coup, he doubled the audience for his products.

Buck certainly believed in and profited from equality of the sexes.

Minutes after assuring himself that baby Doris was in perfect condition, Buck threw open the great front doors of the mansion and started passing cigars to the sea of journalistic sharks swirling in front of the house.

"I am the happiest man on earth," Buck roared in a thick North Carolina accent. "I am a father."

The birth of the richest baby on earth was big news around the world and every newspaper in New York City left no superlative unsaid in descriptions of the birth. The *New York Times* tweaked many a sky-high blue-blooded nose by listing the estimated worth of all of the nation's baby moguls. Baby Doris was easily the richest with $100 million.

The very social W. K. Vanderbilt's son was worth some $60 million while young Eddy McLean followed at $50 million. John Jacob Astor was worth a mere $3 million. "A Duke baby is more than thirty times richer than an Astor baby," Duke said to brother Ben. "I wonder what Pa would think of that?"

The *Times* article continued:

> No child of royal blood ever came into the world amid more comfortable and luxurious surroundings than the daughter of the Dukes. The magnificent Fifth Avenue mansion was turned into a private hospital; no expense was spared in obtaining the best physicians and nurses and the baby's layette represented the outlay of a small fortune. The great wish of a millionaire's heart was to be gratified and no preparations were overlooked.
>
> James B. Duke is to tobacco what John D. Rockefeller is to oil. The immense Rockefeller fortune—while undoubtedly larger than that of the Dukes—eventually will be apportioned among several children and grandchildren. The money of the tobacco king will someday belong solely to this baby—provided, of course, that the stork brings no one else to share it.

Nanaline Duke, nestled in her unenticing twin bed and buried in silk sheets and ermine blankets, read these words with interest. No, there would be no more children. She had accomplished exactly what she wanted by producing that pampered brat in the nursery. But she was determined that the *New York Times*'s flowery prose would be wrong when they mentioned that the money would "belong solely to this baby." To Nanaline Duke, the entire Duke family represented all she detested about the new South.

The Dukes were not people of quality. They worked the soil with their hands while her family set atop proud walking horses supervising hundreds of slaves. The Dukes made their money from selling disgusting tobacco while her family, the arrogant Holts, had been planters of king cotton. The Dukes bought universities while the Holts graduated from them. To Nanaline it was the progeny of generations of aristocrats who understood how to graciously have money.

Nanaline believed that the Dukes were beneath her. To Nanaline the fact that the pampered newborn in the nursery was part Duke meant that the child could not ever be an equal to her Southern aristocrat kin.

Buck, realizing that his austere wife was a snob, knew that she intended to force the useless Walker into his life. He considered the teenage Walker to be a whining drunk who clung to his mother's skirts. He did not approve of the way the boy ordered the Duke servants to perform menial services such as putting on his socks when Buck did not even keep a personal valet.

"I can dress myself without help," Buck told brother Ben. "I don't think that boy could pull on his own britches without two footmen to show him which side faces the front. If this house were on fire he would probably run out the front door with his trousers pulled over his head."

But Buck did have plans for Walker. He decided to send the troublesome boy back to the Georgetown, South Carolina, plantation that Nanaline had purchased in a moment of Spanish moss and magnolia nostalgia.

Angier would head the Duke empire. It would be Angier, a true family member, who would oversee the business and personal affairs of Buck's precious Doris when Buck was no longer around to perform that pleasurable task himself. It would be, as it had always been, Duke taking care of Duke. Meanwhile Buck Duke went about his fatherly duties of protecting his only child as only a wildly creative multimillionaire could. He kept the doctors and nurses on duty for almost a year in the event that the tot should sniffle or cough. Because of his germ phobia, the smell of ammonia greeted all visitors for the next three years in spite of the gallons of French perfume that Nanaline sprayed in the air to mask the stench.

"Whenever I smell ammonia," Doris said years later, "I think of Pa."

He had a private Pullman car constructed and christened it the *Doris*. Then he hired several porters who did nothing but disinfect the car in which Buck's princess would ride. When an epidemic of infantile paralysis felled thousands of children in New York City, Buck rushed baby Doris in a sealed Rolls-Royce to the sterile railroad car and then to Rough Point (which had been sterilized), where she was isolated for the duration of the epidemic. Any servant who was to be near Doris was examined daily by doctors and nurses who also checked their family members and neighbors for any signs of the illness.

Finally, in January 1914, the small Duke family fled to England where the newspapers speculated that Buck was considering moving his fortune following the antitrust action that partially broke apart his business empire. In reality, it was the then epidemic-free environment of London that attracted Buck. Doris would be safer there.

There were also rumors of war. Buck who remembered his father talking about how valueless the Confederate paper money had become during the War of Northern Aggression, believed in gold. During and after the war, gold had been the only dependable means of exchange in the South. He was sure that another war was about to wreak financial havoc with the world economy, so he placed "a very substantial" amount of gold in Switzerland where it could be kept in secrecy.

The threat of war was not the only reason for hoarding of gold. The United States Government had just established the personal income tax and the nation's millionaires were having their financial records exposed to the tax man. Buck had transferred his vast amounts of liquid capital into the gold that would be secreted in Switzerland where it could remain untaxed.

In August of 1914, World War I began and Buck returned to New York. The day his ship landed, Buck got into his limousine and went to at least a dozen banks where he exchanged another

$1 million in currency for gold which was taken that night to the vaults at Duke Farms.

While the world was consumed with the war, Buck was not able to run his international tobacco empire, which meant he had more time to devote to Doris. Buck Duke had again anticipated that accustomed pleasures might become more difficult to find. Thus he had purchased thousands of yards of the finest fabrics and furs, and, as the rest of the world was dealing with wartime shortages and patching clothing, American seamstresses would create spectacular dresses and coats for Doris and an endless procession of ball gowns for Nanaline. The elegant Mrs. Duke did lament that the war had interfered with her constant flow of the latest styles from the Paris designers but she was able to find a few couture expatriates who were sewing out the war in New York City.

Buck always treated little Doris as a small adult. He dressed her in an adult manner. She loved yellow, so many of her silk dresses were various shades of yellow. Her shoes were custom-made with her name imprinted in gold leaf inside of each slipper. The babe had mink, sable, and white ermine coats and wraps. She preferred ermine and would ride her pony with the priceless white fur dragging through the dirt and sweat-stained from the animal. From the day she was born, Doris Duke had her own personal servants. She had a principal nanny, a personal maid, a clothing maid, a laundress, four nurses, endless private tutors, three bodyguards, and a chauffeur for her own Rolls-Royce. Her hundreds of dresses were arranged with their matching shoes and accessories in her room-sized closet. Swatches of the material for each ensemble along with a sketch of the corresponding outfit had been carefully arranged in a large album that weighed almost as much as the child herself. Each day, Doris's maids would carry the tome into the little girl's bedroom and turn each page as she debated what to wear.

"I want to wear yellow," she would say.

"You want to wear yellow all the time," Nanaline would often respond. "Pick something else. Maybe the blue? Or the green?"

Doris's face would turn cloudy and Buck would interject, "Oh for God's sake, let the child wear whatever color she wants. I see nothing wrong with yellow. I like yellow, too. She can wear yellow every day of her life if she wants. It is a lot better than colors that depress me like dark blue or black."

"Are you referring to my clothes?" Nanaline would snap.

"Yeah," Buck would answer. "That is exactly what I am referring to. You used to wear bright clothes for me but lately, you look so dour. I know you are spending enough. I get the bills."

"You would prefer that I dress like that slut Lillian." Nanaline would become irate when her taste was challenged. "Maybe I should dye my hair red and expose my body like a harlot."

"Maybe!" Buck laughed. At this point, Nanaline would usually sweep from the room and retire to her two-story dressing room, which housed sets of the oversized pearls that had become her trademark.

Buck had purchased several museum-quality Gainsborough paintings for his daughter's bedroom because he liked the painter's way of depicting affluent children. When he first saw the Gainsborough *Blue Boy,* he commented that he would like to hire that artist to paint little Doris, and was disappointed to learn that the old master was long dead.

Birthdays were extravaganzas. It was common for Buck to employ an entire circus and order that the big top be erected at Duke Farms where Doris and her cousins (Angier's sons) Angier Biddle Duke and Anthony Drexel Duke would watch the clowns and acrobats and dancing elephants in solitude.

"If Doris tired of a certain act," one servant recalled, "she would tell her daddy to have the performers do something different. She loved the horse and dog acts and would have them repeated until the animals were too tired to continue."

But Doris was a lonely child. The combination of her father's fears of germs or kidnapping and her mother's demand that Doris associate with only the most blue-blooded tykes, limited her friendships to mostly family members and a few of "the right sort" she met at her brief stints at the ultra-exclusive Brearley School in New York City. Still, it is difficult for a child to make friends when her every movement is monitored by a massive bodyguard, looming menacingly in the corner of the classroom. The attempts at private school education had been Nanaline's idea. Buck would have preferred that Doris be taught by the never-ending string of tutors who were brought to the Fifth Avenue mansion, escorted to Doris's second-floor sitting room, and usually fired by young Doris within a few weeks. Nanaline detested the fact that Buck seemed amused when a tiny Doris would dismiss a frustrated tutor, but Buck usually agreed with his daughter.

No matter how busy the old tycoon was, Doris could walk into a meeting where her father was dealing with the most important business people of the time, and he would excuse himself to chat with his young daughter. She often told him about a recently departed tutor.

"You know what that little girl said today," Buck once told his brother Ben. "She said she had dismissed her piano teacher and when I asked why she said, 'He wasn't teaching me anything new. I like having a lot of teachers because I learn something new from each one.'"

Another family story about Buck's ever-availability to his daughter was by his cousin, Laura Delano. "Buck was in a meeting in the library of the Fifth Avenue house with two of the real business titans of the era, my uncle Harry Walters, the owner of the Atlantic Coast Lines, and my other great-great-grandfather, George F. Baker, the president and chairman of the board of the First National Bank of New York (later to become part of the enormous Citibank) when little Doris came to the door. You have to understand that Grandfather Baker was worth about $300 million at the time and was much richer than Buck. Nobody had ever walked out of a meeting with George F. Baker, not ever. When Buck saw the little girl, his eyes lit up, and he brought Doris into the room where she said whatever she had to say in great detail to three of the most powerful men in the world. Doris was more important to Buck Duke than anything or anybody in the world."

She was Daddy's little girl.

# 5

# DADDY'S LITTLE GIRL

The library of Buck's imperial Manhattan mansion overlooked the corner of Fifth Avenue and East Seventy-eighth Street. As a young girl, this was one of the few rooms in that massive pile of stone and marble that Doris liked. She would stand shyly at the towering double French windows that faced Fifth Avenue, her gangly body hidden behind the heavy velvet portieres, and stare at the glittery people promenading on the sidewalk twenty feet below.

She could watch all those interesting people, but she could not touch them. And they, most certainly, would never be permitted to approach the richest child in the world; not unless they first passed careful checks by Buck's detectives and presented the proper social credentials to Nanaline. But few of those who passed such scrutiny were the kinds of people who interested young Doris.

She occasionally was allowed to play with her cousins Tony and Angier Biddle Duke, the young sons of Uncle Ben's boy Angier Buchanan Duke and his extremely socially prominent wife, the former Cordelia Biddle. The Biddles of Philadelphia had been one of the nation's most socially impeccable families for more than two hundred years. Ben's wife, Sarah, was delighted when her handsome playboy son Angier fell in love with the beautiful Cordelia. With this marriage, the Dukes went beyond just merely being rich. They became entrenched in high society. Sarah's delight increased even more when her daughter Mary married Tony Biddle, who was at the time of the wedding only eighteen years of age, a decade younger than Mary.

The Ben Dukes had arrived. They were not as rich as the Buck Dukes, a fact that comforted Nanaline, but Ben did not care as much about money as Buck. For decades, he carried financial responsibility for Trinity College, his father's passion.

Tony and young Angier drifted away from Doris. The little boys were engulfed into the Biddles' energetic boxing, wrestling, and constant sports, lawn parties, and later endless dances. Little Doris was mostly alone.

Nanaline liked it that way. While she approved of the high-society sheen of the little Duke boys, she was afraid of their father, the young, ambitious Angier Buchanan Duke. She would shudder as she watched the two brothers, Buck and Ben, devote thousands of hours to educating Angier in the complex business of the American Tobacco Company and, now Buck's newest project, Duke Power of North Carolina. Buck believed the new industry would be the only stimulus to rebuild the South. He started Duke Power in the hope that he might someday return to North Carolina and his roots.

Buck had even acquired the largest home in Charlotte, complete with a fountain that sprayed so high it was a part of the city's skyline. The ever-competitive Buck wanted a house in his home state that would rival the great Reynolda, the mansion that R. J. Reynolds, the only other potential rival to Buck's title of tobacco czar, had built near Winston-Salem. He had hoped that Nanaline and Doris might someday live in the house but Nanaline would not leave New York City. She considered herself to be the ultimate Southern plantation aristocrat but was not about to live in the South again.

Buck tried stashing an occasional mistress in the Charlotte mansion but his failing health had abated his libido. The idea of mistresses delighted the dour Nanaline who had always believed that sex with men was a revolting and perspiring affair. Nanaline used sex to get what she wanted but she never wanted sex.

However, she was concerned about Buck's health. If he should die, young Angier would be in control of all the Duke assets. He would then run her life. Once Angier Buchanan Duke became the head of the Duke empire, there would be no chance that she would be able to transfer those assets to her darling Walker.

Buck had started taking Angier to Charlotte aboard the *Doris*, the eighty-foot-long luxury private railroad car that slept ten people and had its own chef. The *Doris* was a traveling artery of champagne, gin, and brandy. And there were always women. Young Angier had inherited the Duke sex drive, and quickly filled the voids left by Buck's fading passions. Buck enjoyed the boy and his youthful drives, as if Angier were his own son. "You realize that Angier is the first Duke to ever graduate from college," he would boast again and again. "Ain't that something?" Angier had graduated from Trinity in 1905. "That boy is as sharp as a tack," Buck would continue. "Thank God, he will be around to take care of Doris when I am gone."

Doris would stand at the window of her father's library, pushing her nose into the velvet drapes to smell his cigar smoke. She did not care who would be around to care for her later; she wanted someone to care for her now.

It would be Jenny Renaud who would be her first real friend. Mademoiselle Renaud walked through the great iron double doors of the Duke mansion in 1921. She had been employed to be the nine-year-old Doris's governess. She was French, very French. Jenny Renaud was young and attractive. She had been to night clubs and had traveled to exotic places. She smiled and laughed and would talk to Doris for hours.

Few people had ever been permitted to even speak with Doris. Traveling abroad, Nanaline noticed that servants to English and European royalty were not permitted to speak unless the mistress spoke first. She brought this affectation back to the Duke staff. Servants were allowed to nod but not talk.

"Dammit!" Buck once roared. "If this place were burning

down, you would make the butler wait until you were ready to be told that your ass was about to go up in flames. This is insane."

Still, the servants remained mute and in Doris's case, they had been instructed to answer her shy questions as briefly as possible. Doris had no one. She had no conversations. There was no opportunity for giggling. Laughing out loud was thought to be in bad taste. Jenny Renaud would change that.

Nanaline Duke could not maintain her own standards. While she professed to be revolted by sex, she appeared to be very close to a tall and handsome blond butler—so close in fact that when he once quit and returned to Sweden, the distraught Nanaline threatened to go to Scandinavia herself to make him return. Occasionally, she would drink alone in her room. But she had one habit that completely enraged her husband. She secretly smoked cigarettes. Buck Duke was against his immediate family smoking cigarettes.

In 1917, Buck Duke learned that smoking cigarettes could kill the smoker and probably harm anyone around the smoke. He had always been involved in market research and product testing, and these studies that he had been conducting since the 1880s began to show that his customers were dying younger of heart disease and lung cancer. The death rate was forcing Buck to advertise more to replace customers who were now in their graves.

In the study he received in 1917, he learned that not only were the smokers hacking themselves to death, the persons around them were developing asthma and other lung-related problems. There seemed to be far more problems with cigarettes than cigars or pipe tobacco. The study theorized that there was something in the chemistry of the papers combined with binding chemicals that were added to the tobacco that might be causing the toxic reactions. Realizing that this information could decimate the cigarette business, he ordered the study destroyed and attempted to remove any reference to it from all tobacco company records. But it was Buck himself who would anxiously and repeatedly plead with his loved ones to stay away from cigarettes and cigarette smoke.

There was little love lost between Buck Duke and his rival R. J.

Reynolds (a man who once worked for him before the American Tobacco Trust was ordered dissolved). Duke always believed that it was Reynolds who was behind the government antitrust investigation of the massive Duke empire. Thus when Reynolds proposed to other cigarette manufacturers to investigate ways to make cigarettes more addictive (including using opiates), Duke was repulsed by the idea.

Buck Duke, the biggest cigarette mogul in the world, knew in 1917 that his product was killing his customers. This fact made him physically sick. He decided to slowly liquidate his massive cigarette company holding and look for new investments that would cause less damage and not leave him open to the litigation he was sure loomed in the future of the cigarette industry he created.

"He began to move his assets into Duke Power and the aluminum business. He was an early investor in Texaco," one of Buck's top advisers said years later. "Mr. Duke believed that sooner or later the cigarette buying public would learn about the damages and stop smoking. He predicted there would be massive litigation that could ruin the industry. Some of the other manufacturers were experimenting with opiates and other addictives to make cigarettes more habit forming and harder to quit but Mr. Duke would have no part of that and Ben Duke was adamant that any such action would be morally wrong. Ben and Buck made a decision to get out of the cigarette manufacturing business and started to look for other investments. Buck was sure that cigarette stock would be worthless someday and he wanted Doris's inheritance to be more securely invested."

Meanwhile, Buck knew that Nanaline was smoking.

Needless to say, Buck did not want Nanaline to smoke cigarettes around Doris.

"If I smell cigarette smoke on your breath or on those overpriced clothes I buy you," Buck, who was usually very controlled and polite, would bellow, "I will throw you out of this house. I can, you know. You could be out that door anytime I want!"

Nanaline knew he was right. She understood that Buck had had detectives watching her since the day they were married. If she had secreted funds for her son, he would have been told. If she had ever dabbled in any other forbidden sexual escapade, he would have had all the details. A shiver went through Nanaline's body at that thought.

"I swear," she lied, "I do not smoke."

"I do not care if you smoke yourself to death," Buck thundered. "Just do not do it around my daughter."

(It should be noted here that as soon as she was able, Doris did start smoking herself, although most of the members of the Duke clan never touched a cigarette. Later in her life, Doris, too, would quit smoking.)

At nine, Doris had a different sort of addiction: she loved the piano. Buck moved a Steinway grand piano to Doris's sitting room next to her second-floor bedroom, and when he was home, he insisted that the great double doors to the room be left open so he could hear his daughter practicing her scales. The minute he left the house, Nanaline would order the servants to close the doors, telling friends, "The child has absolutely no talent and her pounding makes my head throb."

Doris would practice for hours behind the closed doors. All the while, Nanaline would lie in her room with a compress on her head and a half-empty sherry bottle on her ornate Louis XVI bedside table.

"The way my wife reacts to Doris's music," Buck would laugh while smoking cigars in the library with Ben, "makes me want to consider learning to play the derned thing myself." Then both men would double over in howls of glee. Ben and Buck were both tiring of the endless efforts of both their wives to entrench themselves in society. Ben detested the endless afternoon musicals, the nights in the opera boxes where society women vied for the biggest emeralds and the most sparkling diamonds, and the endless white-gloved formal dinners. The two old tycoons had reached the point in their lives when they hankered for the old days in North Carolina where the family used to sing around an out-of-tune upright piano or play "Coming Home" on the mouth harp.

"We are so rich," Buck once said, "we cannot afford to enjoy ourselves anymore." It was a flashback to those happy days in an earlier century that came to mind when Buck heard his little daughter stumbling through the old-time music.

Ben Duke still pursued one of his simple pleasures of the past: he loved to sing. This fact was to give Doris her first great adventure.

Nanaline occasionally would bring some bellowing diva or delicate harpist to the ballroom of Buck's mansion and she and Sarah Duke would gather around them the cultured gossips of New York.

Ben would sneak away while the contralto was resting her tonsils and have a drink with his brother in the library. Once he suggested that what he really wanted to do was drive to Harlem to some Negro bar where he could sing the spirited old songs that he used to sing with his family so many years earlier in Durham.

Buck decided to go with him. Little Doris begged, "Oh please, Pa. Please! Please!" And they took her along too.

This was the first time she'd heard black voices harmonizing. Great waves of music swept over the small girl as the Negroes, joined by her uncle Ben, sang hymns like "Go Down Moses" and ditties like "Little Brown Jug" and "Camptown Races." For days afterward, Doris went about the house singing in her delicate little voice, "Yo ho ho, you and me, little brown jug . . . how I love thee."

"Buck," a distressed Nanaline complained. "Where does she learn such things? She sings it all the time. What if someone like Mrs. Whitney or Mrs. Astor should overhear? It would be so humiliating."

Buck would have to stifle a smile.

Doris was given her first real musical encouragement by Mademoiselle Renaud. The first time she heard the little child play, Mademoiselle Renaud sat beside Doris on the piano bench and clapped her hands in encouragement. "*Chérie,*" she bubbled. "You play so well for someone so small. Please, play something else for Jenny." This was the first time in her young life that anyone, other than her father, had ever given Doris Duke a real compliment.

"From that day on," Doris said years later, "I adored the piano. I like to think I have become a pretty fair jazz pianist."

Mademoiselle Renaud spent the morning with Doris teaching her about art and history and music. But the real benefit she brought to the young girl's life was in building Doris Duke's shattered self-esteem.

Doris had been a beautiful baby. Her father had dressed her in the highest of fashion to take his blond-haired and watery-blue-eyed little girl for rides through Central Park in his open car. He beamed as onlookers murmured, "Look at the little princess."

However, there were imperfections even in tiny Doris. She was born with slightly pigeon-toed feet and surgeons were summoned to correct this deformity. After that, she was ordered to wear a heavy orthopedic shoe instead of her dainty satin slippers. Her eyesight was weak, and her mother selected ugly but practical wire-rimmed glasses. Then she started growing until she was taller than any other children her age. Brief stints in New York City private schools often ended abruptly when Doris returned home sobbing.

"They called me a rich giraffe," she wailed to Mademoiselle Renaud. "I am not a giraffe! Promise me that I do not have to go back to that school. I want to stay here with you forever."

"Of course, *chérie,* of course," Jenny Renaud would reassure.

"I cannot understand how Doris grew to be so unattractive," Nanaline would say as she sipped tea from a sterling cup in her private downstairs drawing room. "She will never be a belle. I don't suppose anyone will ever marry someone so gangly."

Mademoiselle Renaud did not agree.

"Why are you still wearing those ugly shoes," she asked Doris. "You no longer need those things. We will take you shopping and buy you some shoes for dancing."

"Dancing? Me!" Doris was amazed. Her mother had told her that she was too tall and clumsy to dance and when she had tried in the privacy of her bedroom, she had tripped over those massive shoes. "Do you really think?"

"I really think." The governess smiled as she hugged the thin child. "There are many ballerinas who are very tall so that they are big enough to be seen from the highest balcony."

"Me . . . a ballerina!" Doris was enthralled. "Oh, Mademoiselle Renaud."

"My child, you can be anything you wish. You are smart and rich and healthy," the governess continued. "You can have the whole world."

"That is what Pa says," Doris answered.

Jenny Renaud taught Doris how to live. When Nanaline said there was nothing to be done with Doris's baby-fine blond hair, Mademoiselle Renaud would take her to a salon for a short bob that made the hair seem thicker and fuller. When Nanaline said that Doris's skin was too pale, Mademoiselle Renaud would say, "Women in Paris would die for flawless white skin like that." She took Doris to Saks Fifth Avenue and B. Altman and Company where the eager girl learned of the treasures and pleasures of shopping. Until that time, everything had been brought to the Duke home where Nanaline, and occasionally Doris, would select what was appropriate. They went to plays and concerts and walked down Fifth Avenue to the Metropolitan Museum of Art. They even started feeding the ducks in the Central Park pond and rowing on the lakes at Duke Farms.

Nanaline was strangely tolerant of Mademoiselle Renaud's effect on her daughter. Buck was delighted. He had been concerned because of rumors that the vivacious French woman had had affairs with both men and women. His detectives had uncovered some ugly stories. There had been a time when he had considered dismissing the woman but Doris became hysterical when he broached the possibility of a new governess to her. Instead, he called Mademoiselle Renaud to the library and warned her that should she ever touch Doris in any unacceptable manner, she would incur his worst wrath. His tone was calm but threatening. He pointed out that there were servants and bodyguards watching Doris at every moment of her life. She could touch the child with affection but not with passion. He made no such request concerning his wife.

Doris's progress on the piano was coming along nicely under the guidance of Jenny Renaud. The pair would practice for several hours each day, and amazingly, Nanaline, who had previously avoided any exposure to her daughter's musical talent, took a new interest.

While the girl and her governess would play at the huge Steinway, Nanaline would silently enter the room and stand behind them. Then she would place her hands on Jenny Renaud's shoulders and the two adults would sway with the music.

"How wonderful," Nanaline would comment.

"Yes," Mademoiselle Renaud would respond.

The Duke bodyguards and detectives whom Buck Duke had employed as servants to watch the events in the various Duke mansions would report that when Doris would retire for a nap, Nanaline would invite Jenny Renaud into her bedroom. Afterward, a maid would be called to put fresh silk sheets on the twin bed. "We never dared to say anything," a retainer said later. "We never even dared to think anything."

Buck Duke didn't care. He was engrossed in building his power plants and teaching young Angier Buchanan Duke how to take over the empire. "It sometimes seems that Angier is more your son than mine," a proud Ben Duke would joke to his brother. The brothers had been disappointed when Angier divorced Cordelia Biddle in 1921 and started filling his own private railroad car with some of the city's highest-quality whores for weekends of champagne and sex at Southampton. These sexual romps saddened Ben but Uncle Buck was more understanding. The boy was just blowing off some youthful steam and the doting uncle was reliving his youth through the antics of his energetic nephew.

Behind the closed doors of the library, Buck would ask Angier, "Tell me about those women of yours. Are they full in the chest? Do they have red hair?"

Angier would tell his uncle things he could never divulge to his own father. He would talk of naked romps in the Atlantic with five women at a time. The proud uncle would encourage his nephew to continue his athletics even though he had injured his arm when he was caught between two railroad cars and never regained the use of it. He had been a superb athlete in every sport from polo to boxing to swimming, and this injury was difficult for him to deal with.

In 1922, Angier and his sister, Mary, donated twenty-five thousand dollars to build a new gymnasium at Trinity College as a memorial to the alumni who died in World War I. Ben Duke, who had been the most generous living member of the family in his support of Trinity College, gave one hundred thousand dollars to Wesleyan College that same year. Buck Duke, who at that time did not share his brother's sense of charitable generosity, gave a mere five thousand dollars to establish a children's ward at the Volunteer Hospital which was named the Doris Duke Ward. He did not take his daughter to see her new memorial because Buck believed that all hospitals were breeding grounds for germs.

"Angier and you are interested in Trinity College," Buck said to Ben, who was encouraging his brother to do more for the North Carolina institution that would later become Duke University. "Let Angier handle that situation later after he takes over the businesses."

Then in the predawn hours of September 3, 1923, something happened that shook the Duke empire, something that Buck and Ben with all their cunning, all their money, and all their power could not control.

Angier Duke along with two male friends and three nubile female escorts was completing a night of wild partying and drinking at a yacht club near Greenwich, Connecticut. Everyone was drinking too much champagne and ready for Angier's favorite pastime, "Diddling at dawn." He invited everyone to make use of the privacy of the *Althea*, his seventy-six-foot yacht, which was anchored in the deep water outside the breakwater that surrounded the docks at the club. The young men, while tipsy, were all fine athletes and in a hurry for the sexual games that were the usual morning event on the *Althea*. They could have waited for the club tender to deliver them to the yacht but someone noticed a rowboat bobbing at the end of the dock.

"I bet I can row better with one good arm than you chaps can with two," Angier boasted. The men ran to the end of the dock with the laughing ladies in tow and started helping the women into the tiny dinghy. As Angier bowed to one of the ladies, his foot slipped from the edge of the rowboat, which tipped over and plunged all six people into the water. One by one the laughing young men and their jazz girls popped to the surface and started splashing each other. Then Angier's date noticed that there were only five heads above the water. At first they thought this was a prank. Angier was an excellent swimmer. He was most likely hiding under the dock in an effort to frighten them. They called his name. He did not answer.

While the wet women ran screaming to the empty clubhouse, Angier Buchanan Duke's two buddies dove into the black water time after time groping in the darkness for their friend. The professional sailors and captains as well as the owners of the other opulent yachts anchored at the club awoke and joined the search. A Duke . . . an invincible Duke . . . had disappeared into the Atlantic Ocean.

Seven hours later, the lifeless body of Angier Buchanan Duke was found wedged under a floating raft. He had drowned at the age of thirty-nine. Investigators believed that he hit his head on the side of the dinghy as it capsized and was knocked unconscious.

No one knows exactly who told Ben that his son and heir was dead. They do know that Ben was at his mansion at 1009 Fifth Avenue, a few blocks away from Buck's marble palace, when he heard the news of the drowning.

"Ben Duke became an old man that day," one close friend said. "His health was never good and as he sat in his drawing room crying, you could watch the man die inside himself."

Sarah Duke suffered a complete nervous breakdown when she heard the news and lay in an upstairs bedroom where doctors had sedated her.

Doris Duke was alone with Mademoiselle Renaud and the servants when she learned of the drowning. The young girl and her governess sat by the piano in silence. It was inconceivable to Doris that something like this could happen. She wondered how her father and Uncle Ben could have ever allowed anything this awful to occur. Doris had begun the habit of playing the piano late into the night. On this night she and her governess would stay in the darkened sitting room and play until nearly dawn.

Buck and Nanaline were in Europe when the cable arrived.

It was mixed with the dozens of business cables he received every hour. When he read of the fate of his beloved nephew, Buck wept.

"I'm so sorry," Nanaline Duke told her distraught husband. "This is just terrible. Terrible!" Her voice was strangely calm. "It must be God's will."

Buck glared at her.

"The funeral is going to be in Durham," Buck whispered. "I don't want Doris to go. There will be photographers. I do not want the funeral to become a circus. I don't know what to say to Ben. He is not strong, you know."

"I know," Nanaline answered.

"We had planned everything so well," Buck continued. "Angier . . . he . . . Angier knew what to do when Ben and I were gone. He was the one who would take care of Doris. I am so old and she is still a little girl." He started to cry again. "Who will take care of my Doris now when I am gone?"

"Why, Buck," Nanaline said with not a trace of warmth or emotion, "I will, of course. Walker and I will."

# 6

# MINE . . . ALL MINE!

Buck Duke's Fifth Avenue mansion had become a mausoleum. While dozens of men came and went from the library, there were no longer peals of men's laughter and booming voices coming from behind the closed double doors. Buck Duke was reorganizing his life.

He had summoned his attorneys, his bankers, and his trusted advisers from every corner of his worldwide empire and one by one they climbed the granite steps to the mansion and were silently ushered into the great hall by hushed servants. There they would sit on Nanaline's oversized Chesterfield couches, which were covered in a green print to match perfectly the green and white marble fireplace, where they would wait to be called into the library.

Those who had been in the enormous room during happier times missed the smell of the fresh flowers that had always been brought from the greenhouses at Duke Farms to the cold stone house on Fifth Avenue. Nanaline had ordered several of the footmen to situate the usual arrangements around the room, but when Buck saw the various bouquets of roses, carnations, and orchids he silently went to each crystal vase, lifted it in the air, and crashed it into sparkling pieces on the gleaming marble floor. Flowers reminded him of funerals: his nephew's funeral in particular.

With the death of Angier, Buck faced his own mortality. He watched as his brother Ben became a frail old man overnight. His leg, which had always been a problem, was hurting so much that Buck Duke had become a cripple. Buck faced the fact that he was going to die. And he knew that Doris, not yet a teenager, was going to be alone.

Buck was the ultimate pragmatist. He most assuredly understood that Nanaline cared little for Doris and would do everything she could to steal the girl's assets to benefit Walker. "That useless piece of work," Buck muttered.

Buck Duke began putting his affairs in order. Not only did he meet with his platoons of advisers at the New York City mansion, he arranged for representatives of Trinity College to come to Duke Farms for lengthy discussions away from the curious scrutiny of Nanaline and her allies. Buck had been very impressed at the reading of Angier Buchanan Duke's will when he learned that his nephew had left two hundred and fifty thousand dollars to Trinity College.

Trinity College had been one of the causes that united the Duke family. Washington Duke had financed the institution's move to Durham and Ben Duke had poured much of his personal fortune into the school. Now the will of young Angier Duke was adding still more Duke dollars to the growing college. Buck Duke's support of Trinity College, in spite of his massive fortune, had been meager when compared to his father's, his brother's, and now, his nephew's. He decided to change that fact.

On December 8, 1924, he established an endowment for Trinity College in the staggering amount of $40 million, making the tiny North Carolina institution one of the richest schools in the nation. Six million dollars was set aside to construct new buildings on the campus. Buck, a man who had never attended college, became the school's creative and financial planner. He wanted to pattern it, architecturally, after the imposing stone buildings of Oxford University in England.

According to records of the announcement of the endowment, Buck was his usual blunt and outspoken self when he explained his reasons for the gift.

"I don't believe that a college education does a man much good in business except for the personal satisfaction it gives him," Buck said. "But when you have a great community growing like we do here in North Carolina, you have got to have five kinds of leaders whose minds are trained. The first is preachers. The second is teachers. The third is lawyers. The fourth is chemists and engineers. And the fifth is doctors."

(It should be noted here that Buck Duke did not insist that Trinity College change its name to Duke University after the endowment. He did suggest, however, that the name change would be a way to honor his father, Washington Duke, and officials of the now wealthy school quickly enacted the change.)

The press and public were so engrossed in the endowment that almost nobody noticed the creation of a second trust, the Doris Duke Trust, of an estimated $100 million that would be given to his daughter in three installments: at age twenty-one, age twenty-five, and age thirty.

Nanaline Duke noticed. And she did not approve. To Nanaline, the purpose of the Duke fortune should have been to endow and restore the fortunes of the proud Holts of Georgia instead of Duke University and Doris. She had secretly rejoiced when Angier was killed and hoped that Buck would finally be forced to accept his stepson, Walker Inman, as the male heir to the "dirt farmer Duke" money. Buck had no intention of doing anything of the kind.

In spite of Nanaline's protestations, Buck had ordered Walker to leave the house and never return. The young man had staggered into the mansion in a drunken and profane state far too many times. He had thrown up on the servants once too often.

The trusts made it evident that Walker would never head the Duke empire and that the Duke empire would never become the Inman empire. While Nanaline was already very rich in her own right and would inherit many millions more at the death of Buck, she was furious that she could leave Walker only a paltry $30 million or so, while Doris was going to be the richest little girl in the world.

Buck tolerated his wife, who feasted on being Mrs. James Buchanan Duke. She had battled her way into New York's high society and enjoyed telling people that Buck Duke married her to gain social position. This comment would make Buck snap, "I do not care a whit about social position unless it helps Doris or business and as for my wife's position in life, I would prefer that she position herself occasionally in bed with me." Buck still carried that Duke passion for the physical joys of the opposite sex and had started to think occasionally about his first wife, Lillian. About the only thing that Buck and Nanaline agreed upon concerning Lillian was that she was indeed a slut. But while Nanaline looked at her predecessor with disgust, Buck considered the possibility that a more affectionate female presence in his life might improve his health and would most certainly enliven his mood.

This worried Nanaline, who was considering the possibility that she could become the second Mrs. Duke instead of *the* Mrs. Duke. It did not help when the poverty-stricken Lillian decided to file her famous and highly publicized lawsuit against Buck and Nanaline, a suit that alleged that Nanaline's wedding was invalid because Buck and Lillian had not completed divorce proceedings at the time of the second marriage. The publicity was unending but the charges were later found to be without grounds.

At this time, Nanaline took an interest in her husband's health. He was a massive eater, and she gave orders to cut his elaborate meals to what amounted to prunes. He was so occupied with expanding his power empire and his new investments in aluminum and oil that he did not argue at this. He lost weight and strength. Suddenly his diet, carefully overseen by his wife, seemed to be starving the large man into a skeleton. More than one member of the family wondered whether he was being poisoned. Buck did not seem to care.

The doctors proclaimed him to be anemic. (Decades later Doris had samples of her father's blood analyzed to learn the real cause of death, but she refused ever to comment on what she learned.)

Early in the fall of 1925, Buck Duke realized that he was seriously ill. He was constantly light-headed and dizzy but worse were the severe stomach pains that forced the tough man to double over in pain. Nanaline had insisted that she and Buck should go to Rough Point, overlooking the Atlantic Ocean at Newport. There she would attend to the health of her husband in the isolation that consumed the mansions of Newport when the summer season ends. But Buck wanted to talk to Ben. He ordered that his private train take him back to Manhattan where he immediately called his brother into a long and secret conference.

While Ben Duke never divulged the topics of this discussion, family members believed that Buck gave his brother the numbers of the English and Swiss accounts where he had stored tons of gold and other assets that had been hidden from the ever-increasing demands of the new Internal Revenue System. Certainly, Buck would not trust his wife to follow his wishes that this secret fortune be the sole property of his daughter. Nanaline, who knew about the gold, was furious, and as Buck deteriorated, she maintained a twenty-four-hour vigil at his bedside should he mumble the precious numbers and codes in his delirium.

Blood transfusions seemed to be working, but after a few more helpings of Nanaline's very special diet, Buck would become sicker still. The doctors were frantic and mystified as to why Buck would improve dramatically after a transfusion, only to regress in a matter of hours or, at the most, days.

In October, the weather turned cold and the outside air was brisk and piercing. It was then that the doctors realized that Buck Duke had developed pneumonia. Buck had very few moments of lucidity, but those moments were devoted to making arrangements for Doris, who was barely in her teens and would soon be alone. Nanaline had proclaimed that her husband was too weak to endure any visits and Doris paced in the second-floor marble hall outside the double doors of her father's bedroom. Finally, when her mother retreated to her bathroom, Doris slipped into the room where she saw her father pale and wheezing in the huge mahogany Victorian bed.

She would later recall what he said. As she placed her hand

over his large clenched fist, the dying empire builder managed to smile at his daughter and say, "Be careful who you trust. You cannot always trust the people who say they love you." He relapsed into a fitful sleep. Doris felt the eyes of her mother boring into her back. She turned and the mother and daughter glared at each other in silence. Nanaline opened the door and stepped aside, indicating that Doris should leave.

Only when mother and daughter were in the outer hall did Nanaline comment, not to Doris but to a butler, "There will be no further visitors. No one!" She walked back into her husband's room and Doris got one last glimpse of her father when he still had some spark of life in his body.

Nanaline called the butler into the room while Doris waited outside. "I have decided that Mr. Duke needs fresh air and I want you to open all the windows and turn off the heat." The butler looked startled. "You did hear me? Now do it! In the South we believe that a sick man needs fresh air."

She ordered that the maid bring her a pile of sable coats, which Nanaline wrapped around herself as her husband lay in the bed with the heavy covers thrown to the floor and his body warmed only by a nightshirt. As snow and near-zero cold swirled through the huge open windows, Nanaline waited.

Buck Duke lapsed into his final coma. As an early winter gale blew from the Atlantic Ocean and turned the streets of Manhattan into wind tunnels, snow gathered on the carvings of the bedroom's ornate furniture. By six o'clock on the evening of October 10, 1925, the last breath of air left the clogged lungs of Buck Duke. Nanaline Duke came out of the room, looked at her twelve-year-old daughter, and commented emotionlessly, "Your father is dead." Then she turned to the butler and said, "Close the windows and turn on the heat."

The servants later told Ben Duke that Doris showed no emotion. It was as if she were refusing to react in any way to what her mother said. Nanaline gestured to her maids to follow her into the huge two-story dressing room where she began selecting the proper black widow's dresses for the occasion. Weeks earlier, she had summoned her dressmakers to prepare the proper wardrobe.

Buck Duke's body was removed to the large drawing room (Doris had wanted the library but Nanaline insisted on the larger room so she could entertain more mourners at the same time) where a ten-foot-high spray of orchids, a tribute from Ben, engulfed the open casket. Doris spent hours looking at the beautiful orchids and the corpse of her father. She later told friends that this last memory of her father surrounded by the flowers is what inspired her to become a pioneer in the American orchid industry. Today the name Duke is attached to hundreds of new orchids that Doris discovered in the greenhouses of Duke Farms. The American Orchid Society credits Doris Duke with being the major force behind the American orchid industry.

On October 13, the body was loaded aboard the *Doris* and taken to Durham for burial. It was and still remains the largest and most spectacular funeral in the history of the city. The schools were closed. The entire population of the city lined the streets. The procession to the grave site numbered in the thousands. Some fourteen hundred students of Duke University formed the honor guard and the football team acted as pallbearers. The body was put to rest in the family crypt in Maplewood Cemetery next to Brodie and Washington Duke. The family did not allocate any space in the mausoleum for Mrs. James Buchanan Duke. Nanaline would, decades later, be buried elsewhere.

Two weeks later, the will was read. The entire estate was left to Doris with Nanaline receiving a lifetime interest in the houses in New York, Newport, and North Carolina. She was also given one hundred thousand dollars yearly for her expenses. Nanaline was furious.

It was true that she was rich in her own right but she had been outsmarted by a series of iron-clad trusts that had been carefully worded so that even if young Doris should succumb to an untimely death, Doris's estate could not be bequeathed to her mother.

With the death of Buck Duke came a massive change in the personality of his beloved daughter, Doris. Not quite a teenager, she seemed to have lost her childhood and transformed herself from a pampered little girl into a serious small adult. She walked silently through the hushed rooms of the Fifth Avenue mansion wearing recently dyed black dresses that seemed to hang lifelessly on her already tall body.

"I knew then what it was to be unhappy," Doris said years later. "My mother and I never spoke. She was busy being a socialite and that did not interest me. I hated the Fifth Avenue house because that is where Daddy died. And my mother loved that place, which also made me hate it." The only person who seemed to brighten Doris's life was her governess, Jenny Renaud, but not even the exuberance of this Frenchwoman could restore a carefree young girl attitude.

Nanaline wanted to exert some authority over Doris but that was difficult as she suddenly found herself financially dependent on the generosity of a thirteen-year-old girl. The mother could give orders, but little Doris could retaliate by opposing an expenditure for an expensive social entertainment coveted by Nanaline.

This was the beginning of the mother-daughter war that would last until Nanaline's death decades later.

Doris Duke might have been a sheltered thirteen-year-old but she had listened well over the years when her father talked of business and the need to be aggressive. When her mother saw a potential financial windfall in a vagary of the will that seemed to allow for the sale of assets of the estate, Nanaline decided to sell Duke Farms, which she considered a white elephant. Doris ordered her attorneys to sue. The houses and the railroad car were auctioned; Doris bought them. She agreed to honor her mother's desire to stay in the houses but she would not be her mother's keeper. The series of suits continued until Doris finally gained complete ownership of Duke Farms, which she immediately began to restore. Her mother always detested Duke Farms and repeatedly said, "I will not go there because I am no picnic girl." This only made Doris cherish the farm even more.

Doris moved to Duke Farms where she dined on one-hundred-thousand-dollar gold place settings and bathed in marble fountains watered through solid gold spigots. She was fifteen years old.

For some time following the death of Buck Duke, the servants continued the habit of censoring Doris's mail. One day, Doris was walking down the grand staircase of the Fifth Avenue mansion when she noticed a footman dragging two bags of mail across the marble floor.

"What is that?" Doris asked.

"Mail, ma'am," the embarrassed footman stammered, looking at the ground.

"Whose mail?" Doris demanded.

"Yours, ma'am," the miserable young man said.

Doris looked surprised. "Do I often get that much mail?"

"Yes, ma'am, you do," the servant answered. "But it is not the kind of mail that you would be interested in reading. The guards look at the mail and send you the letters that are important."

"I want to see them all." Her voice was angry.

"Your father forbid . . ." The footman was interrupted as Nanaline Duke entered the great hall from the drawing room where she had overheard the conversation.

"Perhaps Doris should see the kind of people who are interested in her," Nanaline said in a cold monotone. "Let her have her mail."

The footman moved the heavy bags to one of the couches, and an excited Doris sat cross-legged on the floor as the hundreds of letters tumbled from the open bags.

"Imagine," she smiled, "all these people want to write to me." She smiled as she tore open the first letter. The smile faded as she read it. The letter contained a threat to kill her if she did not send the writer a thousand dollars. She gasped and opened another envelope in hopes of more desirable contents. That letter outlined explicit sexual acts that the writer wanted to force upon teenage Doris. As she ripped apart more envelopes there were more pleas for money, demands for money, and threats.

Her hands were shaking and her pale skin was even whiter but she kept reading. In the next hours, she learned everything that her father had fought to keep from her. She realized she was famous and envied and hated merely because she was so very rich. She understood that she was always in danger. From that day until the end of her life, she had a mania for privacy and security. She placed walls of stone and power between herself and the cruelties of the outside world. Slowly she would become a prisoner of her own isolation.

# 7
# THE REBELLION YEARS

People loved to gossip about Doris Duke. This fascination with her life crossed all lines of society. Her every move was scrutinized. Whom she met. What she wore. What she spent. Where she went. These were all topics of interest in newspapers and magazines throughout the world.

It should be explained that as a teenager, Doris had been fictionalized into one of the most famous people in the world. It was as if she were a combination of today's Madonna and Princess Di. Millions of words were written about her.

"Most of it was pure crap," she explained in a breathy whisper some decades later at Maxim's in Paris. "I would dance with a young man and reporters would speculate on marriage. I might buy a scarf and the fashion press would blow it into some kind of new fad.

"The newspapers had me sleeping with everyone," she laughed. "Just the opposite was true. I had so many people watching me and so many bodyguards that it would have taken quite an exhibitionistic young man to make love to me with such a large audience."

The whole world watched the shy Miss Duke.

"If anything," she lamented, "I was less experienced in sex than most teenage girls my age. If I saw a boy who I found attractive, there would be a committee ranging from my mother to the servants to the lawyers who would have opinions. Nice boys were too shy so all I got were pushy social types and South Americans who were in love with my money."

Like most teenage girls, Doris had crushes. She would fantasize over a young man she found attractive without ever letting him know of her admiration.

"There was this one boy who worked at Duke Farms," she recalled. "I was maybe fifteen, and I was in love with this farm boy. He would work on the lawn or prune the shrubs near the house and I would pray for a hot day so that he would take off his shirt. He was a couple years older and had a wonderful tanned body. I like muscles and a good tan in a man. I used to tell the farm manager that the gardens around the house needed some work, hoping that this boy would be sent to the house. If they did not send him at first, I would keep calling the groundskeepers to send more help until he finally came. Then I was too shy to go outside and talk to him but I would stay in the house and run from window to window with binoculars. I would try to hide behind the curtains so no one would see. Once a footman told this boy that it was improper for him to take off his shirt near the house because 'Miss Duke might see you.' I was listening at the window and I wanted to kill that footman. I fired him as soon as I could find another reason."

Her admiration of the young man continued.

"I was so desperate to see him that I would take one of the cars and drive around the estate looking for him but pretending to learn to drive. I had no idea how to operate the big Peerless and terrified everyone by running off the road and ruining the lawns. When the chauffeurs saw me getting into that car—I usually drove the same one because I did not really want to damage another vehicle—they would go to the phone and warn everyone on the farm that I was driving again. There are miles of roads on the farm and I would race in a cloud of dust until I saw him and then I would usually just become self-conscious and speed away."

It is easy to picture that handsome young man looking at the mistress of the estate in that huge gleaming car as she sped away accompanied by a chorus of grinding gears.

"I never even knew his name," she said. "I was too shy to ask because I thought someone would realized how I felt about him. I am sure that he didn't know." She sighed. "It was probably right that I didn't. The world would have never permitted Doris Duke to date a farm laborer. It would have all been ruined. I would rather remember it as a young girl's fantasy. It is better as a beautiful memory."

So as the newspapers salivated over Doris Duke's romantic life, in reality she was just a shy and sheltered girl peeking at a young boy from behind the silk curtains of her daddy's mansion.

"He was a summer worker and when we went back to New York, I was anxious all winter to see him the following spring. I even ordered that the summer crew be hired a few weeks earlier because I could not wait to look at him. Only he didn't come back. I suppose he got a job someplace else but later in the year I asked the head groundskeeper about the tall boy with brown hair and blue eyes and he said that the boy had wanted to work at Duke Farms that summer but he was in college and couldn't start until the end of May and Miss Duke had ordered that the farm be prepared for the summer season earlier this year so he had to hire someone else."

Doris Duke paused in this story, a story she had repeated many times in her life. "This was the first of many times that I have used my power to try to make things happen for me," she continued, "and everything gets all fucked up. If I had been a normal girl instead of the rich Doris Duke, I might have known this boy, even dated him. But I was never given the luxury of normalcy."

The teenage years of Doris Duke were occupied with her love of the piano, her passion for dancing (she studied everything from tapping to clogging), and dreaming about boys and romance. If she were not worth between $100 and $300 million, she would have seemed to be a typical tall and blond young girl.

By the time she blossomed into adolescence, Doris and Nanaline had reached a touchy détente. Nanaline needed her daughter's bankroll to keep all those expensive houses functioning. So she tried to arrange the "right" kind of social evenings to introduce Doris to all the proper things. For the most part, these parties were disasters as Doris, like her father and her uncle Ben, would much rather sneak away to Harlem bars to sing and listen to spirited Negro-inspired music.

Nanaline went through periods when she tried to exert some form of parental authority over Doris. In a moment of great courage, she packed a miserable Doris off to Fermata, a finishing school in South Carolina where all the girls from the best of the surviving Southern aristocracy were taught to perpetuate a way of life that had ceased to exist during the War of Northern Aggression. Doris's bodyguards were disguised as private detectives.

"The school was just silly," Doris said. "Of course, I detested it. A few of us would climb out a window, walk along the roof, and slide down a rope just to escape. There was no real place to go but it really upset my bodyguards."

Fermata was supposed to instill good Southern values into well-bred belles of the Old Guard. Nanaline hoped that by being forced to make her own bed, Doris would suddenly be transformed into a sweet little ole mistress of the plantation. Doris was revolted by Fermata and many of the other girls, who were there at a great financial sacrifice to their families, whose fortunes had never recovered to match their Southern social positions, resented Doris's millions. These final belles of the Old South detested Doris Duke because she was from the North. They were appalled by the fact that her father and grandfather were Republicans. Doris Duke liked black people and black music and believed that Negroes should be equal to whites. The only thing that Doris Duke had in common with the plantation South was a mother who longed for the days when her ancestors owned other people and ruled with the power of red clay kings.

Doris begged to leave the South and come home. Nanaline refused to respond to her daughter's letters. For the two years that Doris was incarcerated at Fermata, Nanaline visited only once—on business.

On June 5, 1925, Nanaline picked Doris up at Fermata to take her to the dedication of the cornerstone of Duke University. Nanaline was a trustee of the new university and realized that it would be good politics to make sure that her daughter, the only daughter of the benefactor, were present at this moment that would be recorded forever in the history of education.

"Walker was nicer to me than my mother," Doris said. "He would come to the school and charm all my classmates and take me out to a speakeasy and we would drink champagne. We were friends. In a way we were both victims of Nanaline. She spoiled and ruined him with too much love and made me resent her because she never loved me at all."

Doris rather liked her wastrel half-brother Walker, who had been banished to his beautiful plantation near Charleston, South Carolina. He drank and smoked and flew his own plane. Walker was a bad boy and Doris would always have an appreciation for bad boys. She was later equally fond of his unruly son, Walker Inman II.

Doris was allowed to leave the school in December of 1929.

"Mother's private fortune had been damaged by the stock market crash," Doris recalled. "She had hoped to become rich enough so that she would never need my money to keep Walker solvent, so she had become more speculative in her investments, but after the crash, she knew that would never happen. It was to her advantage to keep her daughter happy so she permitted me to come back to New York."

A little more than a decade later when Fermata burned to the ground, Doris threw a party to celebrate the event. To Doris the ashes of Fermata represented the ashes of the segregationist South. The snobbish school was a last refuge of the plantation aristocracy. She had managed to escape the horrors of Southern tradition and arrogance because of her mother's new financial problems that overshadowed the proper racist education of her daughter.

The stock market crash had very little effect on Doris Duke's money, which was protected by trusts and invested in the most secure of stocks and property by her brilliant father. Because so many of her social set had speculated themselves into instant poverty, Doris was even richer than everyone else. She was even more alone in her wealth.

Doris Duke despised being asked for money but she could be very generous. The economic conditions that forced some of her previously pampered friends into poverty shocked Doris. Fathers of her friends jumped to their deaths from the high-rise windows of their walnut-paneled offices. Auctioneers sold off the personal possessions of former millionaires. Debutantes went to secretarial schools. Some of the most social and desirable young men married girls who would never have attracted their attention except for the fact that their fathers still had some money. When Doris had a party, she was saddened to see some of her friends secretly slip claws of lobster and bits of cake into their purses. She understood that this food might feed the friend and his or her family for several days. She would arrange for the best caviar and champagne to be available in abundance at her many small parties during those terrible years following the Crash. And she made it as easy as possible for her friends to take the food.

Very few people realized what she was doing. The press was enraged at these parties. They dubbed her spoiled and extravagant, a person who flaunted her wealth at a time when others were suffering so much.

It would surprise people to learn that Doris could be so very generous. For decades, she secretly made sure that some of her no-longer-affluent friends always had a "suitable" roof over their heads and a stipend of money so that they could live with some dignity. She was quick to open her checkbook for the downtrodden. Doris felt great sympathy for anyone in need, especially anyone who did not ask for help. She was revolted by the number of people in her social set who were "willing to let her in" on some deal that "will make us both more millions." She would offend one member of a family by saying, "I believe that you have mistaken me for a bank" while at the same time she was quietly paying for an apartment for another member of the same family.

"Doris liked to be generous in secrecy," one relative commented. "Gratitude made her uncomfortable. A very private 'thank you' was about all she could tolerate. A public gushing of thanks would actually irritate Doris. There was a reason for that. When other people learned that she might be helping someone, she was deluged by all manner of people who had access to her and wanted money."

An example of her mania for anonymity came as a result of her lifetime passion for Negro gospel music. She thrived on the passionate singing and moving of Negro choirs. When she learned that many of the black churches of the South did not have organs to accompany these choirs, she started donating organs to first dozens and, in the end, probably thousands of small Negro churches across the nation. Only a few people ever knew that these organs, which often cost more than the shacks that served as houses of worship, came from the famous Doris Duke. Since the identity of the donor was kept so secret, there were even several prominent men of the South who hinted that they were responsible for these gifts. When Doris learned that one furniture tycoon from North Carolina had left the impression with a reporter from Raleigh that he was the anonymous donor, she laughed and sent her housekeepers to check every piece of furniture in each house to see if she owned any of the expensive reproduction furniture. When a bed and several highboys were discovered, she arranged a bonfire.

While the stock market crash did not alter the quality of Doris Duke's privileged life, it vastly changed the environment. She realized that she had been lucky because her father had the foresight to protect her fortune. Still a very young girl in 1929, Doris made a decision to watch every dime for the rest of her life.

She considered her life to be a prison. Doris Duke was a pragmatic woman; she knew that hundreds of thousands of people, maybe millions, disliked her because she was rich and they were poor. She understood all too well that even those closest to her, her mother and many of her friends, were there because she was "the richest girl in the world." She knew that she could not escape the prison her money had created, and after seeing the misery that instant poverty had brought to so many of her friends, she had no real desire to be poor.

But she did want to be free.

# 8

# HUSBAND NUMBER ONE

If anyone taught Doris not to trust anyone, that person was the handsome Jimmy Cromwell, her first husband.

Doris never really had a single opportunity to meet a nice guy. Young men of her social circle who had any trace of ethics or honesty did not attempt to romance the tall and somewhat gangly Miss Duke because they did not want to be thought of as fortune hunters. This left only the unabashed fortune hunters to pursue Doris.

Nanaline was panicked that Doris, who very early in her life made it passionately evident that she had inherited the Duke sex drive instead of the Holt restraint, would run away with one of "those greasy South Americans who are always asking her to dance." Needless to say, Nanaline had other plans for Doris's money. She had amassed a substantial fortune herself when Buck died and had earmarked that money for her sulky son, Walker. But Nanaline wanted Doris's fortune to be reunited with her own for the benefit of her family, whom she considered far more deserving and genteel than the Dukes. But Doris was not the only victim of the smothering domination of Nanaline Holt Inman Duke. Walker's first wife, Helene Clarke, had threatened to sue

Nanaline for alienation of affection after Nanaline wrote a check for seventy-five thousand dollars (she later agreed to pay the bride one hundred and fifty thousand dollars annually for the rest of her life if she would agree not to remarry) to get rid of the socially disadvantaged former Kokomo showgirl. Nanaline considered divorce to be a social blemish. This was nothing more than hush money paid to silence Helene and quell the newspapers' demands for Duke gossip, which Nanaline thought would damage her newfound position in highest society.

As the granddaughter of a slave owner, Nanaline did not admire the Duke family sense of democracy when it came to Negroes or any others she considered lower classes. Doris liked Negroes and Nanaline lived in constant fear that she might love a few of them. Thus when Doris would order her Rolls-Royce brought around to the great front door of the New York mansion at the start of an excursion into the world of Harlem jazz and blues and cheap booze, at least one carload of detectives would follow.

Nanaline did not want Doris to marry. Unless she wed someone even richer.

"There is little chance of you finding someone with more money," Nanaline told Doris in one family spat. "You are already richer than almost everyone. While there are some eligible young men with real wealth, why would they look at you? You are not the most attractive girl, you know. It is your cash that so many men find so alluring."

Except for Jimmy Cromwell. At first, Nanaline Duke found much in common between the handsome and popular Jimmy Cromwell and her precious son and heir, Walker Inman. Cromwell was the stepson of the fabulously wealthy stock market manipulator Edward Stotesbury. The Dukes had come to know the lavish-spending Stotesburys through architect Horace Trumbauer, who had designed both the Duke château on Fifth Avenue and the gigantic Stotesbury estate, Whitemarsh Hall, near Philadelphia. Both young men were overindulged spoiled brats but Jimmy was good-looking with classic Nordic features, a great body, perfect tan, and the ability to make charming small talk. Walker was a bore who drank too much.

Nanaline grew to dislike Jimmy. But he was so very rich that, if it came time for divorce, he could not possibly need any of the Duke money, eliminating the possibility of a big settlement with the accompanying bad publicity. At least, that is what Nanaline Duke thought.

Doris was sixteen in 1929 when she met the eternally tanned Jimmy Cromwell in Bar Harbor (or "BaaaHaaba" as Mrs. Stotesbury affected) where the Stotesburys had a summer house. He was supposedly distantly related to Oliver Cromwell, the religious tyrant, but had better manners. Before she married the very rich financial genius Ned Stotesbury, Eva Cromwell had been married to Oliver Cromwell (the Washington financier, not the English zealot), and had been a great social success in the nation's capital. She had three children: Louise, a dark-haired beauty who, during World War I, became the mistress of General Pershing in Paris, and later married General Douglas MacArthur (whom she divorced when she realized that his penis was too small to adequately satisfy her needs); a son unfortunately named Oliver; and Jimmy. When the elder Oliver died of a stroke in 1909, Eva went on the prowl for an even richer husband and landed Stotesbury in 1912. President Taft attended the wedding and the Stotesburys and little Jimmy Cromwell moved to Philadelphia.

"She called her husband Kickapoo," Doris would laugh. "She went from being in bed with Oliver Cromwell to hopping in the sack with Kickapoo Stotesbury. Quite an impressive accomplishment."

From the fifty-room "BaaaHaaba" Georgian cottage, Wingwood, Eva Stotesbury sent "mama's boy" Jimmy to seduce the rich and relatively virginal Doris Duke.

"She was a Frigidaire," the not-too-gallant Jimmy told friends following a unfulfilling evening of groping and thrashing around with the young girl who was sixteen years his junior.

"I thought there must be more to this sex business than I was getting from Jimmy," Doris later confided. "I thought because he had been married that he must know what he was doing. God, was I wrong." But this was a far more worldly Doris Duke making these comments years (and many affairs) later. The devastated little girl who failed to satisfy the Arrow Shirt–imaged darling of American high society was crushed. She just knew it was she who failed. She was too tall. She had an ironing board body and the long pointed chin of a Halloween witch. Or so she thought as she cried alone into her silken sheets.

Jimmy had been previously married to automobile heiress Delphine Dodge. The couple had spent their honeymoon cruising the world on the two-hundred-and-fifty-foot Dodge yacht, *The Delphine*. Jimmy, in his only successful business deal, arranged for the sales of Dodge Motorcar Co. (following the death of Horace Dodge) for $146 million. In 1922, Jimmy and Delphine's daughter, Christine, was born. Delphine had her father's interest in motors and became a champion speed boat racer, winning the President's Cup in 1927. Meanwhile, the newlyweds struggled unsuccessfully to live on a two-hundred-thousand-dollar annual allowance that was never enough. Then Jimmy decided to turn thirty-six hundred acres of swamps between Palm Beach and Miami into "Floranado," the new wintering oasis for the super-rich. He lost $6 million of his wife's and their friends' cash. This kind of business put a strain on the new marriage.

After losing money in a few more of his self-aggrandizing schemes, Delphine dumped Jimmy in 1928. He went to his mother's Palm Beach estate, the forty-room El Mirasol (with an impressive forty-car garage), and busied himself on reviving his tan and plotting the taking of Doris Duke. Meanwhile, Delphine married another good-looking man but that union ended abruptly when she found her new husband in a berth aboard *The Delphine* with one of the handsomest sailors in the crew.

His mother adored and spoiled Jimmy. He was the reigning Adonis of high society. His stepfather was worth $100 million or more. He had homes in Florida and "BaaaHaaba" and the family one-hundred-and-fifty-room palace in Philadelphia (supposedly larger than Biltmore in North Carolina).

Jimmy Cromwell, international pretty boy and witty conversationalist, could take his time wooing the gawky Miss Duke and her estimated $100 million. And who knew? Maybe a better catch would come along! Certainly not even English and European royalty had the kind of money that Doris Duke possessed, steadily gathering interest in ultra-secure trust accounts, but the nobility were rebuilding their fortunes after World War I. The Rothschilds were billionaires again and there were some titled Rothschild women in Belgium and Paris. True, they were Jewish, but their women were more attractive than Doris. It seemed that there was time for pretty Jimmy to look further.

Only there wasn't.

In late October of 1929, the stock market collapsed and with it much of the fortune of banker/industrialist/broker Ned Stotesbury. The foundation of the Stotesbury fortune vanished.

All that remained were the houses, the cars, the servants, and the outer trappings of the rich and decadent. And all that was mortgaged. The Stotesburys were busted but no one would know how their fortunes had diminished for several years.

Doris, on the other hand, was still rich.

And Jimmy Cromwell's interest in Doris Duke grew to instant love.

Eva Stotesbury thought the match was made if not in heaven then on Wall Street and pushed the courtship into overdrive. Still, the wily Nanaline Duke was aware that the Stotesburys might have been damaged by the Crash and was losing any enthusiasm for Jimmy as a possible choice for son-in-law.

Nanaline's growing distaste for Jimmy Cromwell only made him more attractive in the eyes of young Doris. He was inarguably one of the best-looking, most popular, most eligible, and possibly richest young men in America and he was chasing tall, clumsy Doris Duke.

Nanaline decided to occupy Doris's time with her debut into society. At this time in history, rich and prominent young debutantes were "presented" to American high society through a series of parties. In the years before the stock market crash, these parties were so elaborate that they could cost as much as fifty or even one hundred thousand dollars. But postwar manners condemned such ostentation as bad taste, much to the relief of the ever thrifty Nanaline (one could only imagine the grandeur of

Doris's parties if Buck Duke were still alive and throwing them for his only daughter).

Her 1930 party at Rough Point was for a mere six hundred guests instead of the usual fifteen hundred or more. This was partially due to the fact that the debutante list of rich girls had been badly dissipated during the first year of what was to become the Great Depression. Two bands played under a nighttime sky illuminated by tens of thousands of lights (the Dukes did own a power company, remember) and the usual thousands of flowers. The Royal Hungarian Orchestra played under a big top–sized tent.

Doris was standing under an arch of pink and white lilies when she was approached by Jimmy Cromwell. "He was very tall and handsome," she remembered of the night. "We didn't try any sex at all. I wish we had because if I had been more experienced, I never would have married him."

But that debut was minor compared to her presentation to the Queen of England that same year at Buckingham Palace. This was the ultimate social coup for an American heiress and the year Doris was presented to the King and Queen of England only nine Americans were selected, including the Campbell Soup princess Charlotte Dorrance.

Some of Buck Duke's cleverness appeared in the way Doris handled this honor. Part of the protocol was that the debutantes were to be presented in the order in which they arrived, which could mean as much as a two-hour wait.

Doris did not like to wait for anyone and her independent streak did not make exceptions for English royalty. Promptly at 5 P.M., her limousine pulled into the most visible spot in front of the entrance to Buckingham Palace. She was too early.

"The guards told me to scram," Doris recalled. "I simply refused."

An hour later, she was still the first in line. Doris's gown was far more elaborate than the Queen's. She hid her face behind a handful of ostrich plumes as she curtsied before King George and Queen Mary, who were perched on golden thrones.

"I was really rather impressed," Doris said later, "and even then I did not impress easily."

While Doris was partying, Jimmy Cromwell was becoming more desperate for his next rich wife. Eva Stotesbury concocted an elaborate plan to get Jimmy and Doris together. Nanaline had stashed Doris away on "the Continent" where she could meet nobility who, if they could not bring a fortune to the marital bed, might at least add a title to the Duke lineage.

"She wanted me to be a princess or something," Doris said.

Eva Stotesbury began telling people that the impoverished populace was about to revolt against the remaining rich of America (one newspaper columnist had recommended bombing the ostentatious Whitemarsh Hall). She emptied the one-hundred-and-fifty-room house of its antiques and art, fired a few hundred of the servants, and made a run for Europe with Jimmy as her escort. In fact, Whitemarsh Hall had become White Elephant Hall and the Stotesburys could no longer afford the upkeep.

And, surprise, the Dukes and the Stotesburys accidentally met at a Cannes hotel. Even though his mother had issued the ultimate threat to Jimmy, "Marry her or get a job," Jimmy was the eternal spoiled brat and would one minute be the attentive suitor and the next the class catch whose mother had forced him to date the school wallflower. Doris was no slouch in the spoiled department, either.

It was only when the ever-so-debonair Alec Cunningham-Reid, known as Bobbie, joined the party that both Jimmy and Doris began to act more human. Cunningham-Reid was a most civilized man. He was an authentic British aristocrat with all the traits Doris liked. He was tall and dark with thick black hair. A thirty-seven-year-old war hero, he was a Conservative member of Parliament. Doris took an interest in politics.

Cunningham-Reid pursued only heiresses. One daughter of an elevator tycoon had already killed herself by plunging off an Alp when he announced he was going to marry Ruth Mary Ashley, one of the richest women in London. Bobbie and Jimmy had a lot in common. They both were supported by rich women.

Doris was smitten with both men but Cunningham-Reid was married and Jimmy was not. Nanaline decided it was time to take

Doris back to New York and her protective battalion of bodyguards and detectives.

"When I look back," Doris remembers, "it was a wonder that any man ever would try to screw me knowing that he was being watched by all those guards. Most men were so intimidated that they could not get it up and I was still very inexperienced so I couldn't help them."

Jimmy Cromwell had finally committed the ultimate sin that would estrange him from his stepfather and what money Eva Stotesbury had left. The family could tolerate his wasting millions. They could tolerate any kind of romantic scandal. He could lie and exaggerate and victimize his friends. But, finally, Jimmy Cromwell did what no Stotesbury could ever tolerate. He became a New Deal Democrat.

The playboy turned New Dealer wrote a thin book entitled *The Voice of Young America*. Jimmy wanted to nationalize utilities and control overpopulation through sterilization and birth control programs. He recommended that people should eat more hot dogs (all the while he was swilling caviar).

Franklin Delano Roosevelt noticed young citizen Cromwell. He considered him a lightweight, but utilized the young man for his connections with what was left of moneyed society.

FDR greatly approved of the possibility of Cromwell's marrying Doris Duke and wooing the Duke resources into the service of the Democratic Party. Realizing that Doris was his ticket to political power, Jimmy went after her with the fervor experienced only by an underfunded politician when exposed to a fat cat, or rather, fat pussycat.

In June 1933, Doris's sometime friend and ultimate social rival, Barbara Hutton, married Prince Alexis Mdivani and became Princess Mdivani. Doris was wildly jealous and only slightly placated by the fact that the Prince was supposed to be gay. Doris began to take the idea of marriage and the escape that blessed state might offer even more seriously.

Both Doris and Barbara were the stars of the press. Newspapers and magazines recorded their every movement, much as they do today's movie stars. The impoverished public both loved and hated these two very young and very rich girls. While Doris pretended to detest publicity, Barbara happily bathed in the light of flashbulbs. But Doris also kept thick scrapbooks of every item written about both of them. It was a competition.

At this time Doris was the richest and most famous woman in America. And Jimmy Cromwell was flat broke with a hungry fledgling political career to feed.

Nanaline entered into negotiations with King Zog of Albania but Doris was repulsed at the possibility of being Queen Zog, even if it would one-up Princess Barbara.

"Oh my God," Doris rhymed, "I was almost Queen Zog." Sometimes she would sing in the echoing great hall of the New York house, "Hot dog . . . Mama wants me to be Queen Zog. If I ate too much, I'd be Queen Zog the hog. If I ate too much and fell in the mud, I be Queen Zog the hog who fell in the bog!"

"All right," Nanaline would plead. "That will be enough. The servants!" Meanwhile deep in the bowels of the house, the cooks and the footmen were humming the ditty.

In the fall of 1934, at age twenty-one, Doris was no longer legally under the control of Nanaline. All that was left to do was untie the last of the imperial apron strings. She did this by making a trip to Hollywood and returning home with the announcement that she had decided to become a movie star. Nanaline, who considered actors a form of serious social disease, was shocked and terrified. She withdrew her strong opposition to a marriage between Doris and Jimmy Cromwell.

"All right," Nanaline relented. "Marry him. Get it over with but get a prenuptial agreement." This was one bit of motherly advice that Doris wished she had taken.

"At least it will get me out of that horrible old house," Doris said.

# 9
# THE MARRIAGE FROM HELL

It was cold on February 13, 1935, the day before St. Valentine's Day, and Nanaline Duke had a headache. She told her personal maid that she would eat breakfast in her room. This had to be the worst day of her life.

Her daughter, Doris, was about to marry the reputed once-rich playboy Jimmy Cromwell. This was a terrible loss to Nanaline, who was afraid that all that money—money that had been left to Doris by her father, Buck—was slipping away.

"All those millions," Nanaline whined as she sipped a secret morning sherry. Nanaline had far different plans for her daughter, Doris, and the $100 million plus that her late husband had left to his only child in his will. Doris should have remained an old maid, like so many respectable Southern women of Nanaline's era, and devoted her life and fortune to her half-brother Walker Inman and any children he might have. She did not want Eva Stotesbury to gain any control over the money that should be ultimately left to Walker and his heirs.

For these first twenty-two years of Doris's life, Nanaline had tried to guard Doris's virginity. For the most part, Nanaline had not worried that the tall and handsome Jimmy Cromwell had done any deflowering. While he had accomplished a previous marriage and, perhaps, even fathered a child, Nanaline's detectives explained that Cromwell's sex drive at best was unenthusiastic, and was most possibly aimed at a different sex than Doris.

As a last resort, Nanaline had offered to arrange the kind of lavish wedding that very rich girls should have, with ten bridesmaids, an altar of orchids from the greenhouses of Duke Farms, and piles of lobsters doused with cellars of champagne.

Doris said, "No!"

Instead a Supreme Court Justice, Burt Jay Humphrey, would officiate at a tiny ceremony held in the library of the Fifth Avenue mansion. Doris had selected this room because it was the one place on earth where she could feel the presence of her father. Buck's cigar smoke still permeated the walls and the heavy drapes. The leather furniture was still shaped with the dents of his body. The scars of his cigar burns were etched in the mahogany finish of the heavy furniture. This was Daddy's room and Doris wanted her father's spirit to be at this wedding, which was not just a marriage but an escape from her mother's influence.

Doris would have married the devil to free herself from Nanaline. And there was a chance that Jimmy Cromwell might be somewhat better than the devil. He was tall. So tall that Doris, who was nearly six feet and still a little gangly, felt dainty beside him. His waist was small and his arms, which he loved to exhibit in very short-sleeved shirts, were muscular and tanned. His hairless chest was well formed and the muscles in his stomach were defined. This was a rare thing in Doris Duke's world of pampered and unexercised men. It was true that their groping yet unsuccessful attempts at sex had been unsatisfying failures, but Doris thought that such a magnificently bred male animal would have to be fine breeding stock. That was the way it was with the stallions at her farm. The really beautiful ones were always the most spirited and the most eager to breed. A girl could dream, and Doris did.

Nanaline looked at the selection of dresses that her maids had arranged on dress forms in the two-story closet of her bedroom.

She wanted to wear black but that would be in poor taste and Nanaline was incapable of sartorial bad taste. Pink and beige were too cheerful. Maybe lavender? No. Doris had selected blue crepe; imagine that, a light and clinging crepe in winter. No, she would wear something simple and understated in navy blue.

Her dressers slipped the dress over her still lithe body and then gently placed the high-heeled pumps onto her silk-stocking-covered feet. She looked in the huge mirrors and practiced smiling.

"I can do this," she said to nobody.

She walked toward the upstairs landing of the grand marble staircase and paused; Nanaline usually enjoyed the dramatic statement she made descending the two-story drop of the curving stairs, but today she thought of taking the small mahogany elevator, Buck's elevator. She took a breath and started down the stairs.

Eva Stotesbury was already preening in ostrich-plumed finery in the great marble hall below. She was wearing beige and gold lamé. "Well, why shouldn't she?" Nanaline thought. "She had struck gold on this icy February morning, had she not?"

"Nanaline . . . darling," Eva hissed. "Isn't this a wonderful day?"

"I'm sure," Nanaline said icily without extending her gloved hand. "I suppose everyone is in the library."

"Doris could have, at least, used the ballroom and we could have had a small orchestra on the balcony instead of the smelly old room," Nanaline later told relatives.

Doris, wearing the blue crepe, was already in the room, as was Jimmy in his impeccably tailored morning coat and striped pants. Jimmy was smiling his abundant toothy grin and looking for a mirror in which to admire his spectacular reflection. But mirrors were a part of the decor that Buck had never felt necessary for the library, so Jimmy would be denied this matrimonial delight.

The ceremony took less than ten minutes and was traditional with the exception that Doris had stricken the word "obey" from the wedding vows. In a moment of black humor, Doris had selected her half-brother Walker Inman to give the bride away. He was, after all, giving away or losing so much with the culmination of these wedding vows.

Doris was twenty-two years old and inexperienced. Jimmy was thirty-eight. She was a romantic who was hoping that her new husband would show that same kind of passion that her stallions did in the breeding paddocks at Duke Farms, all sweating with tensed muscles biting and throbbing in blind excitement. He was estimating his new net worth.

As the newly wedded couple ran down the granite steps of the mansion to the waiting Rolls-Royce, Doris turned and waved at Nanaline, saying, "Bye-bye . . . Ma!" Nanaline turned and walked into the great hall.

The *Conti di Savoia* was not one of the finest ships but it was sailing at noon on the day that Doris Duke had plotted her escape from her mother. Her servants had spent two days renovating the best suite on the ship into a suitable place for their mistress to be deflowered. Newspaper photos of the couple show Doris looking radiant and smiling. Normally she was too self-conscious to smile in front of cameras but this was a day when she was filled with hope.

This hope lasted less than twelve hours. While an elated Jimmy wired his friends, business associates, and creditors to tell them the news that he had married so very well, Doris and her maids were in the suite selecting the right silk ensemble for the wedding night. This was probably the first time in her life that she thought that she looked beautiful. Her body was slim with breasts that seemed small only because she was so tall. Her almost natural blond hair fell to her shoulders. Her skin was alabaster white and flawless. In spite of the prominent chin (which would later be altered by plastic surgery), her face was almost beautiful. She was ready to make love, oh God, she was ready to make love.

Jimmy entered the stateroom and looked at Doris, who was waiting in bed in her negligee. He seemed very dashing in his morning coat. He looked at his bride as she waited for him to say the romantic words of love that an adoring groom might say on a wedding night. Instead, he lit a cigarette, sat on the side of the bed, leaned toward his excited bride, and said, "My darling, what might I expect my annual income to be?"

Doris Duke's body turned cold. Jimmy realized he had made a

mistake. His mother had warned him not to ask any questions about potential income until the bride was several days at sea and well consummated. But Jimmy had big political dreams and those dreams would require vast amounts of money. He could not wait.

"I told that son of a bitch, and I mean that literally," Doris said with visions of Eva Stotesbury in her head, "to go straight to hell." He went to the ship's bar.

In the bar, Jimmy Cromwell lined up martinis and told everyone in the room, "I have married a frigid woman. I don't think she is a normal female."

Jimmy Cromwell seemed relieved that his new bride rejected him. He devoted his honeymoon days and evenings to imbibing and talking politics in the ship's bar or exercising in the ship's gym. Doris, on the other hand, was contemplating her alternatives. She could annul the marriage and return to Nanaline. No, that would be unbearable.

Jimmy Cromwell might be a dud in the sack but he was her ticket to freedom. With typical Duke reasoning, Doris decided to use her disappointing marriage as an escape from the world of Nanaline and look for passion elsewhere.

The second day of the around-the-world honeymoon was the first day of writing checks for her expensive new husband. Jimmy had planned the entire trip, which was to include tours of the Mediterranean on a leased yacht, climbing the pyramids in Egypt, a sultan's caravan to Baghdad, followed by India, Siam, Java, China, Japan, the Philippines, with the final stop being Hawaii. Jimmy Cromwell had told the travel agents that he would require the very best lodgings and services available in the world. Hundreds of servants were alerted to prepare for the arrival of the fabulously rich Cromwells.

With a flourish, Jimmy had written a check to Cook's Travel, a check that was to cover the first leg of the trip, including the suite on the ocean liner. On their second day at sea, there was a gentle tapping on the door of Doris's stateroom. An embarrassed purser asked Doris, "Has your husband made any arrangements for the check?"

"I don't understand." Doris had never had to personally discuss money before in her life. "What are you talking about?"

"The check that your husband wrote to Cook's was refused by the bank," the purser mumbled nervously.

"Why would the bank refuse a check?" Doris was the one who was now confused. "Who gave them permission to refuse a check? How dare any banker do something like that?"

Years later when retelling the story, Doris would laugh at her ignorance and innocence of exactly how money changed hands in the real world. Until that day, someone else had always provided the checks or letters of credit required to provide for the comfort and whims of Doris Duke.

"I didn't even know what a bounced check was," Doris recalled. She wired her business people in New York who went into action paying the bills and cabling lines of credit to the various destinations of the honeymoon extravaganza.

As the trip meandered from port to port, Jimmy Cromwell would disappear ashore for several hours each time, only to return to the ship where he would regale fellow travelers and the young crew members with stories of his freshest sexual conquests from Monte Carlo to Venice. Cromwell could brag for hours about his sexual talents.

"I am sure he was screwing someone," Doris would later say dryly. "The truth of the matter was that we did try to have sex but there was not much to him. He was small where it would have been nice had he been larger. My experience was very limited so I thought this must be the way all men are. You can imagine my disappointment. But you cannot believe my relief when I learned that some men were far more gifted."

Her occasional friend, Babs Hutton, the wastrel heir to the Woolworth fortune, once explained Doris's affection for men with large sexual organs as "the real Duke endowment."

"Jimmy was no endowment," Doris would chuckle later in her throaty laugh. "He wasn't even a small annuity."

Throughout the seagoing part of the honeymoon, Doris stayed in the suite away from Jimmy and a cadre of newspaper photographers who wanted to chronicle the antics of the world's most glamorous couple. As Jimmy became more and more embarrassed by his wife's pointed rejection, his stories about her alleged frigidity became more elaborate. It was at that time that the first whispered rumors of possible lesbianism appeared. After too many drinks, Jimmy Cromwell, self-anointed super stud, would say that the problem he had with his new wife was beyond even his, or any man's, seductive capabilities.

He told his male buddies that he feared Doris was a lesbian. He further elaborated that he believed she had been seduced by a French governess. "How awful for you," Jimmy's friends would sympathize.

"I will just have to make the best of it," Jimmy would sigh and shrug his well-muscled shoulders. "I am, after all, a gentleman." Then he would flash the famous Cromwell smile and add, "There are always the ports." Jimmy and his buddies would roar, slap each other on the back, and raise their glasses to the ports.

Meanwhile, Doris had nicknamed her husband "the Pope" because "He was very grand and very expensive but he did nothing in bed."

At this time, Doris was directing her passions in a different direction. She was developing into a world-class shopper and she had her father's eye for quality and value. The girl who did not have to concern herself with the cost of anything became the woman who enjoyed haggling with turbaned shopkeepers and street vendors.

While the honeymoon might have been a sexual failure for Doris, it was an education in other ways. When she looked at the white marble of the Taj Mahal in moonlight, she vowed she wanted a home just like that glorious tomb. With the same enthusiasm that Buck Duke had when he built and removed mountains at Duke Farms, she worked with Indian architects to plan her Taj Mahal and ordered spectacular doors that were inlaid with jade, agate, lapis lazuli, mother of pearl, and malachite. It would take a half dozen artisans some six weeks to make each door.

While Doris had found beauty in the architecture of Agra, she was to learn a new nourishment of the soul in the small and empty room where she met Gandhi. It was broiling hot when Doris and Jimmy were given an audience with the emaciated man clad only in a loincloth.

"I wanted to listen to Gandhi," Doris later said, "but Jimmy was set on reeducating Gandhi. Jimmy started babbling about what Gandhi should do to help his people, that whole capitalism bit, and Gandhi was speaking of the importance of nurturing the spirit and soul. Jimmy wanted to talk about politics and industrialization. Gandhi cared nothing about any of those things. He told us of inner peace. Jimmy did most of the talking and didn't listen at all. Imagine, you are granted a personal interview with Gandhi and don't listen to him. It was then that I realized I had married a complete pompous ass. Yet, what I did learn started me thinking about life in a different way."

"I had spoken with a Messiah," Doris later said.

In Bangkok and Shanghai Doris continued her haggling as she acquired priceless antique rugs, the finest of ivory, tiles, and jade. Every ship that sailed west from the Orient that summer carried crated treasures to be delivered to Duke Farms.

In late August, Doris and Jimmy boarded a ship that would take them to Honolulu. A letter from Nanaline was awaiting Doris upon her arrival in the Sandwich Islands, a letter that was supposed to bring the heiress shocking news, but in light of the unconsummated honeymoon (later Jimmy would state that he thought they actually had had sex but this was stated only after his lawyers told him that the marriage could be annulled if they had not made love), Doris found the news in her mother's letter to be wildly funny.

A nude photo with Doris's head crudely pasted over a rather voluptuous body had been delivered to Nanaline with a threat that the picture would be published and her lover revealed if Doris didn't pay an immediate twenty-five thousand dollars. A shocked Nanaline had called the police.

"I enjoyed that photo because of what my husband was saying about my prudishness," Doris laughed, "and I would love to have seen Nanaline's face when she opened that envelope. I will tell you the truth, if I had thought of posing like that to shock my mother, I probably would have done it. But back then I thought my body was ugly."

There was even more irony to the photo. Considering the lack of romance and sex in her life, Doris enjoyed considering the possibility of having had an affair with some cad who would photograph her naked and then attempt to blackmail her with the photos.

She didn't pay the extortionist and the photos were never printed by the press. Many years later, Doris commented, "I almost wish they had been printed and there had been a big scandal. If my reputation had been scandalized earlier in my life, I would have been free to do many things differently a few years later. I would not have been forced to do some of the things I did later to save my reputation. I believe that being infamous gives a person a kind of freedom. My life would have been very different and probably happier if I had been more publicly scandalous."

Doris was ready for a little scandal in her life.

# 10
# OF MEN AND MANIPULATIONS

Doris Duke had been honeymooning with her husband, Jimmy Cromwell, for months and was still what she considered virginal. Jimmy, who had lunged after her with uncontrolled passion only to be stopped by the prying eyes of bodyguards and mothers in the days of courtship, was the king of limp love when the heiress was totally available to the marital bed.

"He turned me against blond men," Doris stated years later. "He was so tall and handsome and he had a great body but that was all he had."

Those who know the Duke family have often teased that every single Duke ever born was oversexed. They marry frequently and tryst even more often. Doris, who was all Duke, was no exception.

"I loved seeing the world on my honeymoon," she said, "but I would have traded it all for a good romp. The more I believed that there was to be no passion on my honeymoon, the more I shopped. By the time my ship docked at Honolulu, there were dozens of other ships steaming toward New York loaded with the things I had bought. It seems that whenever I am miserable, I start spending money."

In August of 1935, the unfulfilled bride and showboat groom arrived in Honolulu aboard the luxury liner *Tatsuda Maru* and moved to the best suite at the Royal Hawaiian Hotel. Doris was dismayed to be met by a horde of reporters but Jimmy was delighted at real, honest-to-God American publicity.

"One reporter remarked about how tan Jimmy looked," Doris said later, "and I told my secretary, Marian Paschal, that he *should* look tan, he spent the whole trip on deck because he certainly was never in our stateroom. Some honeymoon suite!"

If there was one purpose that Jimmy Cromwell served in the life of Doris Duke, it was his ability to talk and talk and talk and talk. This was very useful when it came to the press, who would be lurking to speak with Doris. Husband Jimmy was always available, and Doris would be free to explore the Honolulu area.

With reporters beating on the doors of the suite, Doris was occupied with something more interesting than another bout with the flashbulb set.

One of the great benefits of Hawaii for Doris Duke was the abundance of muscular and tanned young Hawaiian males, wearing the briefest of bathing suits, found everywhere from the beach to the streets to the bars.

"The first few weeks at Diamond Head," she recalled with a smile, "I could not stop looking. There were so many beautiful men and the best part was they thought I was beautiful."

To the easygoing Hawaiians, the fact that Doris was a tall and willowy blonde in a land of dark-haired women was far more interesting than her millions of dollars. She would escape from the hotel early in the morning clad only in her scandalous (for that time) two-piece yellow bathing suit (always her favorite color) and head for the water and the men.

She was escorted around the island by the handsome Olympic swimming star Duke Kahanamoku, a full-blooded Hawaiian and the sheriff of Honolulu. Just as Doris was always attracted by the exotic, this very tall man with his gleaming copper skin, well-muscled body, and almost black eyes brought out the tingles and twinges in her body that had been hidden in the presence of her husband.

Sam Kahanamoku, Duke's brother, offered to teach Doris how to surf.

In the heavy surf of Waikiki or Diamond Head, the blond heiress and the brown islander found themselves in each other's arms. Soon the yellow bathing suit was in a small heap on the sand and Doris Duke finally knew what it was to make love to a man. From that moment on, through the rest of her life, Doris Duke had an abiding affection for the talents of dark-skinned men. For weeks, Doris took more swimming and surfing lessons with Sam; occasionally she actually went into the water.

"Let my husband play tennis with his buddy Bill Tilden (the famous and controversial tennis star), but I like a good plunge into warm water," Doris teased.

She decided to build a house in Hawaii. For a while Jimmy went home to his mother in Philadelphia. Doris opted to remain in Honolulu and continue her newfound appreciation for water sports. Jimmy was sulking because Doris had refused to increase his "paltry ten-thousand-dollar monthly allowance." This would be equal to one hundred and twenty-five thousand dollars today.

Doris Duke was out to prove that her husband was wrong. She most certainly was not a lesbian. In fact, during these early days in Hawaii, she became a virtual man-eater. She rented a small but very private house and would set out each day for the beach, returning with a gaggle of suntanned and well-built goslings in her wake. She introduced the beach boy community of Honolulu to champagne and caviar, and they taught her dirty songs and sexual positions that she had never considered possible.

Jimmy's mother sent him back to his wife with his tail between his legs and not much else. Eva Stotesbury was not about to have her son lose the golden goose he had married, even though the goose had decided to paddle in other ponds.

Since Doris's affairs were very open, Jimmy feared that some Honolulu reporter might write about his wife's beach-boying, which might hinder the development of his nonexistent political career should any of the stories ever get back to the press in New York or Washington. Jimmy Cromwell needed a rich wife to finance his aspirations. Doris wanted an ex-husband.

In less than a year, she had been a young girl, a bride, an unfulfilled wife, a philandering spouse, and a passionate woman. She well understood which one of those categories she liked best. Yes, 1935 had been quite a year. Doris Duke had learned what she wanted from life and she did not want Jimmy Cromwell.

In late December of 1935, Jimmy Cromwell managed to pull his wife away from the Hawaiian beach and its endless attractions and set sail for Los Angeles. As the famous couple debarked at the Port of Los Angeles, they were met by a horde of well-wishers whom Jimmy introduced as relatives.

"What, more nephews?" Doris sniffed. Jimmy winced at the remark that was overheard and reported by the press. He had enough problems without his new wife making double-edged remarks. His first wife, Delphine Dodge, was scandalizing the high society set by having an affair with a married man whose wife was threatening a messy lawsuit. Jimmy was horrified that the antics of his first wife might reflect on his political reputation. His obvious discomfort pleased Doris.

Jimmy Cromwell was not being taken seriously by the power brokers of Washington, D.C. He had learned that his request for meetings and his need for the proper political social invitations were not met with any enthusiasm by the politically significant unless his wife was available.

Doris had power literally. Her North Carolina and South Carolina power plants serviced some of the major military garrisons of the nation. Had she pulled the plug, most of the might of the United States could be in the dark, not that this idea had ever occurred to her.

Jimmy encouraged Doris to take a larger interest in the operations of Duke University. He had hoped for a very public position on the university board as Duke University, with its huge endowment provided by Buck Duke, was transforming itself into an important educational institution in the New South.

In April of 1936, Doris Duke and her longtime secretary and companion, the large and flashy Marian Paschal, traveled to Duke University, but not in the imperial style that Jimmy Cromwell might have orchestrated. Instead the two women climbed into a jalopy that Doris used as a cover and with Doris at the wheel, driving in her usual treacherous style, they headed anonymously to North Carolina.

Calling herself Mrs. Hooper, Doris arrived at the campus where she was recognized by several school officials who promised to keep her secret. For two days, Doris pretended to be a college coed and even threw a quickly catered lunch for the women's dorm. When Doris left the university, she had mixed feelings about her visit. Always a self-conscious person, she was suddenly aware of her lack of a classical education. Like her father, she could walk into a room and instantly know which painting was the best and which Persian carpet was the costliest, but she could not quote Proust. Damn, she didn't even know who Proust was. She had seen the world and bought much of it, but she was not educated. This made her self-conscious around the college students. For years after that, Duke officials worried that her reasons for not coming to the institution were because of some slight that had occurred on this trip, but Doris did not return because she felt uncomfortable to be the daughter of the man who donated the university, yet she did not have the education necessary to be a student.

Meanwhile Jimmy was pestering President Roosevelt for a meeting that had not been forthcoming. He had a plan to revamp the nation's banking system and wanted to submit it to Congress. Roosevelt instructed his underlings to "humor" Doris Duke's husband.

Jimmy decided that he would be wiser to build his political power base in New Jersey and asked Doris to arrange a series of lavish parties to impress the New Jersey political set. He was horrified when Doris's favorite theme for the parties was centered on hula dancers and singing beach boys.

It is difficult to understand exactly what pseudo-economist Jimmy Cromwell proposed for the revitalization of the economy during the Great Depression. He seemed to blame the banking system and the rich for most of the ills but had no qualms about being rich himself. This variance of what he professed and how he actually lived made him seem all the more ridiculous.

Late in the summer of 1936, Doris purchased a choice parcel of property along millionaire's row in Diamond Head. She paid one hundred thousand dollars for what was then considered the finest piece of real estate on the entire island. If she could not be in Hawaii, she could busy herself by designing one of the finest residences in the world for her Diamond Head acres.

As Jimmy made speeches about the overindulgences of the super-rich, his wife prepared to build a Persian palace in paradise. New Deal Democrat Cromwell was furious. Nothing would settle his pique except a donation by his wife of fifty thousand dollars to the Democratic campaign fund for the upcoming presidential election. This was a staggering sum that today would probably have the effect of a $50 million contribution. Amid the depths of the Great Depression money of this magnitude was not readily available. President Roosevelt took a new interest in Doris Duke's husband. (It should be mentioned here that this election was expected to be most difficult for the Democrats and Roosevelt, who was under massive criticism for his policies.)

Roosevelt knew that the wallet was most certainly in Doris's purse. He pondered how to express his gratitude for the financing that just might have kept him in the White House. He had listened to Doris rave about the pleasures of Hawaii and was ready to offer the position of governor of Hawaii to Jimmy. When Cromwell told his wife of the offer, she pretended delight.

But Doris was not delighted with that possibility. Hawaii was her paradise. Her plan was to dispose of the nuisance of her first husband and return to her paradise with its unending pleasures. She made sure that the political grapevine twisted around the President's neck. She intimated that she would consider it a vast underestimation of her husband's talents to exile him to an island isolated from Washington where the real future was. Roosevelt quickly pulled back his feelers. There was no use in angering a woman who could with a flourish of her hand finance a political campaign.

By December, Doris was headed back to Honolulu to refresh her body and renew her spirit. Sam Kahanamoku met her in San Francisco and the reunited lovers sailed for Hawaii. But this was not like sailing on a luxury liner with her husband, who would spend all day on deck impressing the other passengers while she hid from reporters in her suite. Sam Kahanamoku was more than happy to remain below decks with Doris. She debarked in Honolulu a radiant and happy woman.

Doris Duke was intent on building the Persian palace, which she had named Hale Kapu, Hawaiian for "keep out of this house." (When Jimmy learned the meaning of the new name for the proposed estate, he was furious until Doris laughingly said, "All right . . . we'll call it Shangri-La." This name had meaning for her as it was the name of a mythical kingdom in the book *Lost Horizon* where no one ever grew old.)

As tons of marble and a complete bedroom wing of the house gathered on the docks of Honolulu, Doris walked the property with the builders and architects and oversaw every detail of the intricate and complex pleasure dome that was to arise on this land. (Years later she would laugh about the elaborate tiles and jade inlays in the marble that covered the house because the lush vegetation had all but hidden most of these designs from view.)

Meanwhile Jimmy was back with his mother in Palm Beach where he busied himself writing a book, *In Defense of Capitalism*, which was to be a thin volume of his thoughts about the redistribution of wealth. Ironically, he credited his marriage to Doris Duke as one of his efforts to share the wealth because now one of the world's great fortunes would be under his guidance. He would smile knowingly and tell people that he knew how to use "their" money to best benefit the poor and downtrodden.

Since reports of his wife's affairs in Honolulu had reached Jimmy Cromwell, he decided to soothe his pride by being seen with a collection of beautiful women in Palm Beach and New York. When told of this, Doris laughed and said, "Good, I hope they teach the Pope something."

Again Eva Stotesbury ordered her poverty-stricken progeny to go to Hawaii and join his wife. When he arrived, he discovered that not only did he have a separate bedroom in the house Doris had rented but his bedroom was on a different floor.

Occasionally, Doris would leave Hawaii to join her husband

for a political appearance but her habit of insulting people or, worse yet, snubbing the politically powerful, proved more harmful than useful.

She attended the Queen's Ball in London and managed to restrain herself from offending the royal family. Even Doris Duke was in awe of the royals. Still, she would much rather have been in Hawaii on a surfboard or on her back than at Buckingham Palace.

But then her path crossed again with Alec Cunningham-Reid. Cunningham-Reid was probably the most glamorous and exciting person she had ever met. His lineage was impeccable and his reputation was terrible. He made a point of living on the largesse of his rich wife. Not only did he make his wife pay for the honeymoon, he withdrew thirty-six thousand pounds sterling from her accounts to cover his outlay during the courtship. Following a short but expensive marriage, wife number one filed for divorce.

"I simply do not understand finance," he said.

Yet, when it came to a divorce settlement, he graciously accepted one hundred thousand pounds and ten thousand pounds annually for life. He also kept a mansion in the exclusive Mayfair district of London and a yacht he had named after himself, *The Lizard*.

If Cunningham-Reid had a profession it was politics; he was a member of Parliament but he seldom attended a session. When he heard Jimmy lament about his measly ten-thousand-dollar monthly allowance (Doris also paid all other expenses), Cunningham-Reid decided that it was time to pursue Doris.

"Oh . . . I knew he was a lizard," she said, "but he was the most exciting and best-looking lizard I have ever seen. The best part was that he made Jimmy nervous so I gave him a lot of attention."

Jimmy arranged for a long trip to Moscow where Joseph Stalin made no secret of the fact that he wanted to meet the fabulously wealthy Doris Duke. Always wanting to be a center of attention, Jimmy made a point of leaning out the window of the car and taking pictures of everything with his expensive capitalistic Leica. He was promptly arrested.

"I thought my troubles were over," Doris laughed later. "I hoped they would take him off to Siberia but the ambassador managed to get him released. It was a disappointment."

When the Cromwells returned to the United States, Jimmy went to Washington where he astounded the Senate Agriculture Committee with his plan to save capitalism, which included a negative interest plan (the government would loan money to investors and pay them 6 percent for the privilege). He also pointed out that the rich can best improve the economy by freely spending their money. Perhaps he was a pioneer of the "trickle down" economic theories that were to follow decades later. He also felt that the rich should be forced to use one third of their fortunes to build schools, colleges, and orphanages. (He was delighted to say that the appropriate amount of his wife's inheritance went to endow Duke University.)

Jimmy was so strained by having to present his plan to redistribute the wealth to Congress that he decided that Doris should buy a motor yacht as a place to rest and restore his energy. Doris liked the idea.

The result was *Kailani Lahi Lahi* (*Lahi Lahi* was the Hawaiian name supposedly translated into "soft as the wind" that Duke Kahanamoku had given Doris), a fifty-eight-foot teak and cream-colored motor yacht that cost a whopping fifty thousand dollars. This was a record price for such a relatively small boat.

"People used to tease me about that name *Lahi Lahi*," Doris smiled. "It was supposed to mean a person who is so soft and delicate that they can become part of the wind but I think it was just the Hawaiian way of saying, 'Lay me! Lay me!'"

The yacht did not have the expected soothing effect on Jimmy. He was becoming impatient for his reward from President Roosevelt. After all, his wife did give fifty thousand dollars. Shouldn't he be a governor or something by now?

In a letter to one of President Roosevelt's assistants, Jimmy pleaded for a meeting in his usual arrogant way writing: "I should like to have 10 or perhaps 15 minutes of his time in order to point out certain errors in his recent fireside chat which, in my opinion, has laid him wide open to attack from his opponents.

Naturally I am in no roaring rush but I do feel that the sooner the President could see me the better it would be for those of us who remain his friends and admirers."

The letter prattled on but ended with the words that finally caught Roosevelt's attention. Jimmy reminded the President subtly of the power of his wife's checkbook when he wrote: "Doris would like to come along with me as she still has a mighty big yen for the Boss." Jimmy again had played his best card, his wife, and Roosevelt granted the meeting with the result that Jimmy was to be considered as a potential senator from New Jersey.

Jimmy was excited. He had a plan that included spending several terms as a brilliant senator, then he would be selected as Vice President, and finally the Oval Office would be his while he was still in his fifties.

Doris, on the other hand, had a little plan of her own. She had been writing a number of checks to various Democratic Party causes in the State of New Jersey, and giving more Hawaiian theme parties at her estate, but she knew her opportunity to bring the same kind of devotion and happiness to her husband as he had brought to her life was about to occur. With a cunning that she could have inherited only from her father, she began a plan that was designed to make Jimmy Cromwell want to be rid of her in spite of her money. She feared that Jimmy would never initiate a divorce or permit her to divorce him.

Jimmy was thrilled that the White House had asked Doris to accompany Eleanor Roosevelt on a good will trip to West Virginia where they were to meet with five hundred impoverished miners. The two women would be driven from the White House to the West Virginia coal fields. Doris arrived in a full-length Russian mink coat and custom-made walking boots for her trek in the boonies. The cost of the coat alone would have been enough to feed the entire town for several months. Eleanor was revolted but attempted to make the best of it.

At the Tygart Valley Co-operative, Doris swept into the town and walked past the wood and tin uninsulated shacks of the miners as if she were a queen. Many children and some of the adults thought Doris was a movie star and asked for dozens of autographs. Later that evening, Eleanor and Doris attended a square dance and Doris, who would have normally been delighted to be a part of any spirited dancing, feigned boredom with these simple lower-class customs and yawned in a corner. The following day, Doris flew back to New Jersey while Eleanor took the train to New York. The two women had stopped speaking to each other.

The trip was a complete political disaster. It made Jimmy and his crowd appear to be shallow rich kids who were only "slumming" in the Democratic Party. Eleanor said that Doris was immature and insensitive.

"Jimmy was livid," Doris said later. "He could not understand why I dressed the way I did when he knew I had very little interest in clothes." Doris would sometimes shop for sale or even resale clothing and enjoyed shocking her expensively clad friends by wearing a particularly cheap ensemble.

"Why would you dress better for some coal miners in wherever that place was," Jimmy howled, "and wear a made-over nightgown to my parents' ball in Palm Beach? It does not make any sense!"

It made complete sense to Doris Duke Cromwell. The Democratic Party immediately dropped Jimmy from consideration for the Senate seat. Eleanor Roosevelt later commented, "I did not invite her to accompany me. I was asked to do so. I believe her husband was very anxious for her to go . . . I honestly don't know how much of what she saw meant anything to her," the President's wife continued.

Doris and Eleanor Roosevelt might have had much in common. Both were very strong women who used their intelligence to accomplish their goals. While Eleanor said that Doris did not understand the plight of the poor, Doris could have easily remarked that Eleanor had little understanding of the problems of the super-rich. In fact, Doris was deeply touched by the horrid living conditions and the malnutrition of the children and for years secret donations of money to buy food and provide heat were sent to West Virginia.

Doris had made herself out to be one of the jaded and self-centered rich in the presence of Eleanor Roosevelt but the final result was that Jimmy Cromwell was starting to consider the possibility that his rich wife was more of a political hindrance than an asset. He immediately blamed his failure to climb to the top rank of the Democratic Party on his wife.

Doris was headed toward the divorce she wanted but she would have to take even stronger action before she would find herself safely in Reno.

# 11

# THE BRONZE GOD AND OTHERS

Duke Kahanamoku was the first male in Doris Duke's life to transcend that gulf that separates a sexual relationship and an authentic romance. "It was interesting," Doris said years later while in a pensive mood. "My father, Duke, was the only person I was sure really loved me, but another man named Duke would teach me how to make love."

In the beginning, Duke's brother Sam had been the one to launch Doris into the world of frequent climaxes but she actually had a love relationship with the handsome Duke. When Doris was with Sam, Jimmy tried to impress Duke, a former Olympic swimming champion, by telling him how much they had in common. Jimmy would talk of his great exploits as a boxer and tennis player. But it was not sports that Jimmy and Duke had in common, it was Doris.

Doris loved the Hawaiian attitude. Hawaiians were not envious. They were not much interested in money. But best of all, jealousy did not seem to be a part of the Hawaiian philosophy, thus she could move from one Kahanamoku brother to another with only best wishes rather than hard feelings.

Duke and Doris were a beautiful couple. She was so tall,

almost six feet, with oriental blue eyes and the sleek body of a young girl who swam a lot. He was six feet three inches with black eyes and skin the shade of expensive milk chocolate. He had won the hundred-meter freestyle events in the 1912 and 1920 Olympics.

"The Duke taught me the wonders of massage," Doris sighed. "He had these massive strong hands, they were just a little rough from the water, and he would massage me in a strong but gentle way. I would lay on my stomach and he would rub my shoulders and back. Every place. Then he would turn me over and kiss me. Need I say more? . . . He was a man," she remembered with satisfaction.

But Duke Kahanamoku was not the only man who was having a serious relationship with Doris Duke. Another man, a suave British peer who was the exact opposite of Duke Kahanamoku, was the first real romantic obsession in her life.

Since the first time she had seen Alec Cunningham-Reid at Buckingham Palace, Doris Duke had been in love. Her relationship with Duke Kahanamoku was based on real friendship and passion, but her feelings toward Cunningham-Reid went further. Cunningham-Reid was one of those Cary Grant types, a handsome charmer who readily admitted he was a fortune hunter and probably a most disreputable cad. Doris had always liked men with mystique. She would immediately be attracted to a male whose reputation was less than admirable. But she really admired honesty and a man who was honest about his faults was immensely attractive to Doris.

On the outside Cunningham-Reid appeared to be the epitome of the highest-class English gentleman. His tailoring was Savile Row. His body was sleek. His manners were always perfect. And he could say the most outrageous things and propose the wickedest proposals in the clipped and cool accent of a British aristocrat. Doris and Cunningham-Reid actually groped each other minutes after they met, in a linen room of Buckingham Palace.

"In the middle of making love," Doris snickered at the memory, "he paused and wondered whether it was disloyal to the crown to copulate on the Queen's sheets. I started laughing so loud that the only way he could stop me was to smother my mouth with kisses. It was such fun being in love with Bobbie."

In the year 1938, Doris estimates that she traveled more than five hundred thousand miles between her lover in Hawaii and her lover in London. "Flying was considered dangerous by many people at that time," she said. "But I had to fly or I never would have kept my schedules. People thought I was very adventurous when actually I was just a woman in love."

In the period of a few months, Doris and Cunningham-Reid managed to make love in Palm Beach, Paris, Athens, and Cairo, as well as in London.

This blatant affair was obvious to Jimmy, who was licking his political scars back in Washington and threatening to buy a newspaper to get his ideas across to the public since the politicians obviously did not recognize his brilliance. He even produced a short film entitled *Of Men and Money,* which no one ever cared to view. His mother and stepfather, Eva and Ned Stotesbury, had managed to hide the fact that they had lost the bulk of their once great fortune in the Crash of 1929. They still had all the trappings of the American super-rich: the immense mansion in Philadelphia and the house in Palm Beach. Jimmy had always maintained that he was rich in his own right and did not need Doris's fortune.

In the spring of 1938, all that changed when Ned Stotesbury died, leaving the bulk of his dwindled estate to the children of his first wife with a small stipend to Eva. Instead of the $100 million plus that the press estimated Ned Stotesbury's fortune to be, it was only $4 million after taxes and fees. And none of this money went to Jimmy.

The political world suddenly knew that the reason Jimmy Cromwell wanted people to share their money with the poor was because he was one of the poor. At least, that was a joke that made the party rounds in Washington.

Jimmy was turning forty. His body was sagging slightly. He was losing his hair. His political career was in a shambles. People were starting to laugh at him. He was penniless and his rich wife wanted to dump him.

He responded to these problems in a typical Jimmy Cromwell manner: he decided to have a complete face-lift. It is interesting to look into the mind of this vain and shallow man who thought the answer to all his problems would be for him to be as handsome and attractive as he had been a decade earlier. "My ex-husband had two face-lifts before I had my first one," Doris blurted out after an evening of champagne. "Scratch the surface of Jimmy Cromwell," one political watcher said, "and you don't find anything more."

Jimmy's repaired face did not help his career. In an effort to ensure everyone that he was not about to lose his wealthy wife, he would occasionally pinpoint whatever spot on the globe had attracted Doris and her entourage and try to join his wife for a foray in front of the flashbulbs of the press.

While Cunningham-Reid was her love partner and Duke Kahanamoku was her lust partner, Doris did find time for other men such as the controversial movie star Errol Flynn. He did not care about her money and she wanted to bed the star who had bedded and satisfied some of the most famous and desirable women in the world. Doris, who dreamed of being a movie star herself following her brief affair with Flynn, was very flattered that the Australian cocksman would want to add her to the list of the bold and the beautiful whom he had led into bedded bliss.

"He made me feel beautiful," Doris recalled. "We always remained friends until he died."

Nineteen thirty-eight continued to be a great year for Doris.

Shangri-La, her palace on Diamond Head, was in the final stages of construction and, while she was reluctant to leave Los Angeles and Flynn, this $1 million extravaganza in white marble and glass was another of her passions. Like her father, Doris Duke expressed her creativity through extravagant architecture.

The residents of Honolulu were entranced with the epic structure that was changing the view of Diamond Head. Some hundred and fifty men worked more than twelve months to complete the project. The excavation pit for the foundation was large enough to hold the entire Honolulu City Hall. Slowly the tons of Chinese granite and white Indian marble took shape into the

Palace of Duke. It was starting to look as if Doris's Taj Mahal was exactly what she was building on the black lava of Diamond Head.

The driveway was made of crushed white coral. Full-grown palm trees were moved to the site and if they died, they were immediately replaced.

There was a lot of glass, including a twenty-foot glass door in the living room that opened by flicking an electric switch. The floors were inlaid oak that had been stripped from a French château. A stream of water cascaded through the interior and exterior of the house. The bathrooms were jade and marble with water spewing from the open mouths of solid-gold fish. The largest room in the entire house was Doris's personal bathroom, complete with waterfalls.

There was a hundred-foot swimming pool with a hydraulic diving board that raised at the flick of another switch. A guest room was fashioned from an actual sacred Indian temple that had been considered a national and religious treasure back in India. Doris had her own breakwall built at the cost of an additional two hundred and fifty thousand dollars. David Kahanamoku, the brother of Duke and Sam, and his wife were employed as the caretakers.

No house in America, not even San Simeon, the monstrous estate of publisher William Randolph Hearst, was such a treasure trove of fine Eastern art and tapestries.

"I think it was sometime in the eighties," Doris commented many years later, "that some art expert, I forgot his name but he was supposed to be the best, well, he came to Shangri-La and was astounded. I asked him if he thought any of the things I had collected had appreciated much in value. He walked around for a while with a small calculator and then told me, 'This place if liquidated at auction could be worth in excess of $1 billion.' I told him to stop counting. I didn't want to know any more. Why, the dish I was using as an ashtray could have brought as much as four hundred thousand dollars. This is when I decided to turn the place into a museum after I died. It already was."

Although she was elated with her fabulous Persian palace and enjoyed the abundance of new lovemaking places the estate offered for herself and Duke, she missed Cunningham-Reid. So she flew back to Los Angeles and on to New York, where she caught the *Queen Mary* to England.

She needed to get away from Honolulu. The old families of both the white and to a lesser degree the Hawaiian societies of Honolulu were becoming more critical of Doris Duke's blatant affair with the most famous Hawaiian of the first half of the twentieth century. Duke Kahanamoku was considered a black man in a United States where Negroes were still being lynched in some states for even touching a white woman.

Doris had moved him into the new palace and they went from a casual beach affair to a married woman (a famous and rich married woman) living openly with a man of color. Many people in Hawaii, especially those who were lobbying for statehood, feared that should this affair be publicized and sensationalized, the Hawaiian Islands would be known as a place of free sex and free love.

It was obvious to everyone that Doris's marriage to Jimmy Cromwell was and had always been nothing but a sham. In spite of an unusual official statement issued by Eva Stotesbury in which she said: "I would like at this time to publicly contradict the foolish rumors that Jimmy and Doris are not happy," odds-makers were giving the couple only a few months to remain wed.

Now, Cromwell needed his wife's financial backing more than ever. In a foolish move to try again for a nomination for a New Jersey Senate seat, he promised political bosses a three-hundred-thousand-dollar donation in exchange for the job. Doris had all but thrown him out of Duke Farms and Jimmy had begged his mother to spend what little money she had to rent a suitable estate for his image. He still had his ten-thousand-dollar monthly allowance but he felt that "paltry" amount was hardly adequate to sustain his lifestyle if he had to completely support himself. (It would be like living on a $1 million annual income today.)

Doris was not about to spend another three hundred thousand dollars on Jimmy's nonexistent political career. In the summer of 1939, she had other problems, and when Doris Duke had serious personal problems she had no time for anybody else's trials and tribulations.

During that summer, she checked herself into Queen's Hospital under an assumed name, where she was a patient in the gynecological floor in a private room. She later admitted that she had an abortion. Of course, abortions were not legal in New York hospitals in 1939 but the rules were always different for the richest woman in the world.

Shaken, Doris decided to accompany her husband on a trip to London, where she immediately disappeared into the English countryside with Cunningham-Reid, whose divorce had just been finalized. Doris and Bobbie celebrated his freedom by drinking a bottle or two of champagne followed by an afternoon roll in the heath. She told him about the abortion.

He was outraged, more angry than Doris had ever seen him. He believed that the child must have been his. Cunningham-Reid thrived on being thought of as a cad; nonetheless, if a child were his, he wanted it. Doris said nothing.

She had not asked the race or the sex of the child who had been *ripped from her body* but she realized from the shocked and cold attitude exhibited by some of the doctors and nurses that the baby was the result of her nights and days in the palace at Diamond Head with her bronze-skinned lover.

Meanwhile Jimmy was in the Netherlands where he had wrangled a meeting with exiled Kaiser Wilhelm II. He was with the old Kaiser the night Hitler invaded Poland. When Jimmy commented that this action could be a mistake for Hitler, the Kaiser looked him in the eyes and told him that the German army would take Warsaw in less than six weeks and that World War II had begun. Jimmy was anxious to get this news to President Roosevelt and quickly left to meet Doris in France. The two then fled across France to the port of Genoa where they boarded the luxury liner *Rex*, which was bound for New York.

In Washington a week later, Roosevelt smiled at Jimmy and said, "Here comes super-spy." It was a high point for Jimmy, who had not had many high points in the last few years. He preened like a rooster, never realizing that real spies had brought the same information to the White House days earlier.

Doris refused to pay the three hundred thousand dollars that

Jimmy had promised in exchange for the Senate seat and he was instantly dropped from consideration. In Washington, Roosevelt had finally located a political position for Jimmy where, he thought, the political bumbler could do no real damage. For two years, the post of minister to Canada had been vacant. Roosevelt did not know that Doris was, at that very moment, meeting with lawyers to decide just how to unload Jimmy at the least possible cost.

"I was shocked," Jimmy said, which was easily one of the most laughable lies of the decade. "I had no idea that Doris was unhappy. I thought everything was swell."

Jimmy pleaded with Doris to postpone the divorce until he was established in his new post. Reluctantly, Doris agreed. She, too, had been nominated for an honor that seemed most unusual, considering her previous attitude toward clothing. She was to be fourth on the international best-dressed list for 1940 behind the Duchess of Windsor, the Duchess of Kent, and the wife of a tin tycoon. Since becoming enamored with Cunningham-Reid, she had taken more of an interest in her clothing because he was always so impeccably dressed.

From the winter day when Doris and Jimmy arrived in Ottawa, she made no effort to hide her disgust with her husband. Doris had replaced the servants at the official United States envoy's residence with her own servants from Duke Farms. Then she was enraged to find that the beds were too short for her nearly six-foot frame.

"Are Canadians all a bunch of pygmy Eskimos?" she snarled.

Meanwhile Jimmy was making a diplomatic fool of himself. His diplomatic pouches to Washington were filled with plans for grading and spreading manure on the residence's lawns or the results of his haggling over the cost of repairing a fireplace. He requested more gardeners and demanded the use of a government airplane. Doris left Ottawa after only ten days.

She met Cunningham-Reid in New York where they openly went shopping and night clubbing. She moved him to a suite of rooms in the main house of Duke Farms.

Jimmy dragged Doris back to Canada but she would make him

regret that action. Since his wife was always more of an attraction than he, Jimmy wanted Doris to go to an important meeting in the mining region of Val d'Or where there were going to be dogsled races. Doris was less than amused. As the big celebrity of the event, Doris was selected to crown Miss Dog Sled before a crowd of ten thousand shivering Canadians. The speech was to be broadcast on the Canadian Broadcast System over all of Canada. A smiling Doris stepped to the microphone and said, "Hi, Ma. It was a great fight but we won."

"No one had the slightest idea what I was talking about," she said much later. "People thought I was drunk. Maybe I was. It was very cold and I was stuck with the old cold Pope."

Roosevelt decided to call his envoy back to Washington but before Jimmy had time to arrange the trip, he made the stupid remark that began the downfall of his political career. At a speech in Toronto, he chastised the isolationist government of the United States for not supporting and joining the Allies.

He referred to officials of the United States Government as "cynically minded and shortsighted." Canada was supporting the mother country, Great Britain, in its war effort. At this time, Roosevelt was methodically working to convince the isolationists of the United States Congress to give more support to the Allies. Then this upstart rich kid caused international headlines by attempting to bully and embarrass Roosevelt's opponents into supporting the Allies.

"Not very diplomatic, huh," Doris said in her sexiest of throaty whispers.

Still, in an effort not to stir up any more public talk, Roosevelt again asked New Jersey officials to consider giving Cromwell the Senate seat. Anything to get him out of Canada.

Meanwhile, Doris was pregnant again.

The news had somehow been leaked that she was expecting a little bundle of Cromwell. Since there was absolutely no chance that Jimmy could have been the father, Doris had felt no need to tell him the news. He learned the details from Doris's social secretary.

It looked as if Jimmy would have a Senate seat if not a wife to keep him company. Then the heads of the New Jersey Democratic Party reminded him that they still expected that three-hundred-thousand-dollar donation. Jimmy did not have three hundred thousand dollars. Doris was not about to give him a dime.

She was ready to return to Hawaii. Alec Cunningham-Reid had decided to move his family from war-threatened London to the safety of the Duke estate in Hawaii and was traveling toward the islands with his mother and two sons. This was considered to be near treason because he was a Member of Parliament who seemed to be deserting his country during a time of war.

Doris told Jimmy that he was no longer welcome in any Duke residence. He had managed to survive political assassination long enough to make it to the Democratic National Convention where he stood next to Roosevelt for one brief moment of political respect. His hopes were still on becoming a senator.

# 12
# THE SACRIFICE: ARDEN

Doris Duke was alone, except for the servants, in the palace at Diamond Head. She paced from room to room trying to decide what to do. She was pregnant again and she could not be sure who the father was. It might be a dark-skinned scion of Duke Kahanamoku or it might be Cunningham-Reid's. She tried to remember the last time she had made love to Errol Flynn. She lit a cigarette with a shaking hand.

Her lawyers had told her something just before she left New York City . . . a legal fact of life that made her so sick that, combined with morning sickness, she thought she was going to throw up. The lawyers looked at her sternly and explained that Cromwell could well sue for custody of the child and even if it were Cunningham-Reid's there would be no way of proving Jimmy was not the father. Doris did not bother to inform the lawyers that there might very well be an obvious way to determine that the infant was not Jimmy's. If it were born with brown skin, the whole world would realize that Doris Duke was not only the richest girl in the world but the richest tramp in the world.

As the two had not had sex in years, Jimmy would surely know that the child was not his. He and his lawyers would also be shrewd enough to realize that the world would think he was the father and this would provide a lifetime tie to all the Duke money.

Doris Duke knew her husband would swear that he was the father unless, of course, the baby had dark skin. She went to the phone and called Duke Kahanamoku, who had moved back to his own house while Doris was in Canada for her brief stint as a diplomat's wife.

"He understood everything," she said years later.

It would be just as dangerous for Duke Kahanamoku should the world learn that he had fathered a child with a famous rich white woman. Actions that might be overlooked by the tolerant Hawaiians would not go unnoticed by the rest of the world.

Both Duke Kahanamoku and Doris Duke worshiped the sea. He was an Olympic swimming champion and she had won the Hawaiian woman's surfing championship. Silently, they left the house, loaded the surfboards into the Cadillac, and drove to the beach at Waikiki. The surf was high and dangerous.

Together they waded into the surf and paddled beyond the breakers. Doris stood on the board and surfed more recklessly than ever in her life. Spectators gathered on the shore watching the woman with the long blond hair in the treacherous waters. Again and again she paddled out through the heavy surf. Her tall body was lifted into the air and smashed into the curl of the giant waves. She was bruised and battered but she continued surfing.

The crowd on the beach became alarmed. Duke Kahanamoku stood on the beach and watched in silence. She was bruised and cut when she finally left the water.

Doris and Duke drove back to Shangri-La. By the time they reached the gleaming marble mansion, there was blood seeping through the fabric of her bathing suit. Doris screamed in pain. The Hawaiian gods of the sea had agreed to take the infant that was growing in her womb.

At Honolulu's Queen's Hospital she gave birth to a three-pound premature girl. The infant, who Doris named Arden, was small but she clung to life. Doris was in pain but wanted to see the baby so she struggled to her feet and stumbled her way to the window overlooking the incubator. As she looked at the tiny human, she wanted the little girl to live. She wanted to love that tiny creature and how she wanted that baby to love her. Arden's life would be different. Doris would not be an uncaring mother like Nanaline. Oh God, why did she do what she had done? Why did she sacrifice Arden to the ocean? She wanted that baby to live.

Arden, tiny dark-skinned Arden, died slightly less than twenty-four hours after her birth on July 11, 1940. The shades were pulled, making the hospital room as dark as night. When the doctors told Doris that Arden was dead, she asked that the tiny child be brought to her to hold one last time. Then she asked everyone to leave the room. The anxious nurses waiting outside the door first heard a low crying that slowly crescendoed into an animal-like wail. The frantic nurses ran back into the room and had to sedate Doris before they could pull Arden from her arms.

At that moment, something changed in the mind and heart of Doris Duke. The woman who could buy anything had finally wanted something that her money could not procure. She cursed herself for wanting the sea to rid her of this child. This was the start of her search through the mystic religions for the reincarnation of Arden. She wanted Arden to come back to her and would atone to the child for her horrible sin. She would will the reincarnation of Arden.

But for now she would rest.

Soon that rest was interrupted by a somber doctor who silently entered the darkened room. In spite of the heavy sedation, Doris Duke awakened. She had always had a high tolerance to drugs. The doctor and patient conversed for a few minutes and then there was silence. Doris turned her head and buried her face in the pillow. She had just learned that she would never have another child.

Alec Cunningham-Reid, the man she loved, would arrive in Honolulu soon. He would hold her. He would make everything all right.

When reporters started feeding on the story of the dead Duke child, they went looking for Jimmy Cromwell. They found him working on his tan at a Santa Fe dude ranch. Jimmy called Doris, who had immediately returned to Shangri-La to recuperate (she was afraid that Jimmy would come to the hospital surrounded by press and try to play the distraught husband). She told him that if he came to Hawaii, she would refuse to see him. So he did not go to Honolulu.

The press tore him to shreds. He had been the recipient of a lot of bad publicity that had referred to him as a self-absorbed political lightweight. Now the reporters tore to pieces what was left of his reputation for not being with his famous wife when she most needed him. His political popularity and public image died with the death of Arden.

When Cunningham-Reid arrived in Honolulu with his mother and sons, he devoted himself to Doris. He believed that they both had suffered a terrible loss. They had lost their daughter. The thought that the dead baby might not have been his never entered his mind.

Physically, Doris recovered quickly. Doris and Bobbie spent one month of love behind the gates of Shangri-La. She certainly could not have participated in the physical act of lovemaking for much of the time so the two talked and ran along the beach while the children swam in the big pool.

In September, Doris went home to Duke Farms. Bobbie went to New York City. Then Doris decided to make her affair with Cunningham-Reid public. She moved her lover and his two sons to Duke Farms and the boys even enrolled in the nearby Lawrenceville School.

The first week in October, a limousine made the long trek from Somerville to La Guardia Airport in New York City. Doris was sobbing as Bobbie got out of the car and was besieged by the herd of reporters.

"You gonna marry her?" one hard-bitten reporter snarled.

"I have nothing to say about that at this time," Cunningham-Reid said as he pushed through the maze of flashbulbs. Then one of the reporters showed him the headline of a London newspaper that had dubbed him "The Most Hated Man in Britain" because he had deserted his country in time of war. Cunningham-Reid was forced to return to England.

"Get her out of here," he yelled at the chauffeur while banging his fist into the door of the Rolls-Royce.

From the backseat of the speeding car, Doris turned and looked through the rear window at the tall shape of Cunningham-Reid until she could no longer see him. Still crying, she leaned her head back against the soft leather upholstery. Then something flashed in her eyes. A car was driving alongside the Rolls-Royce and a cameraman was leaning precariously out the window in an attempt to photograph her.

"Go faster," she yelled at the chauffeur. "Get them away from me. Get those people away from me. I hate them." She did hate reporters after that experience. She would say later in her throaty whisper, "I just wanted to say good-bye to the man I loved. He was going back to a country where he was hated. He could be killed by bombs or some fanatic. I was scared. Those damn reporters would not leave us alone. I was afraid I would never see him again."

On November 5, 1940, Jimmy Cromwell lost the election to the Senate from the State of New Jersey. He was never again proposed for public office. He went home to Palm Beach and his mother. Doris was on her way back to Hawaii when reporters caught up to her in California and asked her about the status of her marriage. Doris said with a slight smile, "It is very simple. I have separated from my husband. It is a permanent separation."

Then as an afterthought, she turned to the reporters and added, "It is a great pity that my husband lost the election. He worked so hard." She later learned that he had promised the Democrats the $300,000 from his potential divorce settlement to receive the nomination.

Doris was twenty-eight years of age and about to be free for the first time in her life. She had escaped her domineering mother. She was about to divorce a husband who had never been a husband. She was in love. She was rich.

She longed to be reunited with Cunningham-Reid. Doris even considered finding a way to travel to London but due to the war that was impossible. The only possible solution was to make Cunningham-Reid want to risk what remained of his career and reputation by coming to her side at Shangri-La where she would order the gates locked. The outside world would not touch them. She decided to make Cunningham-Reid jealous.

In 1941, she again entertained Errol Flynn in Santa Barbara. She had hoped that the handsome movie star with the ghastly reputation would inspire enough jealousy in Cunningham-Reid to make him want to run back to the United States and into her arms. It was common knowledge in their group of acquaintances that Flynn was bisexual. He himself would joke that not only was he wooing the richest girl in the world, he was also romancing the richest man in the world, Axel Wenner Gren, the Swedish creator of Electrolux (both Doris and Axel had homes called Shangri-La). Flynn was a living scandal. He was also said to be a Nazi spy.

Flynn also fed Doris's need to believe in reincarnation. She would sit for hours and question him about how she might someday be reunited with Arden. He assured her that that would happen. Doris also decided that she and Duke Kahanamoku had been lovers in a previous life when they both were Caucasian. Flynn also inspired Doris's theory that bisexual men made better lovers. The premise was simple. It took longer after an erection for a bisexual or homosexual man to climax with a woman and since women took longer to climax than men, this was a most satisfactory happening.

"It is an absolute fact," Doris would say while puffing on a cigarette. "Gay men who can screw a woman always last longer than a straight man. Well, most of the time. I should know, I have done exhausting research on the subject."

Cunningham-Reid did not run to Doris's side. Even if he had wanted to, it would have been impossible. World War II was starting to really interfere with Doris's sex life.

She was in New York City on December 7, 1941, when the Japanese bombed Pearl Harbor. She thought of the waves of aircraft passing over Diamond Head and her palace. Doris had been scheduled to fly to Hawaii the next day but all travel was canceled. She dialed the phone all night trying to contact any of the Kahanamokus but the lines were dead. The United States was at war.

And Doris found that she was nearly homeless. She could not

return to Hawaii. The government had seized her new motor yacht and military officers were swimming in her pool (the government did not use the house because it was too expensive to maintain). In New Jersey, the tax collectors were demanding $13 million in local income taxes on the $220 million they estimated she had earned in 1941 and 1942. After extensive legal negotiatons, the court agreed that Doris would pay $346,000.

Jimmy was demanding a $7 million settlement and threatening to write a book where he would portray himself as an abused man who was tricked into marrying a lesbian. Doris became furious and screamed, "I hate that liar and will never give him a dime."

She fled to Reno where it was possible to get a divorce after a six-week residency. Jimmy ensconced himself in a cheap New Jersey hotel room and announced that they were both residents of that state and a divorce from anyplace else would be invalid.

He had actually been living with his mother at the Washington home of one of his mother's few remaining friends.

Nanaline was distraught. The newspapers were pouring thousands of gallons of war-rationed ink onto millions of pages of recycled newsprint covering the scandal. The normally frugal Nanaline begged Doris to give Jimmy the $7 million to end the public fighting.

Jimmy even got an injunction to prevent Doris from enlisting in the armed forces or the Red Cross, which would enable her to leave the country. Doris was considering doing just that as a means of reuniting herself with Cunningham-Reid in London. She had received newspaper accounts that told of his having gotten into a fistfight in the House of Commons with a fellow MP who accused him of beachcombing with his paramour in Honolulu while London was in flames.

In December of 1942, Doris was granted her Reno divorce. She threw a champagne party but her celebration was premature because New Jersey would not accept the Reno divorce. Jimmy's lawyers said he would settle for a measly $1 million.

Doris's representatives, at her orders, countered with a final offer of five hundred thousand dollars. The battle was to continue raging for a long time.

Early in 1944, Alec Cunningham-Reid managed to return to the United States and a reunion was planned at Duke Farms. The war had been hard on the elegant and dashing Englishman who was now over fifty, some twenty years older than the woman who loved him so much.

While he had, before the war, enjoyed the image of a roué and a cad, he had become a much more serious man. The war was seemingly going to last forever and his sons might some day have to fight. Cunningham-Reid was devoted to his family. He had ruined his personal and political reputation by taking them to the safety of the white marble fortress on Diamond Head.

He began to feel some guilt about his relationship with Doris. He still believed that he was the father of Arden. The supposedly impervious Cunningham-Reid had been tortured by dreams of the little daughter he never saw. Now, Doris would never have any more children.

After years of wrangling with Jimmy, Doris was at the end of what little patience she had. She had waited years for Cunningham-Reid and he returned to her a tired aging man. She demanded that they get married immediately. He said that he couldn't.

For a brief instant, she lost complete control of her emotions. She stormed across the huge red drawing room with its deep Persian rugs and turned to him in rage and said, "I am glad you were not Arden's father. I wouldn't want your child."

Shocked, Cunningham-Reid looked at her through hollow eyes and said, "If I am not the father, who is? You are not going to tell me that poof Jimmy was actually . . ."

"It wasn't the Pope." Doris knew she should stop talking but she couldn't control her emotions. "It was Duke Kanahamoku. He was a better lover than you ever were."

Silently, Cunningham-Reid glared at her. Then he made a crisp military turn and walked into the great entry hall of the Tudor mansion. His heels clicked across the gleaming floor to the front door of the massive house. Then he paused. He turned and gave Doris a quick bow.

Many months would pass before Doris Duke saw Alec Cunningham-Reid again.

# 13
# THE HEIRESS GOES TO WAR

Her life was a complete mess. With war rationing, Doris could not travel. She was repulsed to learn that even the super-rich had to deal with shortages. She could not even go to the West Coast for a romp with Errol Flynn. There was no possibility of traveling to Hawaii and the ever-dependable arms of Duke Kahanamoku.

In typical Duke fashion, she decided that if she could not escape the war, she might as well enlist and be a part of the excitement. But even that proved impossible. Because of all the publicity about the divorce and her relationship with Cunningham-Reid, the State Department refused to issue a passport to Doris. They believed that the only reason she wanted to travel abroad was to find a way to get to London where she would pursue her former lover. And that was exactly what Doris was planning.

She was absolutely sure that if she could meet with Cunningham-Reid, she could win back his love. She was willing to do whatever it would take to get Cunningham-Reid to marry her. She was eager to seduce him. If all else failed, she would buy him. But first she had to get to him.

In May of 1944, Doris pulled strings at the War Department and managed to enlist in the United States Seaman Service. This service group was established in the early days of the war to set up hotels and headquarters for merchant seamen. Doris's "job" was to entertain the troops, a responsibility she enjoyed as she organized poker games.

"I feel that I am doing something worthwhile," Doris told the press. She made every effort to be dedicated to doing her part in the war effort. Finally in late September of 1944, her efforts resulted in her being assigned to the Egyptian Club in Cairo, Egypt. It was not London but it was a British outpost. She was one ocean closer to Alec Cunningham-Reid.

She spent her days and evenings entertaining the sailors. Doris had lobbied for the Cairo assignment because she had heard that Cunningham-Reid was occasionally in the city, which had a large British community. But Cunningham-Reid avoided her.

It was then that Doris created Captain Henderson. He was a handsome young British officer who, she said, she had met in Cairo where the two had instantly fallen in love in the shadow of the Great Pyramids. She told her friends that "Henderson"—she always called him by his last name—was the man she had always wanted and needed. He was suave and charming and fabulous in bed.

"I know now what it is to be in love," she told anyone who would listen. "We have made a decision to stay completely out of the public eye. That is why I will not reveal his first name or any intimate details about his background. This relationship is very precious to me."

Captain Henderson was a complete fabrication. Doris realized that both the governments of Great Britain and the United States did not want the scandal of the "richest girl in the world" chasing her lover MP through hell and war. Not even Cunningham-Reid wanted his ardent one-time lover to come to England. Thus by concocting the mythical Henderson, she could convince officials of both governments that she was no longer interested in Cunningham-Reid while, at the same time, hopefully making Bobbie jealous. No mere world war would interfere with the love life of Doris Duke.

Only a very few people would ever learn that Captain Henderson (or sometimes when she wanted him to seem younger she called him Lieutenant Henderson) was invented in an effort to make Alec Cunningham-Reid jealous. This was a foolish move. Cunningham-Reid had never loved Doris, so when he finally decided to dump her, he was not about to take her back. The responsibility of war had turned him into a serious member of Parliament who had no time for the demands and desires of a rich oversexed American woman.

On October 27, 1944, Cunningham-Reid announced at a political reception that he had married a beautiful woman who was less than half his age. She was the tall and dark-haired daughter of a naval officer and had no money. She was pregnant and five months after the wedding ceremony, the Cunningham-Reids were the parents of a baby boy.

Doris's wartime romance with "Captain Henderson" was expanding rapidly when the news reached her at her new villa in Cairo. She was devastated and sick of the desert and the dust of Cairo so she transferred Captain Henderson from Cairo and the Desert War to the Italian front. She wanted to go to Italy.

She approached the Office of Strategic Services, a spy organization of the United States Government and the predecessor of the Central Intelligence Agency. General William J. "Wild Bill" Donovan was then the head of the OSS and he liked Doris. In spite of protests from Pentagon types in Washington who believed that Doris Duke was still attempting to finagle her way to London where she could continue her quest for the now married Cunningham-Reid, Donovan hired her. She was now officially Doris Duke, undercover agent and spy, at a government salary of two thousand dollars annually. She was able to travel easier than she could have as a mere entertainer of the troops.

Her code name was "Daisy." She selected this name herself, patterned after the beautiful and leggy Daisy Mae Yokum, the cartoon character who was relentless in her chase after the reluctant to commit to marriage Li'l Abner.

"A rather clever double meaning," she would laugh.

Doris now had Captain Henderson firmly transferred someplace on the Italian front. She would speak of him with tears welling in her eyes and bide her time until she could somehow follow Henderson to London.

Meanwhile, the Secretary of State had a few written comments concerning the antics of his new spy, Daisy. In a coded message, he wrote: "Common gossip Cairo that subject had personal interest in reaching London and she went to Italy on OSS basis as a first easy lesson on how to get to London despite British refusal of a visa. [Cunningham-Reid had ordered that she not be permitted into the country to further embarrass him.] Strongly recommend Washington takes steps to frustrate this if true for good of our agency which is given full credit at Cairo cocktail parties for employment plus special plush plane to Naples."

Doris knew she was about to be ordered back to Washington for "appropriate training." She did not want to return to the United States. So she announced that Captain Henderson had been killed in action. She was appropriately devastated but she told her superiors that she would swallow her misery and continue with her job in spite of her great loss. Many of the officials of the OSS admired her courage in staying on her new post in spite of losing the man she loved.

"And they said in Hollywood," Doris recalled years later, "when I thought I would be an actress, they thought I couldn't act."

Things were going well for Doris. She was receiving great sympathy for the death of a great love who never existed. She was able to stay in Europe and might soon find a way to go to London where she would retrieve Cunningham-Reid from his new marriage. But best of all, Jimmy Cromwell was a loser back in the United States. After years of appeals, her Reno divorce had been upheld. She was free. She was delighted to learn that the judge had lambasted Jimmy for his greed and the newspapers had jumped on the remarks, branding him the worst sort of fortune hunter. When he died at the age of ninety-two, the headline on his obituary read, DORIS DUKE HUSBAND DIES. Doris saved that headline with glee.

Her refusal to pay off Jimmy Cromwell was the first instance of what was to become a pattern of handling anyone who attempted to take advantage of her. She could have had her divorce years earlier (and probably married her beloved Cunningham-Reid at that time) but she would not pay Jimmy $7 million. She would not even offer him $1 million when he said he would settle for that, even though she would spend that much on years of legal battles. In the end, Jimmy got only a few thousand dollars in expenses. When Doris Duke believed she was in the right, she would spend whatever it took to win. This became a philosophy she would continue until her death.

Back in Washington, the state department was pondering what to do with their new superspy "Daisy." "I presented a real problem to the OSS," Doris said. "They wanted to send me home but if I had said anything about Daisy the spy, it would have made a lot of embarrassing headlines for the OSS. In the end, they decided to let me stay in Europe, which was exactly what I wanted." Doris Duke had again managed to get her own way, even in time of war.

One member of the Duke family who was really a high-level member of the OSS said that Doris was merely being "humored" by diplomatic officials who did not want to offend a woman who had so many powerful connections. She was never permitted into any crucial situations that might affect national security or the war effort. While Doris would never be in bed with the enemy, that did not preclude her from bedding down a few of the heroes of the Allied Forces.

Doris Duke became bored with being a spy. She thought it might be more glamorous to be a foreign correspondent. War correspondents stayed in better hotels than most spies. She got a job with the International News Service (INS) and was assigned to the Rome bureau. She interviewed the widow of Il Duce, who she found to be happy in exile in spite of the fact that her husband, the former Italian dictator, had been executed and the country he had ruled was now under the control of the Allies. Doris found slums and suffering in Rome. She visited the remains of the Italian film industry and toured the studio buildings that had been stripped of their glamour.

It was as a journalist that she was finally able to go to London. She forced a meeting with Alec Cunningham-Reid. He was furious and even threatened to have her thrown out of the country if she ever came near him again. Doris had gone to war and suffered the degradation of second-class hotels in an effort to win this man. She was even prepared to buy him. All he had to do was name the price. She even offered to pay in advance. She just wanted him to make love to her, just love her and there would be a deposit of whatever he wanted in his secret accounts. The transactions could be handled in a few hours. Even if he didn't want to divorce his wife, Doris was still ready to negotiate. She would be his mistress. She would be whatever he wanted. She just wanted him to want her.

But Cunningham-Reid didn't want Doris Duke. He was no longer for sale.

Rejected, she went back to Rome and started volunteering for the assignments that nobody else wanted, not because they were boring but because they were dangerous. "She told me," one relative said, "that she did not care if she died. She had lost her daughter and would never have another child and now she had lost that English chap."

In the late winter of 1945, Doris was at the Russian front at the invitation of General George S. Patton. She had known Patton from his days before the war when he was stationed in Hawaii. While he was known as a rash and reckless hero to the American public, "Old Blood and Guts," as he had been nicknamed by the press, was a wealthy aristocrat who played polo and had superb manners.

Patton was at the peak of his fame. He had marched his troops across France and in the process captured seven hundred and fifty thousand Nazi troops. His Third Army met the Russians in Linz, and Soviet Field Marshal Feodor Tolbukhin invited the American four-star general to a celebration at a lavish château near the Czech border that had formerly been the "summer cottage" of Emperor Franz Joseph of Austria.

Following the end of the war in Europe, Doris was in Linz waiting for a plane ride back to Rome when General Patton's plane landed.

"Daisy," Patton said with amusement, using her code name, "what are you doing here? Has the polo season started?"

Doris told him she was a reporter and that her spy days were over. "Hell, write something about me," General Patton said as he grabbed Doris Duke in his powerful arms. Unlike many high-ranking military men, Patton made an effort to keep his body hard. He was tall and strong and, Doris had been told, fully functional in bed.

"This was unusual in a general," Doris said later with the authority of a reporter who has well researched her subject. "It was common knowledge that generals were usually dreadful at lovemaking. For the most part, they are usually underendowed. This is probably what motivates them to become so powerful in other ways. I got it from his wife that General Douglas MacArthur was absolutely tiny. Georgie did not suffer from that problem."

Moments after they met, Doris and Georgie were in his official staff car speeding toward the château. "I just did what any good newspaperwoman would have done," she laughed later. "I knew he wanted to bed me. He liked to be seen with famous and powerful people and I was both. And, if I do say so myself, I was the best-looking and best-dressed woman he was going to find on the Russian front."

Doris knew he was married and had several mistresses. She was not looking for a long-lasting relationship. She just needed some good sex. She had been on a kind of sexual bender since she had been officially and irrevocably dumped by Alec Cunningham-Reid, including several actors and writers, but this was her opportunity to copulate with a future war memorial.

"He wore polished leather knee boots," she said. "I found those boots to be a marvelous turn-on."

At the château, Doris consumed copious amounts of vodka (she could always outdrink most men) and watched an incredibly built Moscow showgirl dance her clothes off. Georgie pulled one of his many medals from the chest of his uniform and tried to pin it on the showgirl but there was no place to stick the medal without inflicting injury so he thrust it into her hand. A drunk Tolbukhin groped at his own nest of medals and immediately went to the tall blond with the great legs and pinned it on Doris's breast. In Russian he honored Doris for being an example of the American working woman and the working-class values that would soon rule the world. Then, as General Patton howled in laughter, Tolbukhin took Doris's face in his weathered paws and kissed her on both cheeks.

She spent the next four days with Georgie at the château. Afterward she said this was some of the best sex she would ever experience.

The war was over in Europe. Doris Duke had failed in her personal siege for the heart and love of Alec Cunningham-Reid. She had experienced passion and romance but not love and Doris Duke was determined to find some man to love her.

Whatever the price.

14

# THE SEX GOD

"It was the most magnificent penis that I had ever seen," Doris Duke said when recalling the legendary part of playboy Porfirio Rubirosa's anatomy. "There has never been anything like it since."

There had been a lot of conjecture about the size and ability of the Rubirosa prick. The length both in times of passion and in times of repose was always in excess of eleven inches. At all times, it was six inches in circumference not, as erroneous accounts reported, six inches in diameter.

The best description is that it was much like the last foot of a Louisville Slugger baseball bat with the consistency of a not completely inflated volley ball.

Doris believed the very rich and the very poor often have the same attitude toward great sex. The very rich can buy almost anything except a perfect climax so when this joyous event occurs, it is vastly appreciated. The very poor have nothing so when they have the opportunity to experience really great sex, it is wondrous. For these two opposites of the social spectrum, sex can be more important than anything. More important than jobs. More important than mortgages or college tuitions or a new living room set. Being poor or being rich gives a person a freedom for sexual indulgence that usually escapes the middle classes.

"Rubirosa the hosa," as Rubi was nicknamed, was the ultimate stud of the 1940s. Within the large social set in which Doris Duke traveled, Rubirosa was the most sensual and exciting, and probably the most dangerous, lover in the world. It was easy for a rich woman to rent Rubirosa. A few polo ponies, an investment in one of his frequent business ideas, some really good jewelry, or just plain cash could be exchanged for a bout with the Rubirosa prick. Only Doris was not a renter; she was an owner and she would settle for nothing more than a complete purchase.

"My success in finding a real love relationship had been disastrous until Rubi," she said. "With the Pope there was no sex and it cost me a lot. Bobbie did not work out even when I was willing to give him what he wanted."

She would not make the same mistake with Porfirio Rubirosa. Very early in the relationship, she decided that she would marry him but she would buy him the way she bought a Rembrandt or an eighteenth-century Chippendale settee. She would deal shrewdly, as she did in all her business transactions, until she got what she wanted at the lowest possible price.

The price might have been very high. It might even have been her life. Early in the relationship Doris was told that the charming and sexually unlimited Rubirosa was also a paid killer. This revelation only seemed to intrigue Doris all the more.

"I believed her when she said that if she could not have Cunningham-Reid, she would kill herself," one Duke relative conjectured. "When Alec dumped her, she did a lot of reckless things but the pursuit of Rubi was by far the most dangerous thing she had ever done in her life." Like Cleopatra with her pet asp, Doris knew that the fortune-hunting yet charming Rubirosa could be a fatal poison.

"I asked Rubi straight out of the blue," Doris remembered while sitting at the bar of the Paris Ritz where she and Rubirosa had spent so many evenings, "whether he would consider killing me to get my money." Rubi looked at her, gently took her hand in his, and said, "I have done much worse." And he had.

He had been a political assassin for dictator and former father-in-law Rafael Trujillo of the Dominican Republic. As a political perk, he was permitted to sell Dominican Republic passports to affluent Jews who were attempting to escape death in Hitler's concentration camps. He would also, for a price, use the political pouch to smuggle jewels and money for Jews who were hoping to salvage some of their assets. More often than not, the valuables would disappear along with their owners. The charming and handsome Porfirio Rubirosa, the man of a million fucks, the darling of the boudoir, like the mythical James Bond (who was said to be patterned after Rubi), had a license to kill. Was Doris dying to be his wife?

The press would babble for decades that Rubi was "the love of Doris Duke's life." This was ridiculous. Alec Cunningham-Reid was the real passion in her existence. Rubirosa was merely one of the unique things that she collected in her search for the very best. At the time, he was thought to be the best lover in the world. He was exciting and dangerous. While he was incapable of being true to any one woman, he was devoted to any woman who could afford him. He was attentive and charming and affectionate and absolutely focused on Doris whenever they were together. He was worth his cost.

After the rejection from Cunningham-Reid, Doris Duke wanted a man who would be true to his contract. She paid and he performed. The Duke-Rubirosa romance was negotiated like a business contract, and Rubi and Doris both adhered to the terms of the deal. He was charming and kept her well laid, and she kept him well paid. Even after the relationship ended, Doris and Rubi remained friends until the day he died.

In the early days of the relationship, Rubirosa might have had other ideas of the benefits he might ultimately acquire from the union. But Doris was smarter than Rubi. She had researched her new romantic acquisition.

He was at least four inches shorter than her nearly six feet. His skin was mahogany in color and he was rumored to be a mulatto. This was an attraction to Doris, who liked dark-skinned men. His one-time wide and flat Negroid nose had been reshaped by plastic surgery. He was slightly bow-legged but that was said to make him an even better polo player than his lanky English and American competitors.

"His purpose was to satisfy women," Doris would say in a matter-of-fact tone. "He was sterile and probably impotent but his prick was so large that it seemed to be in a state of eternal erection. I don't think that he really felt anything when he was making love but he was able to do whatever I wanted for endless hours. I was always the focus during sex. All that mattered was that I be satisfied. He simply wanted to make every woman on earth experience the ultimate climax."

Scientists would later refer to the Rubirosa lovemaking method as "retarded ejaculation." In reality, he was like no other man in that he had this marvelous appendage that could always function on automatic pilot. All he had to do was to point his fabulous penis in the direction of a willing woman and this oh-so-dependable appendage would perform. His was the Rolls-Royce of genitalia in a world inhabited by sexual Chevettes. He was an erotic powerful sexual streamliner in a world where most males were traveling the tracks in a hand-powered pump car. Rubi would even ask a woman what she enjoyed before initiating sex. She might want her ears kissed or her breasts nibbled. His tongue was available to every part of the female form. He could and would do anything any woman wanted. Doris, as always, wanted it all.

The one-time sheltered heiress had learned a lot about sex and satisfying a man. She realized that her long and fabulous legs could clamp a man in a trap of almost painful eroticism. She was not afraid to sweat, thus lovemaking was usually extremely physical. After a few hours of passion, she would race to the shower ahead of her partner. When Rubi was her paramour, he would usually follow her to the water jets where his famous rudder would relaunch the lovemaking. Wet or dry or any state in between, Rubi and Doris were equals in passion.

"He would even fake an orgasm," Doris laughed. "Women have had to fake orgasms for centuries to make men think they were better than they were but Rubi's dry runs were absolutely charming. The world would be a better place if more men were capable of faking an orgasm but all other males I have ever known have been basically interested in only satisfying themselves. There is nothing as useless as a man who has just climaxed."

She had once discussed this theory with General George Patton. "I told him," she said, "that if women were generals we could win battles easier than any man who had studied military strategy at West Point. I suggested that a thousand beautiful naked women be marched into the oncoming male army and within a few minutes every fighting man would be exhausted and ready to go to sleep. Didn't the Greeks do something like that? Perhaps that is why Alexander the Great did so well with a gay army. Georgie did not think this idea had much merit."

The son of a Dominican Republic general, Rubi was educated in Paris. As a child, he was puny. "It was all his little body could do to grow that marvelous magic wand," Doris would joke. His hobby of boxing developed his body as a more appropriate setting for the "Rubber Hosa."

General Trujillo took a liking to young Rubi, who was a good polo player and had acquired European manners. Soon Rubi had attracted the attention of Trujillo's sixteen-year-old daughter Flor de Oro (flower of gold). Soon he had deflowered Flor.

"Imagine being a sixteen-year-old girl and your first experience was with Rubi," Doris philosophized years later. "She probably thought that all men were able to make love like Rubi. It must have been a horrible shock to learn that Rubi was the best and that it was all downhill from there."

General Trujillo was not a happy dictator when Flor de Oro insisted on marrying Rubirosa in 1932. For the next few years, Rubi bedded Flor and became a professional killer for her father. He was stationed in Berlin where he found profit in marketing passports to Jews, and was later he sent to Paris. His need to bed every woman in the city of lights enraged Flor de Oro, who divorced Rubi in 1936.

In 1942, he married Danielle Darrieux, who was the reigning siren of the French motion picture industry as well as a Nazi sympathizer. Danielle found herself so unpopular following the war that she and Rubi were even ambushed in Paris by partisans seeking revenge against her because of her Nazi past. Three bullets hit Rubi in the area of his kidneys when he threw his body over his wife in an effort to protect her.

"It could have been so much worse," Doris said of the shooting. "He could have been hit in the groin. After all, he did have two kidneys. He might have lost one of the great treasures of the civilized world."

Immediately following her first evening with Rubi in liberated Paris, Doris started writing checks. She followed him to his new post in Rome where she arranged for a newspaper interview (she had decided to be a reporter again) at his hotel where she met both Rubi and Danielle. Instead of interviewing the superstar, Doris negotiated with Danielle for the purchase of her husband.

The exact words that were exchanged by the two women (as Rubi sat on a Louis XV settee in silence) have remained a secret but Doris proved that she had, indeed, inherited Buck Duke's ability to negotiate for what she wanted. Doris pointed out that Rubi would probably leave Danielle sooner or later. She also called attention to the fact that the once-adored actress was now a pariah in France and fans would no longer be willing to pay their francs to be entertained by a traitor. Her career ruined, she should consider liquidating some of her more expensive assets, of which Rubi was the most expensive. Danielle waited for an offer.

Rubi, who always went with the most money, would have left Danielle for Doris but Doris had learned from her bitter and costly divorce from Jimmy that it is better to reach an amicable financial settlement first. The two very sophisticated women continued to negotiate.

Danielle suggested that $5 million seemed fair. Without taking a breath, Doris offered $1 million, not a penny more. She pointed out that $1 million in American dollars was worth a lot of francs in the ravaged postwar French economy. All French women are very pragmatic when it comes to matters of money and Danielle was no exception. She took the million. Doris, who would have paid more, was so pleased with the deal that she gave Rubirosa an additional five hundred thousand dollars as a signing bonus. He bought a coffee plantation.

Rubi was ready to earn his money. Besides the sex, he always tried to match her generosity by giving her gifts that were as tasteful and carefully selected as the presents she gave him. She gave him a sapphire-studded solid gold cigarette case and he gave her diamond earrings and a ruby-encrusted compact, the most expensive gift that any man other than her father would ever give to Doris Duke. In gratitude for the cigarette case, Rubirosa never permitted Doris Duke to light her own cigarette when she was in his presence for the rest of his life. All she needed was to reach for a cigarette and he would be on his feet. Then with a quick bow, he would flick his solid-gold lighter into action.

"It was the kind of attention that Doris loved," a family member commented. "She felt that she was getting a good return on her investment from Rubi. She wrote checks and he adored her. It was exactly what she needed after that beastly Cromwell, who was emotionally abusive, and Cunningham-Reid, who dumped her."

The State Department brass were starting to worry that Doris's relationship with the unsavory Rubirosa could be a potential threat to national security. Doris Duke was the most powerful woman in America as she controlled vast amounts of power and energy. Duke Power provided much of the electric energy for a large part of the South, including some of the largest military installations in the country. She owned much of Texaco and had interests in aluminum, the basis of the growing aircraft industry. If she should marry Rubirosa, he could be in a position to inherit this empire, which would be ostensibly under the control of the Dominican Republic. The possibility of some banana republic dictator being able to potentially pull the plug on Fort Bragg sent shivers through the cold hearts of the Pentagon.

The State Department ordered Doris to return from Paris to the United States alone in the summer of 1946. She went to Rough Point, the damp and cavernous immense Newport beach cottage where Nanaline loved to reign over what little remained of the glory days of society before the Crash. After nearly five years away from her mother, Doris had finally become completely independent. The two strong-willed women immediately discovered that they detested each other.

Doris headed for Hawaii and Shangri-La. Duke Kahanamoku met her plane and drove her to the closed white marble palace. As they walked through the darkened and echoing rooms and looked out over the giant breakers that crashed on the sands of Diamond Head, Doris could not escape the memories of her dead child. The adoring Duke Kahanamoku tried to entice her back into the romance that they had shared a half decade earlier and they did have sex. But she kept thinking of Rubirosa.

In March of 1947, after taking a job with *Harper's Bazaar* as a fashion writer in an effort to convince the State Department that she was devoted to her newfound career, which coincidentally required that she spend time in Paris, Doris arrived in France. Rubi was in Paris waiting to continue to fulfill his part of the contract with Doris Duke.

By June, the divorce between Rubi and Danielle was finalized. Doris had spent a considerable fortune in acquiring Rubirosa and decided to culminate the deal in marriage. He thought this to be a terrific idea and rushed the trip to the altar.

Again the State Department and Doris's associates at the OSS were horrified. The White House debated what to do in the few hours that remained before the wedding. There were some OSS officials who suggested killing Rubirosa. Calmer diplomats suggested a premarital agreement which would probably be about as painful to Rubirosa as a volley of ammunition from an untraceable rifle. Representatives of the United States Government went to Doris and expressed their desire for a premarital agreement protecting all those electric plants and oil wells from Rubirosa.

Doris was no fool. She had become the ultimate realist. She knew that her adoring husband was a murderer and that there was a chance she could become a victim. She told the officials to take care of the problem without harming Rubi or any of his precious appendages. The stern-faced men of the OSS met with Rubirosa and suggested that he sign the prenuptial agreement on September 1, 1947.

Rubi found their suggestion to be wildly humorous. He, of course, refused, returning to the party that Doris had arranged as a prelude to the wedding ceremony. Rubi had arranged that the wedding be held at the Dominican Republic legation where, he believed, he would be safe. Just as the American officials were worried that Rubi might kill Doris and take control of her fortune, the officials of the Dominican Republic were equally concerned that the OSS would kill Rubi before he could ice the heiress.

There was an ongoing debate as to who would survive the honeymoon night. But Rubi was charming; he drank champagne and downed two whiskey highballs. Like most men of Rubirosa's ilk, he was proud of his drinking ability. On this occasion, however, he was woozy. Only minutes before the wedding, two lawyers (looking more like OSS officials than representatives of some white shoe law firm) arrived with a briefcase holding the agreement.

Sign it or die was the message. A stumbling but angry Rubirosa signed and the wedding continued. Attempting to regain his composure, Rubirosa smoked a cigarette while the vows were being recited. His hand shook as he slipped the small ruby wedding band on Doris's left hand. She smiled and very calmly placed a heavy gold band (she had ordered it designed to resemble a single handcuff) on his ring finger.

At this point, Porfirio Rubirosa, international playboy, lover, man's man, and political assassin, fainted in his wife's arms. A strong and physically powerful woman, Doris Duke stood at the temporary altar smiling with her expensive new husband unconscious in her arms.

Rubi slept through most of the wedding night. In the morning, he awoke in the wedding suite of the exclusive Eden Roc Hotel on the Riviera. He was one pissed playboy.

"I thought it was funny," Doris recalled. "Big Boy [her nickname for her new groom] was so upset that he just paced around the suite smoking cigarettes."

Rubirosa told Doris that he was a man who would honor his agreements and was shocked that the government (and Doris) would drug him into signing that damned prenuptial agreement. Doris sympathized, but she also refused to destroy the agreement, which was already in a diplomatic pouch headed for her lawyer's vaults in New York City.

Rubirosa fired his ultimate weapon, or rather, he refused to fire his ultimate weapon. He refused to have sex with Doris for the entire honeymoon. Doris was appropriately contrite and atoned for her actions by buying Rubi a mansion at 46 rue de Bellechasse on Paris's Left Bank.

Rubi was somewhat mollified and his penis was again primed for action. A second honeymoon was celebrated in the mirrored rooms of the hundred-thousand-dollar (a huge sum to pay for a house in postwar Paris) house. It was a three-story seventeenth-century townhouse that was surrounded by a high white stone wall.

But Doris soon became bored with even the best sex the world had to offer. The excitement and the danger in the relationship with Rubi had lost their luster in a matter of months. She had amused herself with Rubi and he had given her the calculated adoration that she had needed so badly. But he was a plaything, a sexual toy like the leather mechanical bull she had installed in the garden of the Paris house. In much the same manner, she would wrap her long legs around the man or the bull and ride.

"He did whatever I asked," she would say, "and I was losing respect for him. I had used Rubi as a marvelous distraction. He always kept his part of the bargain but . . . I wanted more."

Doris Duke wanted real love. She had been adored by Duke Kahanamoku. She had experienced passion from Cunningham-Reid. Most assuredly she had felt every sensual thrill possible from Rubi.

Somewhere, she thought, there must be a man to love her. Doris realized that she could not buy love. She could only wonder how it would feel to hold a man in her arms, or be held in his, and know that he would love her if she weren't Doris Duke and didn't have all that damn money.

Rubi served his purpose with Doris. "He made me get over Bobbie [Alec Cunningham-Reid] and that was worth every penny he ever cost me," she said.

# 15

# NEW INTERESTS . . . NEW MEN

Paris was recovering from the war and life was exciting again. It was almost impossible for Doris to believe but she was tiring of really great sex. She had a new interest . . . jazz music.

Since her days in the mansion on Fifth Avenue, she had loved the piano and had developed into a competent pianist. But it was in the smoke-filled jazz joints of Paris where Doris Duke discovered her new passion. She wanted to be a jazz pianist.

"If Doris could have done whatever she wanted in life," one family member commented, "she would have opted to go to some cheap bar every night and play piano jazz for anyone who was willing to listen. She used to do just that; go places where no one had ever heard of Doris Duke and play nonstop until the bar was empty. She was so pleased one time when the audience filled her tip jar. She was amazed and told everyone, 'They paid me to play. They actually paid me to play.' I think it was the only money she ever earned entirely by herself."

Instead of going to Rubi's bed, she would sit at the keyboard of the massive Steinway in the drawing room of the Paris mansion and play jazz until dawn. Sometimes she would venture onto the cobbled streets of the Left Bank where she had become known in the tiny and usually dirty jazz joints where she would smoke cigarettes and drink cheap booze until dawn.

After her therapeutic fling with Rubi, Doris Duke began to look for ways of defining herself other than being very rich and very good in bed. She had learned the difference between passion and love and was seeking satisfaction.

Rubi's calculatingly agreeable nature was tested when she started bringing band members home to the Left Bank mansion for all-night sessions loud enough to keep the entire neighborhood awake.

Since his own house was turned into Doris Duke's personal cabaret, Rubi headed toward his old playground, the nightlife of Paris, for entertainment. He would leave the house and return days later. Rubi was ready to escape from Doris.

He approached his former father-in-law Trujillo, and soon the offer of the position of ambassador to Argentina arrived at the Paris house. Strings were pulled and the United States Department of State refused to grant permission for Doris to go to Buenos Aires. Government officials feared that should Doris find herself on South American soil, she could also be convinced to change the prenuptial agreement, which most probably would result in her death.

Forced to return to the States but not quite willing to completely give up Rubirosa's marvelous screwing, Doris bought a war-surplus B-25 bomber and refitted it as a luxury plane for Rubi to use to fly to her side should her need for him to arise . . . arise.

The State Department finally relented and Doris was permitted to join her husband in Buenos Aires. She brought her own furniture, china, and his French servants.

As usual, Rubi used his best talent to assure his success. One member of the Duke family who held a diplomatic post in Argentina at the same time commented, "He bedded every woman of any importance from every embassy including Eva Peron. He was a popular person in that most men liked him and all women adored him."

Following a particularly enthusiastic marathon of Rubirosa

copulation, Doris suggested that he should consider being more discreet or consider paying his own bills. A contrite Rubi flew back to Paris and Doris headed for Hawaii for a return to her old dependable romance with Duke Kahanamoku.

Rubi's fabulous prick went into high gear in Europe but it ventured into a forbidden zone when he rediscovered Flor de Oro and reportedly struck gold on the polished surface of a Rome bar. Both Trujillo and Doris were enraged and it was difficult to determine whose anger worried Rubi more.

Doris had brought to Paris her three German shepherd attack dogs, which were trained to devour anyone who touched their mistress. "She told people she had beaten the dogs with a pair of his unwashed underwear," one friend recalled. "We knew this was impossible because she would never beat an animal. Rubi maybe, but not an animal."

Two final things happened that convinced Doris to rid herself of her Latin lover. First, she had a fight with him during which she was injured enough to bleed all over the bedroom of the Paris mansion. And second, the B-25 crashed mysteriously in New Jersey when Doris was supposed to have been aboard. At the last moment she had decided not to fly. Rubi then rushed a supposedly distraught Doris, who was mysteriously unconscious, to a remote rest cure hospital where she might have remained as an inmate for years had not her old OSS buddies rescued her. Doris realized that there were people who would gladly murder her for her money and one of those people was that marvelous prick Porfirio Rubirosa.

Doris Duke headed for Reno. Part of the terms of the divorce was a twenty-five-thousand-dollar annual allowance to Rubi if he agreed never to marry anyone. The pair parted as friends, Rubi was after all a professional diplomat, and Doris and Rubi went back to being lovers instead of husband and wife. For the next two years, Doris kept Rubi and his fabulous appendage on call should she have a need for the best sex in the world.

The Mocambo was the hottest night club in Los Angeles in 1950 and it was there that Doris went to hear Joey Castro, perhaps the world's finest undiscovered jazz pianist. He was young and swarthy, and they soon ended up in bed, but Doris was looking for "the right kind of man." Castro was most definitely wrong. Still, she trundled Castro and his musician friends from Los Angeles to Honolulu to New Jersey and even took them to the New York mansion where Nanaline lived alone with her fifteen servants. (When Castro arrived at the front door, he was admonished and taken to the downstairs servants' quarters by mistake.)

Doris also was taking a more intense interest in her financial empire and her trusts. She started looking at Duke Farms, her father's place, the place for which she sued her mother to prevent its sale, and applied herself to restoring the thousands of acres. Her orchid greenhouses were the most famous in the world. But Doris had recently devoted more attention to her love life than to the sprawling Duke Farms. She needed someone to advise her on how to rebuild her father's private kingdom. She found Louis Bromfield.

Of all the men whom Doris tried to love, Pulitzer Prize–winning fiction writer Louis Bromfield was the only person who met her on equal terms. He was not as rich as she. Nobody was. But for all but the last year or so of his life, his income from his books provided everything he wanted. He had no need for Doris Duke or her fortune. Doris was very rich but Louis Bromfield was a success.

Louis Bromfield was born into a poor family in Mansfield, a small farming city in central Ohio. As a child and teenager, he was entranced by the wealthy families of his affluent hometown and as he explored more of the state, he stored memories of the nouveau riche steel and industrial dynasties of Youngstown, Canton, Akron, and the Cleveland mansion suburbs of Cleveland Heights and Shaker Heights.

His early years were a study in rejection. As happened with many poor but smart and ambitious young men of his age in those years before World War I, he was enticed by the blond hair and ivory skin and arrogant attitudes of the girls of the families who aspired to breeding. He was rejected as a bumpkin who wanted to climb the hill to the mansion. He developed a kind of callousness and disdain toward the new rich who mistook snobbery to be a sign of sophistication and position.

Too many people in Mansfield laughed at his announcements that he would be a great writer. He was a hick. His family had no money.

Young Louis was grateful for World War I. He went to war in France driving an ambulance even before the United States officially entered the war. He both detested and thrived on the violence and excitement of the war as his many-layered psyche stored memories of people and places he would later use to populate his books.

His first book, *The Green Bay Tree*, was published in 1924 and went immediately to the best-seller list. It was a cathartic not-so-disguised requiem of his young years in his family's tiny house in Mansfield where a window overlooked a green bay tree. In 1926, he won the Pulitzer Prize for *Early Autumn* and in 1928, he was awarded the O. Henry Short Story Award for "The Apothecary." A prolific fiction and screenplay writer, he published thirty books, each one of which went immediately to the top ten best-seller list. Most of his books were published by Harper Brothers, including *The Rains Came, Wild Is the River, Mrs. Parkington,* and *Night in Bombay*, which were made into hit feature films.

With each success, Bromfield became more desirable in the expensive new Midwestern mansions of Ohio. But he was a bitter young man and chose to disdain his new popularity by snubbing the very people who had snubbed him. He took his new fortune and wife and moved to a large house outside of Paris where his uniqueness was more understood and appreciated by the aristocracy and the literati of Europe. He might have happily remained in his French country house had Hitler not decided to march across France and through Louis Bromfield's new place in the Old World.

In 1939 Louis Bromfield, his wife, and four daughters came back to the United States. His American bank accounts were bulging with years of unspent residuals. Hollywood producers, fists filled with money, wanted his screenplays and advice as well as the rights to bring his words to film.

Nanaline Holt Inman Duke was delighted that her only child by Buck Duke was a girl. She thought this would protect the interests of her son by a previous marriage, but she was wrong. In her will, she left her grandson $35 million and her daughter a ratty fur coat of horrific significance. (Culver Pictures, Inc.)

"Do not tolerate disloyal people," Buck Duke taught his daughter. He was the most powerful man in the world tobacco market. "I got my sex drive from Daddy," Doris said. She also got $100 million and was the richest child in the world. (Author's Collection)

Washington Duke was a North Carolina dirt farmer. His fortune could be traced to a single fifty-cent piece, which he used to bankroll the American Tobacco Company in 1865. (Duke University Archives)

Tobacco was mostly a male product until Buck Duke doubled its audience. He believed in the equality of women—while being rabidly opposed to smoking for reasons of health. (The Bettmann Archive)

Buck Duke's close friendship with President Taft prevented his going to jail when his American Tobacco Trust was broken in 1909. (AP/Wide World Photos)

Lillian McCredy was Buck Duke's first wife. She caused trouble for him long after their divorce. "Lillian was always in heat," Doris said. (UPI/Bettmann)

Ben Duke married the socially prominent Sarah Angier of North Carolina. He encouraged his brother Buck to marry a woman of similar "quality," the opposite of Lillian. Angier Duke *(right)* was groomed to run the Duke empire. He took after his Uncle Buck and met with an untimely end. (Author's Collection)

Doris Duke was a lonely child. (UPI/Bettmann)

The Fifth Avenue mansion was as quiet as a tomb. Nanaline Duke had learned that in English royal households servants never spoke, and she adopted this rule of silence. (UPI/Bettmann)

Duke Farms in Somerville, New Jersey, was built to rival the epoch Biltmore House that George Vanderbilt constructed in North Carolina. (Culver Pictures, Inc.)

Throughout the twenties and thirties, newspapers and magazines ran countless stories on the children of the super-rich. Gloria Vanderbilt is at the center. Doris Duke, to her left, was by far the richest and the most famous. (UPI/Bettmann)

Doris laid the cornerstone for the newly named Duke University. Buck's will gave the university the largest endowment of any college in the country. Doris never felt comfortable there. (Duke University Archives)

Doris was wildly jealous of Barbara Hutton's marrying Prince Alexis Mdivani. She began to take marriage seriously as a way out of her mother's clutches. (Culver Pictures, Inc.)

Doris married Jimmy Cromwell in 1935. He was the reigning Adonis of high society, and he confirmed Buck's admonition to Doris not to trust people. "I thought there must be more to this sex business than I was getting from Jimmy," she later said. (AP/Wide World Photos)

Hawaii was Doris's paradise. She built her Shangri-La there. (AP/Wide World Photos)

"Another man named Duke would teach me how to make love," Doris said of Olympic swimming champion Duke Kahanamoku. (Author's Collection)

Duke's brother Sam *(center)* shared Doris's favors. She loved her "beach boys." (Author's Collection)

During the Depression, Doris toured the poverty-stricken coal fields of West Virginia with Eleanor Roosevelt. She played the grande dame in public to get revenge on Jimmy Cromwell. Privately, she sent money anonymously to help ease the miners' suffering. (UPI/Bettmann)

Doris's half-brother, Walker Inman, never gained control of the powerful Duke empire. (UPI/Bettmann)

Doris became an undercover agent and spy during World War II in order to get to England, where she hoped to rekindle a love affair. Her code name was "Daisy," after L'il Abner's Daisy Mae Yokum. (UPI/Bettmann)

Doris asserted that General George S. Patton was one of the best lovers she'd ever had. (AP/Wide World Photos)

Porfirio Rubirosa possessed the Rolls-Royce of genitalia. Doris bought him for $1 million. The price might have been her life had the U.S. government not intervened. (AP/Wide World Photos)

Errol Flynn boasted he was having an affair with the richest girl in the world, in America, and with the richest boy in the world, in Sweden. He kept both happy for a time. (UPI/Bettmann)

"I don't know what I loved more," Doris confessed, "Malabar Farm or Louis Bromfield." Both changed her life (here Bromfield sits atop "Mount Jeez"). (UPI/Bettmann)

Doris believed Joey Castro *(right)* was a musical genius, perhaps the greatest jazz pianist in the world. He sued her for a divorce settlement over a marriage that never really happened. (UPI/Bettmann)

"I wanted to leave a legacy of beauty," Doris said. Edward Tirella *(right)* was the set designer for *The Sandpiper*, which starred Richard Burton and Elizabeth Taylor. He was the creative key to Doris's obsession with beautifying her surroundings. Life with him was an adventure. (UPI/Bettmann)

Rough Point, in Newport, was the freezing barn of Duke mansions. Tirella restored the house to its original look during the heydey decades preceding the Depression. He and Doris then undertook the restoration of downtown Newport (in the 1960s, her expendable income was $1 million a week). Historic preservation is one of Doris's lasting legacies. (AP/Wide World Photos)

On Friday, October 7, 1966, Doris was behind the wheel of this car when it crushed Edward Tirella to death against the gates of Rough Point. (AP/Wide World Photos)

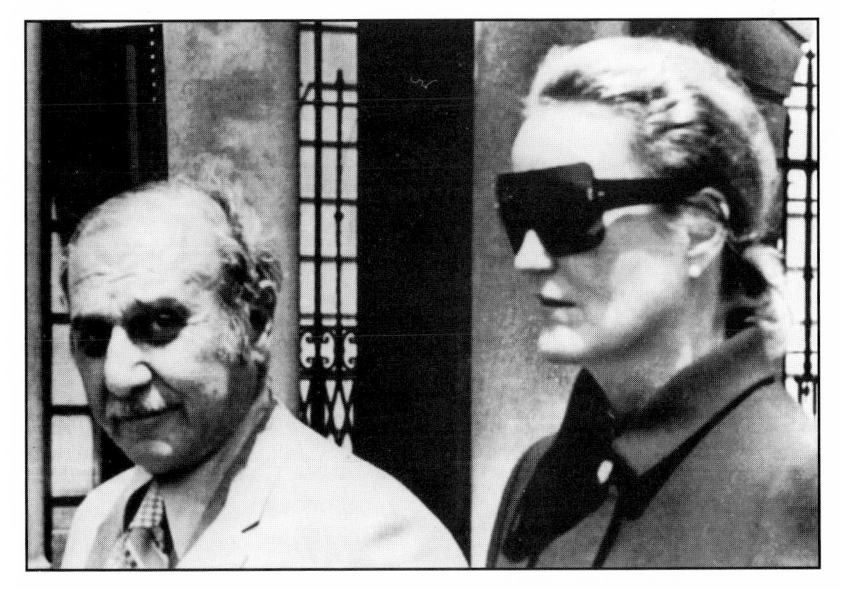

Doris with her attorney after Tirella's relatives brought a negligence suit against her. Newport was reminded that Doris was its only hope for refurbishment; no official records of the investigation can be found. (AP/Wide World Photos)

Angier Biddle Duke, Doris's closest relative, was chief of protocol for JFK's White House. (UPI/Bettmann)

Ari Onassis often used Doris to make his famous wife jealous. (AP/Wide World Photos)

Doris had a great passion for music. She particularly loved gospel singing. Here she sings with the Reverend Lawrence Roberts and the Angelic Choir. (AP/Wide World Photos)

Doris and Franco Rosellini visiting Elizabeth Taylor in her dressing room at the Martin Beck Theatre in New York. Bernard Lafferty's appointment of Taylor to the Doris Duke Charitable Foundation board gave him high-powered celebrity clout. (AP/Wide World Photos)

Doris, Imelda Marcos, and Chandi Heffner. Doris did everything in her power to keep Imelda Marcos out of jail (and Ferdinand Marcos alive). She considered her adoption of Chandi to be the greatest mistake of her life. The truth about Chandi was far different from the fanciful image she successfully presented to Doris. (Dennis Oda)

Falcon's Lair was Valentino's Hollywood home before it became a prison for Doris. (UPI/Bettmann)

Tammy Payette, a former navy nurse, came forward with her knowledge of what really happened to Doris. (Dan Groshong/SYGMA)

Former Doris Duke butler Bernard Lafferty with Nannerl O. Keohane, the president of Duke University and a board member of the Doris Duke Charitable Foundation, after he presented her with a $10 million endowment for the school. (Chuck Liddy/*The News and Observer*/SYGMA)

But now there were Nazis in his house in France and Louis Bromfield was shaken. He told friends that it was difficult to accept that the new life he had created for himself in Europe was so fragile that it could be smashed under the heels of goose-stepping young soldiers.

He looked at the beautiful rolling hills of central Ohio, where corn and wheat appeared annually from the black and moist soil. Louis Bromfield did what he had sworn he would never do, he went home to Ohio and bought nearly one thousand acres of some of the finest farmland in the world. He wanted to become a real farmer. He studied the latest conservation and natural farming techniques and was soon considered to be one of the nation's first and foremost conservationists.

He took a simple farmhouse and remodeled it into a graceful white clapboard Western Reserve–style mansion that was to become the heart of Malabar Farm. On the day he moved into the rambling house, he placed a statue of a Malabar elephant in an alcove above the entry porch to the house. The Malabar elephant was his talisman for luck and happiness and success.

In 1941, he and his family and a continual parade of friends and the famous began a twenty-year involvement with Malabar Farm, which was later to be described as "the most beautiful farm in America."

Louis Bromfield treasured nature and the land and built his farm around the focus of the fields, hedgerows, cattle, horses, and barns. The purpose of Malabar Farm was defined by the beauty of the land. Malabar Farm was nothing like Duke Farms.

Doris Duke loved architecture. She built great stone rooms with floors pulled from European palaces and marble from around the world. Louis Bromfield built a house from oak and wide pine floors taken from the trees of his land. Louis Bromfield loved the land.

Kings and movie stars came to Malabar Farm, where they were all loaded into the old hay wagons and towed around the fields by the John Deere tractors. Louis's best friend was Humphrey Bogart, who unlike his tough-guy image was actually a sophisticated product of an upper-class upbringing. In the spring of

1945, Bogie married Lauren "Bette" Bacall (who was even then an international star) at the base of the double stairway in the entrance hall of Malabar Farm. Unlike the cavernous entrance halls of the various Duke mansions, the entrance hall at Louis's house was a more modest setting with the famous but underscaled double staircase that seemed even smaller because it was the only place in the house where Louis could locate a grand piano. Guests stood in the mirrored living room or looked down from the second floor. The honeymoon night was spent in the guest room that jutted over the main entrance of the house.

Nobody is sure about exactly what brought Doris Duke to Malabar Farm. Doris later said it was Dutch elm disease. In the early part of the 1950s, Doris found herself, at forty years of age, with a new appreciation for her father's farm.

Bromfield had published the books *Pleasant Valley* in 1945 and *Malabar Farm* in 1946, which were immediately embraced as the conservation guides for anyone interested in the new farming theory that Louis dubbed conservation of the land. As Doris watched hundreds of beautiful Dutch elm trees slowly die along the hundreds of once shaded miles of roads on her estate, she read the books.

Doris was not one to settle for advice from a book when she could probably buy the author. She had her secretary contact Louis to inform him that a plane would be sent to take him to New Jersey where he could explain to Miss Duke what she could do with her trees.

# 16

# THE MAN FROM MALABAR FARM

Louis Bromfield ignored Doris Duke's request. He was far too busy with the development of Malabar Farm to bother with the whims of what he then considered a spoiled heiress who could always get what she wanted by writing a check.

Doris wrote a more personal handwritten note of invitation to Louis. He responded by sending some of his own writings on conservation and included a note in his own hand to the effect that the trees were no longer good for anything but kindling and should be destroyed in order to slow the rate of infestation into what few trees might survive.

Doris decided to invite herself to Malabar Farm. Just as it had happened with everyone who had come to the farm before her, the beauty, the natural combination of land and plant, earth and trees, and gently swaying acres of corn, oats, and wheat, overwhelmed her. Doris had flown into Cleveland, where a limousine was waiting for the three-hour drive to Lucas, the tiny hamlet that nestled at the edge of Malabar Farm.

As she sat in the rear seat of the expensive car that churned a soaring cockscomb of dust in its powerful wake, Doris realized that there was a world of nature, a living painting in greens, blues, and browns, that was as beautiful as anything she had ever bought or built. As the car passed the farm wagons as she neared the compound of barns and houses that formed the farmstead, she was embarrassed by her own ostentation.

Louis Bromfield, a bear of a man with a bawdy sense of humor and an often loud voice, bounded out of the big barn that was less than one hundred and fifty feet from the house.

"He reminded me of Papa," she told friends later in her little-girl whisper of a voice that became even more delicate when speaking of Bromfield. Doris Duke was no longer a girl but a woman who had had too many lovers and not enough love. But she looked better than she ever had in her life, thanks to a chin reduction and other plastic surgery she had undergone during her stint in Hollywood.

On her first visit to Malabar Farm, Doris Duke quickly adapted to the lifestyle and her quick mind absorbed every lesson in agronomy that Louis Bromfield was willing to teach. Wearing jeans, canvas shoes, and a flowered silk shirt, she walked for miles along the lanes that were lined with twenty-foot-high walls of fragrant multiflower rose hedges. Doris took notes and asked questions with an insight that impressed Bromfield.

Together they strolled with his favorite unruly boxer dogs, Prince and Baby, through a new-growth forest that would later be named Doris Duke Woods. They climbed the hill that overlooked the entire farm, a spot that was called Mount Jeez because every time Louis climbed it he would say, "Jesus what a view."

Doris had her own version of the naming of Mount Jeez. She used to tell people that it was atop Mount Jeez where she and Louis first had sex and it was named after her echoing cries of "Oh Jesus!" as she reached climax.

Louis Bromfield was more a man of emotional passion than physical sensuality. He was, like most writers, an observer of people and their imperfections. His relationship with his wife had settled into a drone of unemotional but cordial ennui. It was true that there were four daughters but Louis would tell friends after his usual nightly dosage of too much scotch that he seldom ventured into his wife's bedroom. He usually slept on a leather couch in the library, the room where he wrote, instead of on his twin bed in his wife's domain. His fondness for scotch was so well known that when Prince and Baby appeared in a scotch ad that ran in the *Saturday Evening Post*, readers instantly knew the boxers must be Louis Bromfield's famous pets.

In an effort to entice his longtime agent and business manager to Malabar Farm from his Manhattan penthouse, Louis re-created the New York apartment on the floor above his library and installed a secret stairway behind the paneling so that the man could go to the apartment without using the main staircase. The agent was gay before the word gay meant homosexual, and the astonished townspeople in Mansfield referred to him as "Bromfield's pervert."

There were many rumors about Louis Bromfield, including rumors of affairs, which Bromfield would sometimes sadly hint had some basis in truth. Louis Bromfield had left Ohio as a poor and insecure boy but had returned as a famous and admired author. In the early forties, he took a perverse delight in the piles of invitations to visit the great estates of the industrial rich of Cleveland and Youngstown and Akron where newly married debutantes were eager to bed the ruddy-faced, crew-cut, lumbering writer. In a kind of delicious revenge, he allowed himself to be seduced by the WASPy blond wives and daughters of the blue-blooded society. But like most revenge, his sexual raiding of the mansions where he had once been rejected resulted in a new pain for his delicate writer's ego. Several of these women became pregnant with children whose faces Louis Bromfield later closely scrutinized for familiar features.

"I love my daughters," Bromfield told Doris, "but I have always wanted a son. Now I think I have one and his father is some rich and spoiled tennis player. No matter what I do, these people will not let me have what I want." Louis Bromfield, tortured by the demons of his life which were nurtured by his immense creative imagination, looked for escape in his farm and his scotch.

"I remember standing on the front portico of the wood house where the paint was always peeling," Doris said, "and I would look out over those hills and trees; the willows would be barely moving around the lake and the branches drooped into the water. The swans used to swim through the willows. And I thought of how easily and naturally beautiful this place was. Shangri-La was impressive and magnificent. It was a beautiful place, too. But I started to realize that there was more beauty in what nature could create effortlessly each season than the glorious structures all my money and imagination could create. I don't know what I loved more, Malabar Farm or Louis Bromfield."

In 1952, Louis Bromfield's wife died. Doris Duke wanted to be the next Mrs. Bromfield. She dreamed of springs and snowy winters in the white frame house with her instant family. Even the idea of being the mother of four daughters delighted her.

Louis loved her in his own way. His health was failing and he drew strength from the driven spirit of Doris Duke. She felt stronger and more powerful as a person with Louis Bromfield than she had ever been with any person in the past. He needed her strength and determination more than he could ever need her money. He had every comfort he wanted at Malabar Farm.

Louis Bromfield knew that liquor was shortening his life but he kept drinking. Each day, another bottle of scotch would challenge his swollen liver.

Doris was determined to save him. Without his knowing, she investigated every possible medical discovery in hopes that she would find something that would help him. Scientists and quacks went through the gates of Duke Farms to present their theories to Doris. She later estimated that she spent several million dollars in search of something that would help her Louis.

"People started thinking I was crazy," she would recall. "Everyone was making jokes about all the strange people and idiotic medical treatments I was financing. They didn't know that the man I loved was dying and I was ready to try anything and spend anything to save him. There was so little time, so I tried everything. I even asked some of the doctors at the Duke Medical Center whether it might be possible for them to transplant a liver. They were polite but made me feel that they were merely patronizing me. I always felt that they looked down their noses at me because I never went to college. I never forgave them for that attitude."

Louis Bromfield was not a cooperative patient. Doris understood that she could not arrive at Malabar Farm with a procession of men in white jackets and healers in turbans. "Louis was not the guru type," she laughed. "There wasn't enough room in the house for all my entourage so I needed a way of getting Louis to come to Duke Farms." Battalions of swamis and entire hospitals of medical theorists could be stashed in the many guest houses of Duke Farms without attracting too much attention from Bromfield.

She convinced Louis to help her repair the ecological damage that had been done to Duke Farms by decades of careless mountain building and swamp filling. She had her fabulous greenhouses filled with orchids that could be transformed into a horticultural extravaganza. She wanted a thriving herd of milk cows like the docile and contented animals that fed on the timothy and clover pastures at Malabar Farm. She needed Louis Bromfield to do this for her.

In the years immediately following the death of Louis's wife, the Duke plane made frequent trips between Mansfield and Somerville. Louis and Doris instructed her troops of gardeners and farmers in the methods that would transform Duke Farms into a real working farm.

"One of my basic premises of farming," Louis would say, "is that a farm should be able to support itself. In the past, farmers raised their food and made their clothing from the bounty of their farms. A farm should be able to provide everything needed to feed and shelter its people. Otherwise it is nothing more than a hobby. A working farm is beautiful in the purity of its function."

Louis Bromfield tried to purify the excesses of Duke Farms. New crops were planted on land that was being restored to productivity with natural fertilizers. Doris found herself studying the bloodlines of her cattle with the same enthusiasm she had previously felt when buying priceless art and antiquities.

In the hours when Louis was not designing land terraces and irrigation systems, they would return to the massive and forbidding Tudor mansion where the latest purveyors of potential cures dined in the great dining room. They would subtly try to examine a slightly amused Louis Bromfield over drinks in the drawing room.

"He always really knew what I was trying to do," Doris said. "He made a joke of it but I think he secretly hoped that I would find something."

After seeing Duke Farms, Louis Bromfield was somewhat more reluctant to marry Doris. He loved her but was afraid of what this strong-willed woman and her endless supply of money might do to the delicate natural balance of Malabar Farm.

"He was afraid that I would install an Olympic pool behind the house in the hillside," she laughed, "and he had a positive fear that I might install a wall around Malabar Farm like the one at Duke Farms."

"I like people," Louis would roar. "I want to look out the window and see new people coming up my driveway. I am not going to live in any goddamn cage."

In the late winter of 1956, Louis Bromfield mentioned to a few friends that he was planning to marry Doris Duke. But he worried that he might be considered just another fortune hunter. His own fortune had diminished during his years of ill health and alcoholism, years when he had been unable to write. There was a six-hundred-thousand-dollar mortgage on Malabar Farm.

"I think my last name would have been Bromfield," Doris Duke commented years later, "if it had not been for that damned mortgage. Louis didn't want people thinking he was like Jimmy or Rubi. Louis Bromfield wasn't a user."

There was a late winter snow on the ground in mid-March of 1956 when Louis Bromfield doubled over in pain in the library where he had written so many words on the ancient typewriter that rested amid the clutter atop a wobbly card table (he seldom used the grand hand-carved desk). The pain was worse than he had ever experienced and he told his houseman to get the car. He died hours later in a Columbus hospital.

Doris Duke stood by the window of her delicate yellow bedroom at Duke Farms, holding her picture of Louis Bromfield, and looked out at her empire, which had been so changed by this man. She had a strange pang of helplessness in her chest, a twinge she had felt only once before in her life, on the day when Buck Duke died.

"I wish Louis could have seen one last spring at Malabar Farm," she whispered in a voice that was heard only by herself.

Of all of Doris Duke's lovers, Louis Bromfield was the one she would later be the most reluctant to talk about. Family members recall that she always kept a picture of him someplace in her bedroom, often on the table next to her bed.

There was much criticism of Doris Duke in the days following the death of Louis Bromfield. She did write a check for sixty thousand dollars to halt the sale of the trees in what would later be called Doris Duke Woods to a timber company in an effort to hold off the creditors, but people called her cheap for not merely paying off the mortgage.

People, gossiping vindictive people, did not know the entire story. Louis had told at least one close friend in the weeks before his death that, if something were to happen to him, he did not want his closest friends, and most especially Doris Duke, to save the farm. He had a different plan.

He had one last bit of revenge for many of the moneyed set of Mansfield, the very people whose families had snubbed him as a boy and fawned over him as a famous writer. His farm was left as a legacy to the Bromfield ecology foundation headed by "some of my closest friends." In fact some of the people selected to perpetuate the Bromfield name were individuals he most detested. Just as Louis had hoped, they were so honored by "their close friend Louis Bromfield" that they dug into their own pockets to save the farm.

"His enemies paid for his legacy," one old friend commented.

Doris Duke made one last secret trip to Malabar Farm and the grave of the only man, other than her father, who she was sure loved her. The modest stone over Louis Bromfield's grave in the tiny untended family cemetery is carved with the following epitaph:

To him who in the love
of nature holds communion
with her visible forms,
She speaks a various language.
Bryant

The only sign of Doris's return to Malabar Farm were dozens of wilting Duke orchids, found scattered in front of the simple marker. Alone she had driven, after selecting each perfect bloom in the greenhouse of Duke Farms, across New Jersey and Pennsylvania to the hills of central Ohio and the place where she had what was to be her last chance at real happiness. She would never again return.

Today Malabar Farm still exists. There are still traces of Louis Bromfield in the house, which is now a museum. The scratches from the paws of Prince and Baby are still on the doors to the library. The old typewriter is still on the rickety card table. There is a souvenir shop now attached to the kitchen where lobsters once boiled in a huge black kettle. The original barn has burned and been replicated with exhibits and access for the handicapped.

The house and land are now the Malabar Farm State Park and anyone is welcome to drive up the dusty driveway and knock on the front door. Visitors can also walk through the Doris Duke Woods on the Doris Duke Nature Trail, the only real honor that, as yet, has been awarded to Doris.

Louis Bromfield only knew Doris as a woman. She came to him, a person whose life had been centered on money and possessions and passions, and he taught her to appreciate a kind of beauty that cannot be bought . . . it can only be nurtured. If he had lived, she might have been happy to become an Ohio farmer's wife. But no matter what, Louis Bromfield had changed Doris Duke. She would view the rest of her life with a new awareness.

Doris knew Louis Bromfield had been her best chance at real happiness and she realized, for the first time, that her money could not always make the impossible happen. Louis Bromfield was dead and no check with its infinite parade of zeros could bring him back to her side.

Doris once reflected, "In 1974, I read in some preservation magazine that Malabar Farm had been designated as a national historic site just like the Duke farm in Durham. He was a man like my father and uncle and grandfather. He came from the soil and he loved the earth. None of the other men in my life left the world any kind of legacy. Other men came to me because they wanted my money to help them define themselves. Jimmy needed money to become President. Bobbie wanted my money to buy every luxury. Rubi was after security. Even Duke Kahanamoku was little more than one of my possessions. Louis detested my world. He wanted me to come back to Malabar Farm, me on an Ohio farm in the middle of nowhere. God, how I wish I could have done it."

# 17
# THE JAZZ MAN

Whenever Doris Duke was upset, she would go to her Steinway and play her precious jazz. After the death of Louis Bromfield she sat at the piano in the great house at Duke Farms and pounded in anger on the keyboard. And she cried.

"I am not the kind of woman who cries," she said. "I thought I had cried out all my tears as a girl. But I cried over Louis." While holding a picture of Louis encased in a sterling silver frame, she sobbed.

And Joey Castro was always around as a means of distraction. His dark Latin features and thick black hair were attributes that Doris had found so attractive in the past. She believed him to be a musical genius, perhaps the greatest jazz pianist in the world. He tended to agree with her opinion of him. They had sex but Doris Duke was looking for more emotional satisfaction as she neared her fifth decade on earth. Doris Duke wanted to do something with her life.

She very secretively started to create a plan that would establish a school of ecology connected to Duke University; this would be a curriculum that would continue the ecological and environmental efforts of Louis Bromfield. She had already done much to improve the thousands of acres at Duke Farms by following Bromfield's concepts.

Her plan was to incorporate Duke Farms, Malabar Farms, and a ranch she had in Hawaii. Then she would purchase land in North Carolina and a ranch someplace in Montana, Wyoming, or the Dakotas. Each of these facilities would become working laboratories in the study and improvement of the ecology of the United States.

Already considered the world's leading expert in orchid growing, Doris was, in the late 1950s and early 1960s, far ahead of the agricultural science curve. She theorized that hundreds of new breeds of pasture grass, corn, soybeans, wheat, and oats could be discovered in these various agrarian incubators. This plan had been presented to Doris by Louis Bromfield and she was going to continue with its development through Duke University, the educational institution that bore her family name.

Advances in all aspects of farm life would be made by the new school of agriculture, which she had decided to name the Louis Bromfield School of Ecology and Agriculture. The finest of livestock would be bred and perfected. New machinery would be invented and tested. Doris even spent hours designing new farm structures that would use the latest materials to improve the quality of life for the farm family from Hawaii to Billings to Omaha to New Jersey to Durham.

She told almost no one of this plan. It was very precious to her and she wanted the concept to be perfect before she presented it to the officials at Duke University.

She also wanted to know what all this was going to cost. Doris's godchild, Pony Duke, a recent graduate of Duke University who shared her love of the land, was one of the few people she told. Her whisper of a voice was barely audible but shaking with enthusiasm when she spoke to him about this project.

"It sounded great to me," Pony said later. "I suppose I disappointed her by not offering to help her with the school but my mind was on going to Wall Street to make my own fortune. Today I can think of nothing I would rather do but I was just an ambitious kid out of college then."

The agriculture school never happened. Because of her own lack of a college education, Doris Duke was self-conscious around the academicians at Duke University. "They never even offered me an honorary degree," she would say with more than a trace of sadness in her voice. "I could not help but have the feeling that they looked down on me."

When she mentioned this plan to a relative with close ties to Duke University, the relative scoffed at the whole idea. "I was told not to be ridiculous and that Duke University was a place of serious study and was not about to be turned into some farm school." The relative pointed out that Doris knew virtually nothing about the university and had no appreciation of a university's higher purpose since Doris herself was close to being completely uneducated.

Believing that her plan for a school of ecology and agriculture would have been unwanted at Duke University, she dropped the plans for the school. This was a catastrophe for our world because had the Doris Duke foresight and fortune been focused on ecology in the sixties instead of decades later, today's world could be a vastly better place.

Doris turned over the management and responsibility for her father's legacy at Duke University to her cousin Mary Duke Biddle Trent Semens, who had moved from her mansion on Fifth Avenue to Durham, where she was raising a huge family. Cousin Mary, although publicity-shy, is the second richest member of the Duke family (after Doris) with a personal fortune in the vicinity of $300 million. In all ways, Mary was the exact opposite of Doris, conventional rather than exotic, unknown rather than famous, motherly rather than worldly. Mary Semens reveled in filling the void that existed when Doris, the only daughter of the founder and benefactor, neglected her responsibilities at the university. Mary continues to serve as chairman of the board of trustees of the $1.4 billion Duke Endowment that was established by Buck Duke.

"It was as if Mary were really the daughter of Buck Duke," Doris remarked dryly. "There was no place for me at Duke University. I suppose it was better that way. Mary was a graduate of Duke and fit in better with those professor types. She was like them. I was too notorious for their tastes."

Doris was too much like her father Buck to be accepted readily into the stratified atmosphere of the academic community in Durham. She believed that the only thing she had to offer, that the powers at Duke University wanted, was her money. Every time Doris Duke heard of Mary Semens receiving another honor from the university, Doris would feel a sharp pang of jealousy.

As always, Doris was pragmatic about her complex relationship with the fine school her father's money had built.

"If you want my money you also get me," Doris would joke. "They were better off with Mary. She has a lot of money, too, so maybe she will be the next member of the Duke family to be a benefactor of my father's school." Then she smiled and said in a loud stage whisper, "I was like my father. I didn't want to attend college, but I might have liked to build one."

In the early 1960s, Doris Duke was looking for new purpose and meaning in her life. She not only helped Pony Duke skyrocket to success on Wall Street, she hoped to rebuild long-ignored family relationships. It was too late.

While she was always included at her aunt Cordelia's Thanksgiving dinners, her highly public escapades were viewed as an embarrassment by most members of the Duke and Biddle families. Ambassador Angier Biddle Duke was the chief of protocol at the Kennedy White House and feared reading the paper each day lest Doris's antics be reported on the front pages. Earlier in his career, he had briefly considered dropping the last name of Duke and becoming Angier Biddle as Doris dragged the Duke name through the headlines during the 1930s.

There was a lot of difference when comparing the Duke and Biddle names. The Biddles of Philadelphia had been blue bloods for three hundred years. The Dukes were newly rich. While the Biddles were aristocrats who married into great fortunes, the Dukes were empire builders who amassed great fortunes.

Opportune marriages had kept the Biddles among the wealthiest Americans since before the Revolution without any member of the Biddle family actually having to work for a living.

The Biddles were appalled by Doris Duke. Doris was not too fond of them either, although she did care for Angier and his brother, Tony Duke. When she would write to a member of her family who was tainted by the Biddle strain, she would change the name of Biddle to Little, making them into Little Dukes. Doris Duke did not tolerate or forgive rejection and the Biddles would always be "those Little people" to her.

Still, she would have enjoyed being included in Kennedy's Camelot and made a lifetime effort to cultivate Jacqueline Kennedy (who always permitted herself to be cultivated by very affluent people). While she was basically a Republican like her father and her enthusiasm for the Democratic Party was not expanded by Jimmy Cromwell's attempt at political empire building, Doris was envious of Angier's inclusion in the beautiful and exciting world of the Kennedy Democratic White House.

"When I didn't write checks," Doris would hiss, "the Democrats didn't want me."

So Doris went looking for new friends and interests to replace the rejection she received from her family and the powers at Duke University. And Joey Castro was still waiting patiently.

Doris was nearly as interested in the arts as she was in ecology. Castro would join her in the all-night piano sessions. She even wrote a piece that was inspired by the memory of her tiny dead daughter Arden.

A few months following the death of Louis Bromfield, Joey Castro asked Doris to marry him. She liked his music and he was not that bad in bed, and he certainly attracted interesting people into her life, but Doris was not about to be married again. Still, the fiery Castro was insistent that the millionairess make an honest man of him, so Doris orchestrated a strange sort of marriage ceremony that was not really a marriage ceremony. Everyone involved, with the exception of Castro himself, knew that the ceremony was a sham and it was certainly not legal.

"Joey later sued me for a divorce settlement over a marriage that really never happened," Doris said. "It was hard for me to believe that he never realized that we had never really been legally married. I had no intention of ever actually marrying him. It was not going to happen but I did what I did to stop him from coaxing and threatening. I took good care of Joey as long as he stayed with me but I always made it clear that the day he left would be the day the money ended. I had supported all the men I ever intended to support."

Doris's family was aloof and removed. She had no real friends. Her only satisfaction came from her agricultural successes at Duke Farms and her music. She had no one whom she believed really cared about her, including Nanaline, her cold and critical mother. Soon their relationship would come to an end.

Grande dame Nanaline Duke lived in baronial isolation surrounded by her servants in the echoing château on Fifth Avenue. One by one famous families had sold their immense mansions along Fifth Avenue and bulldozers had leveled gilded ballrooms and marble staircases so that expensive high-rises could be built on the valuable lots. But Buck's and Ben Duke's houses remained untouched.

Doris Duke seldom visited her mother's residence, even though she owned and maintained the costly property and staff. To Doris, this house was nothing more than an austere and cold setting for an austere and cold woman. Nanaline had been badgering Doris to inspect the house because there were some expensive repairs that the old woman wanted her daughter to order done, including a new copper roof.

The mother and daughter, as usual, could not agree. Doris commented that if Buck had felt a copper roof was necessary for the house, he would have installed one when he built it.

"You just want a shiny copper roof so that everyone on Fifth Avenue can see it shining," Doris snarled. "If my papa had wanted copper he would have had copper."

"I don't care what Buck Duke did," Nanaline, who was now confined much of the time to a wheelchair, screamed. "He has been dead for almost forty years. I am sick of listening to you babble about Buck Duke."

"At least Papa loved me." Doris glared at her mother as the

two argued in the upstairs hallway outside the double doors of the room where Buck had died.

"Your father . . . your precious damn father. What a laugh. I could tell you something about your great Buck Duke." Nanaline's voice was crackling like an aging cat.

Suddenly Doris did not want to hear what her mother was going to say. She turned away from the once beautiful old woman and almost ran down the long marble staircase. Nanaline wheeled to the top of the stairs, her screams echoing through the halls of the great house.

"Don't you walk away from me, missy, don't you dare walk away from me until I am finished talking to you. Do you hear me?" Nanaline was nearly hysterical.

Doris halted at the turn of the staircase and glared at the quivering bundle of silk and bones that seemed to be sinking deeper into the wheelchair. She looked at her mother but said nothing.

Nanaline tried to compose herself. She lowered her voice to a stage whisper. "I should have told you a long time ago. I don't think Buck Duke was really your father. He was too old and too sick and we almost never . . ."

"You bitch!" Doris spat the words at her mother.

"Look at yourself. Do you look like your father? Where did you get that blond hair? Why are you so tall? You look Scandinavian to me. You look like . . ."

"Shut up!" Doris ordered. "You shut your goddamned mouth." Doris would listen no more to her mother. She would never really speak to her mother again. She had heard the stories about her mother's obsession with the tall, blond Nordic butler. Doris had been told that her mother had even tried to follow the man back to Europe the first time he left the Duke mansion, and that Nanaline had finally enticed the man to return to her service. Quickly Doris walked the last few steps, gliding in long strides to the center of the dimly lit huge entrance hall. In the middle of the cold marble room, she turned toward her mother and said with a strange calmness, "Nothing you can say matters. Buck Duke was my father and he will always be my father."

Then Doris Duke turned and stormed through the double

inner doors and shoved open the heavy iron and glass double outer doors, leaving them both wide open to the outside world. As Nanaline Duke whimpered at the top of the stairs, servants silently appeared from the shadows and pulled the cryptlike doors closed.

Within days, Doris had made arrangements to dispose of the house. She believed that if Nanaline could suggest that she had dishonored Buck Duke, she should have no right to live in the mansion he had built. She offered the house to the Museum of Modern Art but was refused. Then nervous officials of the New York University Institute of Fine Arts approached Doris Duke to ask for the house to be used as their headquarters. Quickly, she gave it to them.

Her mother and several servants were moved to a suite at the Stanhope Hotel. Nanaline pretended that she was glad to be away from the gloomy house but whispered to friends that Doris was being beastly in evicting her. To the outside world it appeared that the arrogant Doris Duke had thrown her feeble mother out of her home merely because she was too cheap to fix the roof. Newspaper gossip columnists snipped at her.

New York University officials hoped that Doris would continue an interest in the altering of the mansion into a school of the arts and, in the beginning, Doris intended to provide the funding that could have made the project successful. She approached her own architects to design plans for the remodeling. Doris Duke fully intended that she would use her money to make the house a proper monument to her father. Then one day she returned for a tour (with her checkbook in her purse) and was shocked to see that her mother's two-story dressing room with its dozens of doors and abundant mirrors had been buried under a new superstructure of shelves for books. She had wanted that room to survive as a grotesque monument to her mother's excessive narcissism and vanity. She wanted everyone to see the extravagant room and now it was hidden by a massive steel framework filled with books and boxes. Doris walked out of her father's house for the last time.

On April 12, 1962, Nanaline Duke died in her suite at the

Stanhope Hotel, only three blocks from the grand house where she had been a titan of society. She was ninety-three years of age. A very stone-faced and tearless Doris attended her mother's funeral and interment in the family crypt at Duke Chapel in Durham. Her cold blue eyes were even icier as she listened to the eulogies. She declined to say any words about her mother. It was as if she had come only to be sure that the old woman was really dead. Later at a gathering of the family, she seemed unemotional and disconnected. Doris looked almost radiant and glamorous in her black close-fitting dress and veil. She walked the long graceful strides of a woman who suddenly had found herself to be free.

In her will, Nanaline bequeathed $5 million to the Duke University Medical Center with the rest of her $40 million estate going to her eleven-year-old grandson Walker Inman, the orphaned son of her beloved Walker, who had drunk himself to death a few years earlier.

Her bequest to Doris, her only living child, confused everyone who learned of its strange nature. Nanaline Duke, a woman who owned dozens of mink, sable, and ermine coats, left one aged fur to her daughter. But Doris Duke knew what her mother meant by this unusual gift. The pile of rotting fur had once been the coat that Nanaline Duke had wrapped around herself as she sat in the freezing room alone with a dying Buck Duke. It was the coat that kept Nanaline warm while the shaking body of the incoherent tycoon was being decimated by pneumonia. Doris Duke burned her mother's last gift.

The only person with a blood tie to Doris Duke who was willing to be a part of her life was the young orphan Walker Inman. Doris Duke accepted her responsibility and tried to be a kind of mother to the young boy.

But young Walker could be impossible. He had been raised with almost no supervision and absolutely no discipline. Whatever little Walker wanted, little Walker was given. The child was impossibly spoiled. He had been reared as the pampered young master of a five-thousand-acre South Carolina plantation where he was permitted anything he wanted from setting off Roman candles in the drawing room to waking the servants in the middle of the night to fix him a snack. He was enrolled in boarding school each year, only to be thrown out within weeks.

"He was the ultimate little hellion," Doris recalled. "But he was my hellion and I loved him. He called me Aunt Doris." Much to Joey Castro's misery, in 1965 she decided to have young Walker come to live with her and invited the boy to Shangri-La.

Little Walker had developed his talent as a fire lover. He started small by burning two crates of rare and valuable teak in the driveway of the house. The fire department estimated the damage at ten thousand dollars.

Castro took off his belt and prepared to beat the hell out of the little hellion. A menacing Doris explained that Joey Castro would not now or ever lay a hand on her rowdy relative. Doris Duke, of all people on earth, could understand the complex mind of a pampered rich child.

Soon her patience would be pushed to the edge. As she was floating on a rubber raft in her pool one morning, it seemed that all of Hawaii was experiencing an earthquake. There was a massive blast and it seemed as if her eardrums had been shattered. A funnel of water exploded more than a hundred feet in the air. Her whole body ached. Hysterical servants screamed at the edge of the pool that the Japanese were bombing the island again.

But it wasn't the Japanese; it was a teenage Walker, who had somehow come into the possession of several ancient hand grenades left over from World War II and decided to surprise his dozing "Aunt Doris" by exploding one in the pool.

Doris Duke was furious with the boy but minutes later when the police arrived at the gates to investigate the explosion that was heard and seen by dozens of boaters and neighbors, she told them there must be a mistake and that everything at Shangri-La was as blissful as usual.

"The police didn't believe me," she said, "but they left without investigating." Her main concern was to locate and dispose of the small armory of weapons and ammunition before "the little darling blew the whole place to hell." While she was impressed with young Walker's resourcefulness in procuring illegal weaponry, she was starting to believe that she might not be the right person to oversee him. (She always loved him and years later he was designated as the executor of many of her wills. Knowing he had no understanding of money, she always made a provision in her wills that would provide an annual stipend for him as an adult.) "Walker might have been spoiled but we were the ones who did the spoiling," she would confide to family. "It was easier for us to give him whatever he wanted than for us to be forced to take a real interest in teaching him what he would need to survive. We were all too self-centered to be bothered with a problem child."

At one point, Joey Castro told Doris to decide between him or the kid. She refused to make the decision, but Castro decided to wait even if it took a few years.

It was always amazing to Doris Duke that so many of the people whom she accepted into her upholstered life would later complain of her cheapness. She bought Castro the finest clothes and cars. She financed a record company to promote him and his many talented friends. She would fly people anyplace in the world and pay their hotel bills with her only request being that they entertain her or, at the very least, be nice to her. Doris Duke spent millions of dollars on her friends.

"I am living proof that money cannot buy friendship," she said while sipping champagne one afternoon on the terrace of Rough Point. "I have become an expert on the venom of ungrateful people. I am reluctant to admit it but I keep trying to find real friends. That is why I go to such extremes to help people who are in trouble. Papa used to say, 'You help a man who is in trouble and he will be a true friend,' but I am afraid that Papa was wrong. I would have done anything or paid a fortune for one real friend who I could trust."

Joey Castro was a prime example of her lament.

While she would always adore jazz, her interest in the jazzman was fading. Doris was now focusing much attention on Asian art. She created a foundation to build an eighty-acre Asian cultural center. She had bought an exact copy of the Royal Golden Pavilion where Bangkok royalty had trod for centuries that was to be erected at the site. Other historical and sacred buildings had been purchased throughout Southeast Asia, dismantled and moved to Honolulu where they waited in crates. There were Buddhist shrines and temples that had been pulled from their four-hundred-year-old foundations now residing in numbered crates for reassembly in the new museum.

But there were problems. While the corrupt government officials of Thailand and other Asian countries were delighted to exchange their nations' treasures for Duke bank drafts, there were religious groups who were furious about what they rightly considered desecrations. Doris could not grasp the reasons for their religious outrage. What had she done wrong? The government officials had approached her to buy the treasures and she had bought them. A savvy business deal. Now there were threats from outraged zealots who saw Doris and her proposed Asian cultural center as an affront to their beliefs and a desecration of their sacred sites. It seemed that both her plans for a cultural center and her relationship with her jazzman were doomed. Joey Castro was worried that his time on the Doris Duke gravy train was about to end.

Doris kicked Joey out of the Falcon's Lair mansion she had bought in Beverly Hills. Castro countered with the first of the palimony suits, saying the pair had married once in Providence in 1956 and again in Philadelphia in 1960. He was amazed to learn that no records of either wedding existed.

Their battle, as usual, made headlines, but this time it was Castro who was damaged by the publicity. He was painted as a thirty-six-year-old unemployed musician who had never earned more than a hundred and fifty dollars per week before he attached himself to the rich Miss Duke. Castro, knowing this was true, panicked.

Doris had fled to the Far East to escape from reporters and Joey found her in Tahiti where the reluctantly reconciled couple stayed in a house near Marlon Brando's compound. Castro arranged for the return-trip tickets to be in the name of Mr. and Mrs. Castro but they were charged to Doris Duke. The on-again-off-again relationship between Castro and Doris dragged on for months while she financed his record album.

Slowly she stopped most of her financial support right down to his car repair. She had already shut down the record company.

Joey Castro went crazy.

He smashed the kitchen of Falcon's Lair and chased the servants and some house guests through the mansion with knives he had retrieved from the ravaged kitchen.

Doris made the mistake of confronting Castro, who had been drinking, and told him to leave the house. Castro was so enraged that he pulled off his pants.

A shaken Doris Duke later told family members, "He was still wearing his shirt but he was naked from the waist down. He kept yelling something about the fact that he had done his part and I should do mine."

Then he hit her, knocking her to the ground and breaking her jaw. She locked herself in the bedroom while Castro roamed the house screaming and raving until Duke employees arrived and took him to the Beverly Hills Hotel and put him to bed.

The following morning, Doris had fled to Newport. There she would be safe because the estate was surrounded by water and her guards could secure the street entrance in case Joey Castro might try to get to her in an effort to do more damage. She also had immense power with the Newport Police Department as she was single-handedly paying for the entire urban renewal of the town. The police were given orders to immediately arrest Joey Castro should he arrive in Newport.

Finally Joey Castro just faded out of Doris Duke's life.

When asked about him in later years. Doris would say, "He was a very talented piano player. He knew his jazz. I think he works for a hotel in Las Vegas."

# 18
# DEATH AT THE GATES

In the mid-1960s, the gossip about Doris Duke no longer centered on her romantic life but on her supposed eccentricities. It is true that there was a procession of quacks and charlatans making pilgrimages to worship at the altar of the Duke fortune but Doris was not a foolish woman.

She enjoyed the challenge of outsmarting the never-ending parade of con men and scam artists who approached her. She found them to be entertaining and held the hope that one of their preposterous proposals or outrageous contraptions might somehow benefit mankind. "I am not afraid of wild ideas," she would say.

One of the wildest of those ideas was the cancer-curing machine. Doris had become acquainted with a man who said he had invented a machine that could remove all forms of cancer from the human body. Doris had watched many people die of cancer and, while she thought that this ponderous and odd-looking machine was probably a fraud, she decided that she wanted the machine to be properly tested. She asked the Duke Medical Center for help.

The president of Duke University "declined" to make a laboratory available to test the gadget. When Doris was told that her request had been treated with what she considered contempt by the Duke administration, she was furious.

"It was a direct insult to me," she fumed. "The least they could have done was to permit me to send the machine to Duke. All they had to do was look at it and tell me it was a farce and I would have accepted it. Instead they treated me with arrogance and that damn academic attitude of superiority. I was merely the ignorant daughter of Buck Duke who was making a request that was beneath their academic dignity. It made me question the value of a formal education where you learn a lot of facts but know nothing about how to behave in the real world. I knew then that the powers at Duke had nothing but disdain for me so I would never again force myself upon them." And she never did.

For three more decades, the powers of Duke University would besiege Doris with invitations to come visit the rarefied atmosphere of higher learning but these requests were all refused. Broad hints of programs that might interest Doris and her unlimited funding potential were ignored. Decades would pass before any project connected to Duke University would receive a check with Doris's signature.

Doris Duke became even more reclusive. She isolated herself with a colorful group of Hollywood types whom she'd met during her period with Joey Castro. These were talented artists and musicians, the most talented of whom was Edward Tirella.

Eddie Tirella was the perfect ornament. He was tall and tanned and handsome. His conversation was always stimulating and witty. His taste was flawless, in fact, he was a fine interior designer and motion picture set designer who left nothing but beauty in his wake. Tirella was the mixture of masculinity and taste that Doris Duke found so very attractive. He was also openly gay.

Because theirs was a relationship that was so very tragic, Doris Duke was always reluctant to speak of Eddie Tirella other than to tell family members that there was never a physical relationship.

In her fifties, Doris Duke had begun to replace men with beauty. She saw her fine mansions as settings for her exquisite collections of furniture and art. She loved color, especially red and yellow. For decades she'd bought millions of dollars worth of art, especially Asian religious art, and had accumulated warehouses filled with superb pieces. Tirella had the ability to take these treasures from their crated tombs and make them an aesthetically pleasing part of Doris Duke's day-to-day life.

Doris was a dramatic woman and Edward Tirella was a designer whose background was based in the entertainment business. Both of them thought in grandiose terms. Theirs was a world of sweeping staircases, twenty-foot ceilings, Indian white marble, and oversized paintings.

"I wanted to leave a legacy of beauty," Doris Duke would tell friends.

Tirella had famous and powerful friends, including Peggy Lee (who years later would employ Doris Duke's controversial butler Bernard Lafferty) and Elizabeth Taylor (whom Bernard Lafferty would later appoint to the board of the various Doris Duke foundations). But Doris Duke did not want Eddie Tirella because of his famous and powerful friends. Although she enjoyed meeting them, she wanted Eddie for his ability to transform Rough Point, that cold and drafty white elephant on the Atlantic Ocean, into a place that might be livable for a few months every summer.

Far from being a carefree beach escape, Rough Point was a cold place, both symbolically and in actuality. Even during moderate weather, the overworked furnaces had to consume entire veins of coal and oil to keep the temperature at a chilling fifty-five degrees. Doris Duke believed that the house was haunted by the souls of the corpses of African slaves who were washed ashore after the sinking of a slave ship during an Atlantic northeaster. It was these souls who roamed and chilled the halls of Rough Point.

The walls were hung with huge but dark tapestries and looming paintings. Everything inside of the mansion at Rough Point was oversized except the people.

Even noises were eerier at Rough Point. A slight noise in the house could echo down the hallways. A tree branch scraping against a window would be amplified into a terrifying invasion. And there was always the crashing of the waves, a sound that was so calming at Shangri-La but seemed invasive and menacing at Rough Point. Doris Duke might have opted to sell the house but there were few buyers for Newport mansions in the 1960s. These Gatsby-era palaces were out of fashion in a decade when many people were moving toward antiestablishment thinking. Additionally, Doris was considering the restoration of the village of Newport as her next project.

Newport was an odd place. Along the Atlantic Ocean stood some of the most elaborate and costly residences in the world while only a few blocks away stood slumlike structures formerly inhabited by the platoons of servants who had been needed by the summering rich. It was these streets of shabby and peeling clapboard houses that Doris decided to beautify. Her reasons for doing this were simple: she didn't like having to look at slums as she came and went from Rough Point and decided to raise the real estate values of her neighborhood.

She looked for someone with infinite imagination and expansive vision to help with the project. She needed Eddie Tirella.

Tirella had superb taste. He had started his career as a hat designer at Saks Fifth Avenue and he had been a set designer for the 1965 film *The Sandpiper*, staring Richard Burton and Elizabeth Taylor (he created Miss Taylor's artist shack, which was a forerunner of the American sophisticated rustic look that is so popular today). He even appeared in a cameo role in the film.

While he was very talented, he was a terrible businessman and barely earned more than four thousand dollars a year although his client list included some of the most famous names in the world. He wanted to be a part of the movie colony and not a purveyor of services to the stars, so he often did vast amounts of work as a no-charge gift for a friend.

He badly needed Doris Duke and her checkbook.

He first was hired to redesign the ancient and dingy kitchen of Rough Point, which reminded most people of the kind of scullery that would be found in the bowels of a medieval castle. Tirella would appear, all virile and masculine in a turtleneck pullover and tight-fitting jeans, and Doris would wonder what he would be like in bed.

"He let me know very quickly that a woman had no chance in his life," Doris told a family friend. "He reminded me of one of the bulls at Duke Farms. The bull had wonderful conformation and the bloodline of a champion but whenever we tried to breed him to a heifer, he had no interest but he would jump over a fence to hump one of the steers. I decided my advances were scaring him. I decided I could always find a man who would be good in bed but a really great interior designer was a treasure."

When the kitchen was successfully glamorized, Doris hired Tirella to redo an old hotel near Pasadena, California, that was to serve as a main headquarters for the Self Realization Society, one of the many yogi-inspired groups that attracted her attention. Tirella was very impressed with the infinite depth of the Duke bank accounts and their ability to finance his abundant creativity.

Tirella was with Doris Duke on July 5, 1965, when she learned of the death of Porfirio Rubirosa, who smashed his Ferrari into a tree following still another all-night reverie in the clubs of Paris. Doris was devastated. She had truly liked Rubi because he always did what he had promised.

It was Tirella, who had recently changed his name to Eduardo, with his wicked sense of humor who started the rumor that Doris Duke had arranged to have the legendary Rubirosa penis preserved for fornication history.

"She was very sentimental about that prick," Tirella said in his mocking manner. "Doris had planned to keep it for herself, something like the body of Lenin, and display it with her other treasures but she could not find an electrician to wire it for batteries. I think she finally donated it to the Smithsonian Institution. It is now considered the eighth wonder of the world."

Friends gasped when Tirella said this in front of Doris at a breakfast (he was eating a sausage at the time) at Rough Point. "We were ready for Doris to chew him to pieces," one friend said. "Instead she laughed and said it sounded like a good idea."

Life with Tirella was an adventure. He convinced Doris to buy a penthouse at 475 Park Avenue (Penthouse B) and taught her the joys and economies of buying designer copies at a fraction of their cost at Ohrbach's. Tirella gave Doris a new kind of freedom.

She learned that by wrapping a scarf around her head and wearing huge sunglasses (soon to become one of her trademarks) she could often wander around the streets of New York without being noticed. They would explore antique shops and art galleries and Doris would have a marvelous time bartering with the proprietors for the lowest possible prices and then watch their faces when they were told to bill the Duke offices.

Doris paid Eduardo well for his efforts. But Eduardo had a problem: he was a gentleman. Whenever he and Doris would go out to dinner or an evening on the town (which was frequently, because Doris loved being on the go) he would pay the checks. Doris never carried any money. She was one of those people who would go to the best restaurants anyplace in the world and walk out without paying. Of course, the bill would be sent to the Duke offices (after an enormous tip was added) and checks would be issued. But Tirella was of Old World stock and believed in paying a tab when it was presented. Thus he spent much of his large salary on his benefactor. He could have rebilled Doris for the entertainment costs as part of his expenses but this was against his nature.

Thus Tirella found himself making more money than ever before in his life, yet he was going broke. "If Eddie Tirella was going to spend evening after evening in the company of a woman," one Hollywood insider recalled, "he would have to be making some money."

Doris Duke had the cash Tirella found necessary. In the 1960s, Doris Duke's fortune had grown under her skillful management until she was considered the third-richest woman in the world, topped only by Queen Elizabeth of England and Queen Juliana of the Netherlands. Her spendable income was approximately $1 million per week. She decided to spend much of this money (and provide herself with a whopping tax shelter) on the historical preservation of Newport, a town where everything had become just a bit seedy.

Eddie Tirella became a detective as well as a designer as he began the restoration of Rough Point. Restoration would require finding much of the original furnishings of the house during its heyday decades prior to the stock market crash of 1929. Until he began the Newport redevelopment project, Eddie Tirella's main function was to assist Doris Duke in creating the fabulous Duke Gardens at Duke Farms. But he was mostly an assistant on that project, which was a creation mostly of the mind and soul of Doris as a monument to her father. Rough Point would be the project that would bear the Tirella design signature.

Even with this project under way, Doris had become depressed. She was unhappy about her terrible relationships with the men in her life. A woman on the edge of late middle age, she realized she was alone. Plastic surgeons and special treatments could help her hang on to the illusion of youth but they could not give her a family. Doris had begun to understand this when tiny Arden died so many years earlier and along with her, Doris's chance at motherhood and perhaps the only opportunity to have someone with Duke blood who would love her. She wanted someone to call her "Mother." Her only escape from her sadness was her projects. And Eddie Tirella was the creative key to this obsession.

Doris Duke's slender form, crammed into the tightest of toreador pants and usually wearing a white shirt, would seem to appear at the gardens of Duke Farms and Rough Point at nearly the same time barking orders. (Or so it seemed to the employees.) Eddie Tirella was a calming influence and the handsome Italian became very popular with the harassed Duke staff.

Only Tirella was tiring of Doris Duke's mood swings. He was worried that his motion picture design career was suffering because all of his time was being monopolized by his rich employer. Worse yet, his sex life, which had been abundant, was now minimal because of Doris's social demands.

He was making Doris Duke's life beautiful. His exquisite taste had left its mark on the Beverly Hills house as well as Rough Point and Duke Farms. He could not do enough, fast enough, to beautify her life. Doris could always write checks faster than Tirella could create beauty. Eddie was tired and burned out.

Then he got another job offer. Producer Martin Ransohoff offered Tirella a design job on the Tony Curtis and Sharon Tate film *Don't Make Waves*. Doris was panicked when Eddie told her that he was considering the job (he had actually accepted it). Her entire life revolved around his ability to make things—her things—look beautiful. She pleaded with him not to leave her. He made up an excuse that he needed to return to Los Angeles to have some dental work done. Doris immediately started making arrangements with the best dentist in New York City to do whatever work might be needed—at her expense. But Tirella went to Los Angeles.

Doris made a series of pleading calls, begging Tirella to return to her. She offered him more money and was even ready to reconsider her financing of the Big Sur park project. He could have anything if he would only come back East.

In early October of 1966, Eduardo Tirella returned to the world of Doris Duke and the dramatic mansion of Rough Point, a gothic novel setting with its crashing breakers and rocky beaches, its austere brick-gabled house with French doors and leaded windows. Doris again had Tirella and she did not intend to lose him this time. Unlike her lovers, Tirella was indispensable to her life because he gave her purpose. She could visualize a project and she could most certainly finance a project but Tirella had the talent to make a project into perfection.

On Friday, October 7, 1966, all this beauty and perfection ended. Only Doris knew what really happened that afternoon. Unlike her lovers, whom she delighted in discussing, she never mentions the events of October 7. Her lawyers had theories. Her family had theories. Her friends had theories. The police and the press had theories. Only Doris Duke would ever really know.

Sometime around three in the afternoon, Doris and Eddie got into a rented car (Newport insiders later whispered that the car had been rented because Doris had premeditated what would soon happen and did not want to risk damaging one of her own cars), supposedly to attend to the business of the Newport Preservation Society. They were not going to be gone long. Doris had left instructions with the servants for dinner to be served at eight in the evening. Doris was driving.

The massive iron gates at Rough Point were nearly twenty feet high and weighed more than a ton each. They were always kept closed and there was no electronic opener.

Tirella got out of the car and walked toward the gates to open them. Just as he placed himself between the car and the gates, the car jumped forward pinning him. The engine continued roaring until the stately gates shook and then slowly toppled toward the street. Still, the car kept moving ahead while the body of Tirella remained caught between the automobile and the crumpled gates. As his body was ground to pieces by the combination of scraping iron, machinery, and pavement, the car kept pushing until the wreckage, both human and mechanical, stopped on the other side of the street, jammed against a large tree.

Witnesses who came upon the accident at first thought that Doris was the only person involved. Most of Tirella was unrecognizable as having once been a human being. In shock, Doris got out of the car and walked toward the house in a daze. Then she started to scream. It was the fierce scream of a wounded animal with no trace of the usual Doris Duke sensual whisper.

"Eduardo!"

"Eduardo! Eduardo! Eduardo!!!"

She continued screeching his name as she climbed the great staircase and went to her bedroom. Out in the street, horrified onlookers were realizing that what was strained through the gates and ground in little puddles of flesh and plasma into the pavement, that collection of entrails had once been human. The head had been bashed against the concrete like a broken melon and features such as the nose and ears were gone. Gloved police would later gather bits of brain and lost eyeballs from the street.

An ambulance rushed through the gaping opening where the iron gates had been only a few minutes earlier. They were there to take Doris to the hospital. There was nothing that could be done for handsome Eduardo Tirella, whose life had been a statement in beauty and whose death had been the ultimate in ugliness.

Never before had the Duke lawyers had to work so quickly. The story of what happened at the gates was worldwide news. Doris was kept in isolation in the hospital overnight. Servants had packed all of Tirella's things at both Rough Point and Duke Farms and had them removed. Groundskeepers spent all night scrubbing the skid marks and bloodstains from the road.

Landscapers from Duke Farms restored any lawn and shrubbery that might have been damaged so that there would be no sordid photo opportunities for reporters the following dawn. The gates were taken away to be repaired and rehung as quickly as possible. The rental car disappeared from the face of the earth. Politicians were called from Providence to Washington and deals were made.

The lawyers and Duke retainers knew that there was a good chance that Doris could be charged with manslaughter or, perhaps, even murder. It was no secret that she was enraged with Tirella for refusing to remain an important part of her privileged life.

The political power structure of Newport, including the police department, was reminded that Doris was the only financial hope for the redevelopment of their town.

The following afternoon, awed police investigators who had lived lifetimes in Newport but had never entered the Rough Point mansion had the opportunity to question the sedated Doris. After a twenty-minute interrogation, the police were escorted from the mansion and the investigation was completed.

The police drove through freshly repaired and painted gates as they exited the grounds—never to return. Today no official record of the murder or investigation can be found. All that is known is what was written in the newspapers, which was incriminating in itself.

Those closest to Doris think they know what happened. When Tirella came that last time to Rough Point, Doris was determined to convince him to stay. She offered him money. She tried to explain that the work he would do at Duke Gardens and for the Newport Preservation Society could not only make him a rich man but give him a place in history. She plied him with promises and champagne.

The two had been drinking heavily for almost two days before she slid behind the wheel of the rental car. Eddie Tirella was staggering when he climbed from the passenger seat and struggled with the padlock at the gate. Doris was close to drunk when she joked to Tirella that his alcoholic condition was such that he could not open the lock. She laughed and pushed her heel into the accelerator to make the motor roar in an effort to startle Tirella, whose handsome face was caught in a sheepish and inebriated grin as he pretended to push away the car. The motor roared again. And he was dead.

It was probably an accident—a drunken and foolish accident.

The Tirella episode officially ended in 1971, when Doris Duke paid a $96,000 settlement to his family, who had sued her for $1.2 million. Gossips criticized this trivial sum as still another example of Doris Duke's cheapness.

In reality, Doris Duke had pleaded with her lawyers to make a larger settlement. She was willing to pay millions of dollars in an effort to avoid having to go to court but her lawyers said that an out of court settlement would be the same as admitting guilt so they would not permit her to write the check. In court, she winced as her lawyers painted Tirella as a financial failure who probably never would have made much money. The jury deliberated only six hours before deciding on the meager settlement.

Doris Duke's lawyers were elated. But Doris's face was frozen as if she had turned to stone. She would have paid any amount to have Tirella back in her life. She would have gladly written a check for millions of dollars. But she had learned that money could not buy immortality.

She would find some way to atone for those she had hurt. Somehow, it seemed as if she had brought misery to everyone who cared about her or for whom she cared. It was as if her life had never had any meaning.

# 19
# THE DUCHESS WILL BE AMUSED

If any woman detested growing old more than Cleopatra, it was Doris Duke. She spent millions of dollars in an unsuccessful effort to keep her body and face from aging. Her face had been through so much plastic surgery that her eyes were pulled back toward her scalp, resulting in a slanted-eye Asian appearance. Her chin had been shortened and reshaped. She had traveled the world in search of youth preservatives that ranged from hundred-thousand-dollar treatments of sheep embryo injections to strange machines that promised to stimulate sagging skin and regenerate weakening internal organs. Doris Duke could not buy youth but she tried.

She once raged to a family member about the catty comment of a fellow dowager (God, how she hated the term "dowager"), "The old prune told me that I looked fabulous for my age. She said I must be doing something right. Damn, I have done everything right. I don't want to look good for my age. I want to be young!"

She exercised. She took more and more dance lessons. She was massaged and oiled and acupunctured. She was dipped in expensive oozes that promised therapeutic miracles. Her elbows and heels were pumiced and her legs were waxed. Bags under the eyes were cooled by sliced cucumbers and when that was unsuccessful, they were snipped away under a surgeon's scalpel.

Since she had tried everything to keep her body young and was failing, she decided to add a human zoo of exotic people to her life to at least keep her spirit youthful. However, because of all the publicity surrounding the death of Eddie Tirella, Doris had become even more publicity-shy. Her life began to reflect the decadent lifestyles of the ancient Asian potentates whose treasures she had collected and warehoused for so many decades. Beautiful people, brilliant people, bizarre people, and a constant onslaught of people after her money began to pass through the gates of her walled estates to entertain Miss Duke. She appeared to the outside only in what her family called "her moments of atonement."

One such moment came in the late 1960s. At the height of the civil rights movement and following the Newark race riots, she made a public appearance singing in a black church choir. It was her way of promoting the Duke family belief in integration. She was revolted at seeing herself exposed in the press but she still went to the church because she believed that her presence might somehow set some sort of example.

Following the death of Eduardo Tirella, Doris, always a woman with a strong libido, decided to make some pragmatic but possibly dangerous adjustments in her sex life. There would be no more emotional relationships. It would be pure slam-bam-thank-you-sir.

In her forays into black culture, Doris Duke discovered an abundance of what she liked: muscular and dark-skinned men with gigantic sexual organs. She would venture into the dark and dangerous clubs of Harlem looking for her satisfaction, willing to pay a collection of studs and hustlers. Thus she would be satisfied and, most of the time, still have her privacy.

"It is wonderful how few black people have even heard of me," she told family members. "When I am with them it is as if I have a new life to live."

Needless to say, Doris was very secretive about her brief

encounters (and they were brief, seldom lasting more than thirty minutes). Even though she was far beyond her youth, her body was still good (except for a skin condition caused by too much exposure to the Hawaiian sun that caused a blotchy discoloration) and her daily naked appraisals in her full-length bedroom mirrors showed that her legs and breasts and rear end were still firm and well placed, a testimonial to modern plastic surgery.

She was delighted when one of her thirty-minute romances would ask her if she was forty or even fifty. She also liked the fact that she could give explicit instructions to a paid sexual performer as to exactly what she desired. "A lot of us thought she was doing something unusual," one family member said. "It was not unusual to run into some dark-skinned stud coming out of the Park Avenue penthouse. Some of these people looked awfully dangerous. She was smart enough to have them come to the Park Avenue place where she had a lot of close protection. We never saw anybody like that at Rough Point or the farm or the Honolulu place. You have to realize that Doris thought like a man. She was always more than equal to any man on earth so if a man could buy sex, so could she. I think it seemed sensible to her."

In fact the entire purpose of the Park Avenue penthouse during the 1970s and 1980s seemed to be to provide a playpen for Doris Duke's sexual fantasies. Unlike the magnificent other residences with their priceless art and rare carpeting, the penthouse was done in what one family member dubbed "disco bordello." This was because at the time, Doris Duke spent many evenings dancing in the shadowy lighting of Studio 54, only a few blocks away from the penthouse, where the rich and the beautiful and the coked-out nested and liaisoned. On many nights a tall, thin blond woman would dance until dawn and then invite whoever she found interesting back to the Park Avenue penthouse.

The penthouse was an odd-looking place in the sexually free decade of the seventies. The place was a mass of silver wall coverings and black-enameled floors (not unlike Studio 54) with lots of mirrors and huge ornate couches covered in fake fur. It was as if the entire place had been designed to harbor some uninhibited alter ego of Doris Duke. "I think of it as the trollop tower," Doris would joke occasionally. It was the place where an aging woman dwelled while she fought for the last memories of a youth that had already passed.

It was at this penthouse where she had hoped to seduce famed Russian ballet dancer Rudolph Nureyev. She had no misapprehensions about him; she knew he was nearly exclusively gay but, if the possibility existed that he might have some long-forgotten heterosexual yearning, Doris had hopes of nurturing those emotions. She did not want a relationship with Nureyev. She merely wanted his magnificent body. Doris adored dancers and took thousands of hours of dance lessons to improve her own abilities. And Nureyev was the most famous dancer in the world.

Nureyev was aware that Doris Duke was interested in more than the point of his toe and carefully avoided her lair. Instead he would take her on the rounds of the nightclubs (she wore the fabulous Duke emeralds) with the evenings usually ending at Studio 54.

Doris would not be denied. She was prepared to spend as much as $3 million to lure Nureyev to the penthouse. She agreed to provide the $3 million necessary to finance a movie based on the life of the legendary dancer Nijinsky, which would star Nureyev, and sent a token hundred-thousand-dollar payment to the producers, requesting that Nureyev come to the penthouse to discuss the film. When he arrived, according to a family member, Doris, who was enthusiastically studying belly dancing at the time, was dressed in a collection of veils with tiny clacking cymbals attached to her fingers. She offered to dance for him and proceeded to undulate suggestively around him as he roosted nervously on one of the fur couches.

At the first opportunity, Nureyev fled the penthouse as if his tights were on fire. Doris's seduction of the famed dancer was a failure. He even arranged to have the hundred thousand dollars returned to Doris Duke, explaining that they could not work together because of artistic differences.

(Later when Nureyev died of AIDS-related illnesses, gossips hinted that Doris might also be suffering from the illness because of her supposed relationship with the dancer. As no one on the inside ever entertained the thought of the two of them leaping in passion in her enormous mirrored bed, most family members discounted this possibility. But it was true that one of the main reasons Doris, years later, gave $2 million for AIDS research to the Duke Medical Center, was as a partial memorial to the great dancer.)

Rudi was one of the few people at this time from her café society set whom Doris tried to lure into her web of hormones (she was taking shots of sheep placenta at sixty thousand dollars a treatment to keep those hormones trickling if not flowing.) It was still more common when that gleam appeared in her blue eyes, for her to look toward the endless and nameless studs of Harlem.

Black hustlers do not have friends who write for the *New York Post* or *Daily News* gossip columns. Black male prostitutes had nothing to gain socially from linking their names to the Doris Duke fortune. The dozens of interior designers, actors, producers, lawyers, and the smattering of broke socialites who alleged that they had affairs with Doris during her last two decades on earth were probably lying.

"Gay interior designers were always trying to enhance their bisexual images by spreading the rumors that they had bedded Doris. She had the kind of café society reputation for being good at sex that was usually associated with males. You might say that she was the female version of a stud," a family member said. "There was the tiny little twerp from Morocco who hung around for about six months and managed to stay connected to the payroll for a few years. Anyhow, this poofter has made a career of bragging about his physical relationship with Doris. It was a laugh. He was such a mousy little creature that she would most likely have killed him in bed. There were a lot of little pricks like that around Doris. She liked them but she never fucked them. They never had a chance of satisfying her."

Doris, especially during the 1970s and 1980s, was not idle. It was as if she had an obsession with keeping herself entertained and occupied for every moment of her life. She collected unusual people and unusual things. She had projects. She spent thousands of hours on self-improvement. What she could not stand to do was be alone with her thoughts. The memories of death filled her mind unless she kept herself occupied. There was the death of her father and her mother's part in it. Arden was gone before she ever had the chance to live. Rubi was dead. Louis Bromfield was dead. Her mother was gone. And then there was Eddie. Doris did not want to think about death but she seemed to be surrounded by it. She herself was no longer young and was haunted by her ultimate terror: her own death.

She looked for reassurance from a parade of psychics. They spoke to Arden, whose essence sent rapping spiritual messages to her mother that indicated her dead daughter would someday reincarnate and mother and daughter would be together again. Buck Duke was frequently conjured for advice. The aura of Rubi recalled nights of passion. Eduardo forgave her. Doris Duke's well-paid mystics were adept at bringing her the words she wanted to hear for the right price.

She was still looking for the reincarnation of her lost daughter Arden and she was nearly positive she had found her when she met actress Sharon Tate. While Arden had been a baby of darker skin, Sharon Tate was tall and blond like Doris Duke. She was also extremely beautiful.

Doris would take the young actress on expensive shopping trips on Rodeo Drive in Beverly Hills where she would spend thousands of dollars buying mother-and-daughter designer ensembles.

When a pregnant Sharon Tate and her houseguests were murdered in 1969 in their rented Beverly Hills mansion by the infamous Charles Manson cult, Doris became hysterical and screamed, "She was taken from me because of what happened to Arden!" Ashen, Doris listened to reports of the butchering of the beautiful Sharon, who was stabbed dozens of times while she begged the invaders not to harm the child inside her body. Neither Sharon nor the baby were spared.

Doris saw a horrible connection between Arden being pounded to pieces inside her uterus by the huge and violent waves of Hawaii and the stabbing of Sharon and her unborn baby. "Both babies never had the chance to be born," Doris Duke said once as she drew the comparison. "I am being punished."

Following the Sharon Tate murders, Doris Duke again retreated into her own private world behind iron gates. Her only outings were to the midnight crowds at clubs like Studio 54 where she would dance under the strobe lights as artificial fog arose from the floor and a glittering half moon drifted above the crowd. She was, of course, invited into the very private lounge where the superstars did lines of cocaine and consumed dishes of uppers and downers. Doris Duke probably did some drugs but she preferred vitamins. She once attempted to convince a drugged-out Judy Garland to exchange her uppers and downers for vitamins and a low-fat diet back in the 1950s. (Doris Duke had had most fat removed from her food since the late 1940s, which was decades before fat-free diets became popular.) One family member said, "Doris survived on the lobster and beluga caviar washed down with La Ina sherry or champagne. Her diet cost more in a week than most families spent in a year. But she was healthy and thin." She had even quit smoking, which would have made her father happy.

Actor Marlon Brando, who was also known for his obsession with privacy, sought Doris's millions for his American Indian projects. Of course, Brando, whose once magnificent body had not then turned completely to flab, was lured to the penthouse. He was even seen at Duke Farms. He eventually convinced Doris to purchase more than two hundred and fifty head of breeding cattle for the Rosebud Indians in the Black Hills of South Dakota.

She financed many Indian programs, including studies to record the history and language of various Indian nations. If Doris is to be remembered for any great contributions to society, they will be the development of the American orchid industry, restoration of historic structures, and the preservation of Indian history. There were many sides to Doris Duke.

At this point in her life, Doris developed a new philosophy, one that her father had understood well: money is more powerful than fame. She adored movie stars, musicians, and artists. She also realized that all that was needed to bring them to her was for her to ask them to come. A woman who had experienced a lifetime of fame could summon Andy Warhol, the artist who penned the axiom that every person had fifteen minutes of fame in each lifetime, to come to her to pay homage to her billions. Elvis Presley courted her favor. When she sang at the same black church for several Sundays in a row, singer and future psychic network tycoon Dionne Warwick would suddenly decide that she too wished to be a part of the choir. Even Greta Garbo would accept a dinner invitation from Doris Duke although she did not receive many such requests for her elusive presence because Doris found her to be stuffy. Jacqueline Kennedy, who was on the board of the Newport Preservation Society, was also usually eager to accept an invitation.

Jacqueline Kennedy Onassis, who was always attracted to anyone with a vast amount of money, courted Doris Duke, at that time the single-largest holder of United States Treasury bonds in the world. Doris Duke was envious of Jackie's image, beauty, and style, so she was delighted when she found herself being used by Aristotle Onassis, the Greek shipping billionaire, in an attempt to make his famous wife jealous. Ari and Doris were an even stranger-looking pair than Jackie and Ari on the international social scene. Doris Duke was more than a head taller than the little Greek, whose nose would nestle in the middle of her surgically uplifted breasts when they danced.

Like many women, Doris found the little Greek with the big nose and even bigger wallet to be infinitely attractive. He was supposedly a master in bed but it is doubtful whether he and Doris Duke ever tried sex. Instead they were the kind of equal friends that only two billionaires who do not need each other for any reason except friendship could be. They enjoyed each other.

In 1973, Doris accepted an invitation from Ari for one of his legendary trips aboard his fabulous 325-foot yacht, the *Christina*, named for his daughter. After flying to Puerto Rico, Doris joined a glittering crowd aboard the ship including Jackie and young John Kennedy.

A trip with Ari Onassis never cost a guest a dime. When a guest went shopping, an Onassis aide would arrange for payment for any items that the guest might have expressed even the least passing interest in, whether it was a pair of sunglasses or a gold Rolex watch. Doris was intrigued with being on the receiving end of this kind of generosity for the first time in her life. She was also thrilled to learn that Ari admired her taste in art and antiques and felt that her instincts were far superior to those of his trophy wife.

Ari Onassis wanted to be a man of taste and style and was determined to buy that distinction if he had to do so. If he decided to have a formal dinner in the grand dining room of the ship, the men would find perfectly tailored tuxedos in their staterooms. Onassis kept a tailor on board to alter the stock of the most expensive Italian and French garments that were laded aboard just as were the cases of champagne and Château Lafite wine. Of course, the recipients of these tuxedos were expected to keep the garments, which usually cost more than a thousand dollars each. Sometimes Onassis would decide that it would be fun for all guests to dress in white or pink or yellow for an afternoon and the appropriate designer clothing would be gifted to his guests. In fact, he had several full-time employees on his payroll whose responsibility it was to select the perfect garments for his guests.

Ari was so thorough that when one male guest accidentally dropped a solid-gold Dunhill lighter over the side of the ship, an exact replica of the lighter appeared on the man's dresser that night complete with the engraved message that the guest had happened to mention was on the lighter.

This was the same attention to detail that Doris possessed. She could go to her small New York City offices in the middle of the night and read the thousands of pages of business transactions done on her behalf and immediately recognize any new or unusual transactions. It was also possible for her to scan the dozens of rooms of the particular house she was leaving and mentally record the thousands of valuable items that were about to be covered by sheeting until her return. Both Doris Duke and Ari Onassis had an exacting eye and memory for detail.

Doris later invited Jackie, Ari, and his daughter Christina to Duke Farms for Thanksgiving. Ari accepted without consulting Jackie, who wanted to spend the holiday with her children. When Jackie refused to attend, Ari ended up arriving at Duke Farms alone, and he and Doris Duke dined on turkey stuffed with oysters and caviar washed down with Château Margaux from wine cellars stocked by Buck Duke.

Ari died in March of 1975, leaving his daughter, Christina, the richest woman in the world. Christina died in 1988 after years of drug abuse, leaving her tiny daughter, Athina, whom the press immediately dubbed, "the richest little girl in the world," a title once created for Doris Duke.

Holidays were always a sad and lonely time for Doris Duke. For years Doris had attended Duke-Biddle family holidays but in the late 1970s the families were pulling apart and she found herself alone with just her servants. At Christmas, she often came back from Hawaii to see the snow at Duke Farms and present her gifts to the staff. She had a tradition of giving each employee fifty dollars to buy a single luxury gift for each child in the family. On Christmas Eve, she would summon the several hundred employees of Duke Farms to the elaborate decorated big house where she would present each child with a gift which was more often than not the best present the child would receive. Doris loved doing this and thrived on the smiles of the children, but their parents often resented it, feeling that their rich employer was stealing their Christmas with her wonderful presents.

Doris couldn't have cared less. She wanted to give presents at Christmas and those presents must be absolutely perfect. It made her Christmas and that was all that was important.

# 20
# THE USERS

Doris Duke was one of the richest and loneliest women on earth. She had nearly estranged herself from her family, partially due to her actions, but also because of the never-ending trail of people and projects that monopolized her attention.

Her life during the last years of the "disco decade" of the 1970s was a nomadic odyssey where she traveled from one fabulous pleasure palace to another. She could remodel and redecorate her environment hundreds of times to occupy her time.

When she was not redesigning her environment, Doris was fine-tuning her portfolios of investments. She had simplified her vast empire into a series of investment areas. There were real estate and art, which were probably worth more than $1 billion. Then there were her liquid assets, which consisted of another $1 billion in government and very safe high-yield bonds. No one but Doris knew the actual extent of the holdings in gold that Buck Duke had placed in European vaults almost eight decades earlier but the weight of the bullion was measured in tons. Her greenhouses, most especially the superb Doris Duke orchids, had become far more than a hobby and were highly profitable. It was not unusual to see this tall woman walking into the brownstone offices in the middle of the night where she would remain until dawn reading the ledgers alone with her empire. "Money is power," she would say, "and my money is real power."

Doris had an obsession that seemed to infect the entire Duke family: the need to create the image that she was poorer than she actually was. While she was probably worth several billion dollars, both she and her cousin Mary Semens (who has a personal fortune estimated in the $300 million area) enjoyed tricking their associates into underestimating their worth.

This is when she started manipulating Malcolm Forbes, the eccentric owner and publisher of *Forbes* magazine. He would sit on the terrace at Rough Point and probe Doris about the extent of her fortune and she would lament as to how she had lost so much money because of the charlatans who fed on her bank accounts. Later when Malcolm would publish his "richest Americans" list, he would vastly underestimate the size of the Duke fortune. Doris would read "Malcolm's mistakes" with a combination of joy and contempt. "Silly little Malcolm has been fooled again," she would delight. "Maybe that will help keep all those people who are after my money away. They might think they should go somewhere else."

At the start of the 1980s, it seemed that Doris Duke had everything. She was still immensely rich when many of her once-affluent childhood acquaintances had disappeared into the anonymity of the middle classes. She looked to be in her forties when she was actually twenty years older. Her Newport Restoration Society was completely successful. She amused herself by dangling her money in front of the eternally greedy and toadish entertainment-mogul types of Hollywood but she never really intended to give them millions of dollars to finance their fanciful projects; this was done to provide her with a never-ending array of strange and entertaining characters for her human zoo. But Doris Duke did not have everything she wanted.

She wanted Arden.

She got Chandi Heffner.

Doris knew that she would never give birth again but still believed that someday the reincarnation of Arden would return to give her another chance at motherhood. It was this hope that fostered her interest in Eastern religions with their beliefs in reincarnation of souls.

Doris thought that she was going to love Chandi Heffner more than she had ever loved anyone but, instead, she ended her life hating Heffner more than she had ever hated anyone in her past including Jimmy Cromwell and Nanaline Duke. "If anything ever proved to me that she did not murder Eddie Tirella that day at Rough Point," one family member recalled, "it was the fact that she didn't murder Chandi Heffner or have her murdered. She hated her that much for what she did. The fact that Chandi Heffner is walking the streets today and spending vast amounts of Doris's money is evidence that Doris was not capable of murder. Doris believed that she would return from the grave and if she does, Chandi had better start worrying."

Doris was positive that Chandi Heffner, who would become her adopted daughter, was the worst mistake in her life. She died believing that Chandi was behind the illnesses that caused her deterioration. In her last years, Doris was positive that Chandi was nothing more than a "lying little con artist" who launched a plan to extract as much of the Duke fortune as was possible. "She lied to me from the first day that we met," Doris said. "I hope that there really is a hell so that she can burn there."

This was a dramatic change in attitude from Doris's opinions of Chandi in the early 1980s. At that time, Doris was delighted to have the tiny and tanned Chandi with her thick dark hair as a part of her life. "I believe that is how Arden would have looked," Doris told one family member. "Arden would have had a Polynesian look."

Later, Doris would say that Chandi had begun her quest for the Duke billions back in the 1970s when she first learned of Doris in Honolulu.

Chandi Heffner was not Polynesian but Baltimorean. Had Doris hired the same private detectives that she used to research other business and social acquaintances, Chandi would never have made it to the inner workings of the Duke empire.

The truth about Chandi Heffner was far different from the fanciful image she presented to Doris Duke. Charlene Gail Heffner was raised in a nice, middle-class area of Baltimore. She graduated from a private Catholic girls' school. Her father was an attorney and bank vice president. Her mother was a surgical nurse. She had two sisters, one of whom would later marry the very rich Nelson Peltz.

"I believe she was jealous of her sister's rich husband," Doris theorized years later. "She was competitive and wanted to be richer than her sister."

In the early 1970s, tattooed and peasant-dressed Heffner was a part of the hippie movement that migrated toward the gentle climate and tolerant attitudes of the Hawaiian Islands. She was soon absorbed into the Hare Krishna movement. She wore the saffron gowns and veils and became a vegetarian. She claimed to reject money and material possessions. But she was fascinated with super-rich Doris Duke. Charlene had affected the name of Chandi and was living in a filthy shack with other Krishna followers just as Doris was lounging in her white marble palace in Honolulu.

During a trip to India, Chandi was supposedly married to a fellow Krishna and they returned to Hawaii where they lived on a spartan sixty-acre ranch and had a few horses. But a life of poverty was wearing on Chandi.

She began to re-create herself. She lost weight and headed for the polo matches where she said she was an heiress (sometimes she said she was related to Hugh Hefner) who had little regard for the immense fortune that would someday be hers.

In the late 1970s, Chandi Heffner launched a plan to become a part of Doris Duke's life. She returned briefly to the East Coast where she attempted to move in with her former model sister, Claudia, who was living in luxury in Nelson Peltz's mansion. She learned that Doris Duke was interested in belly dancing and went to a dance company that had once been funded by Doris.

For a while Chandi took the name Phaedra.

By the end of 1984, Chandi was ready to leave New York and return to Hawaii. She planned a belly-dancing seminar in Honolulu and hoped Doris might appear in her class. Just before leaving for Hawaii in 1985, Chandi broke her leg in a riding accident but she decided to continue with her plans even though she had to teach while wearing a massive cast.

In January of 1985, Doris was en route to Shangri-La.

She had been visiting with President Ferdinand Marcos and his wife, Imelda, in Manila and had cut the trip short after having to listen to Imelda sing one time too many. "I cannot stand that woman's voice but I like Ferdinand," Doris would comment. The powerful and cunning Marcos reminded her of Buck Duke and she sometimes hinted that she had trysted with the little president of the Philippine Islands.

"I thought Imelda was a lesbian," Doris would tell friends. "She was boring but Ferdinand was different. I felt something from him. We had things in common." (Chandi seemed to have some sort of early connection with Imelda and told people that she and Imelda were close friends.)

According to information that Doris learned later, Chandi had ingratiated herself with an acquaintance of Doris and begged to ride with him to Shangri-La one evening. He was to be at the house only briefly and Chandi was supposed to wait in the car. Instead, a few minutes after he entered the house, she walked into the drawing room, unannounced, and began her emotional assault on the psyche and fortune of Doris Duke.

"It seemed that we had everything in common," Doris told family members. "She had done her homework well." Within a week, Chandi Heffner had become an important element in the complex chemistry of the life of Doris Duke.

"Rumors began to circulate that she and this girl were having a lesbian relationship," one family member recalls. "We didn't believe it because Doris was crazy about men and touchy about the previous Jimmy Cromwell–inspired rumors."

"I now believe that Chandi herself was behind those rumors. I believe that she was considering some sort of palimony extortion plan. She seemed to delight in being discovered with me in some sort of compromising position. We might be having breakfast in my bedroom and just before the servants would come to take the trays, she would climb into bed and hug me. Then she would giggle when they entered the room," Doris later recalled. "I was a fool for not realizing what she was doing."

In February of 1986, the Marcoses were overthrown and the former President and his wife became Honolulu neighbors of Doris Duke. Imelda and Chandi had much in common and soon Chandi and Imelda were both extracting large amounts of money from Doris. It is interesting to note that Chandi suddenly was able to pay $1.5 million cash for a Hawaiian ranch that she later listed as a longtime asset of hers in an effort to prove she was not destitute when she was adopted by Doris. It was at this ranch that Doris became convinced that Chandi was the living incarnation of Arden.

Chandi had begged Doris, who was very fond of her usual luxurious environments, to go alone with her to the extremely rustic ranch. It was there, Doris would later recall, that she, after smoking some unusual pot and ingesting some hallucinogenic "herbs" provided by Chandi, witnessed the girl go into a trance and begin "channeling" the long-lost daughter, Arden, back from the dead. For one of the few times in her life, Doris was stunned.

"And probably stoned," she said later. But this was her opportunity to atone to Arden through the medium of Chandi. Doris was delighted and then came the biggest surprise. Arden told Doris through Chandi's lips that Chandi was the incarnation of Arden. Chandi was, indeed, the lost daughter of one of the richest persons in the world. Doris was delighted. She would have her second chance to be a mother.

Chandi, the self-depicted nonmaterialistic Krishna, was more than eager to become Arden, the spoiled heir to the manor. Instead of saffron, she wore Chanel. From here on out, it would be only the best for Chandi (Arden). This was to include a jet plane.

It seemed that Chandi's sister, Claudia, had a jet and Chandi wanted something bigger. Imelda Marcos was anxious to help Doris and Chandi find just the right aircraft, an eighteen-passenger Boeing 737 that belonged to international arms merchant Adnan Khashoggi.

In November of 1987, Doris paid $25 million for the airplane.

This transaction would later start the downfall of Chandi when Doris was told that the plane had only been worth $10 million and that Imelda and Chandi split a $2.5 million "commission" for abetting in the sale of the airborne white elephant to Doris. Doris believed that she was being conned, and she detested being cheated of fifteen cents, let alone $15 million for a gas-hog aircraft.

When Doris's pilot saw the plane, he was suspicious of the deal and suggested that Doris hold out some $2 million in case of problems. This seemed to Doris to be a practical idea but Chandi was anxious that this amount, which was so close to the alleged under-the-table commission, not be withheld. Chandi also wanted two Mongolian humpbacked camels and a Saudi-Arabian polo cap. (The camels were later named Princess and Baby, which was later compared to Prince and Baby, the famous Louis Bromfield boxer dogs.)

By 1987, it was evident that Chandi Heffner was starting to take control of the Doris Duke empire. Longtime business advisers were replaced by former Nelson Peltz associates at the recommendation of Chandi. Sister Claudia's former butler, Bernard Lafferty, was brought to the household because he professed to be loyal to his beloved Chandi. He undermined the power of the Duke employees who were of the opinion that they answered only to Doris Duke. Doris did not care for the often soused Bernard, whom she purposely called "Rafferty." She said he was a sloppy drunk and extremely effeminate. "The silly fool gushes and makes me nervous," Doris told a family member. "But Chandi seems to like him."

In the meantime, Imelda and Chandi were spending more and more time together. They enjoyed massages and would spend hours having their bodies rubbed. Sometimes they took turns massaging each other. They devoted hours to plotting both of their futures.

Imelda told Chandi that she was worth more than Doris and had $14 billion hidden away in gold bullion. Then on October 21, 1988, Imelda and her husband were indicted on fraud and racketeering charges in New York City. The Marcoses' assets were frozen.

Ferdinand Marcos, age seventy-one, was deemed too sick to go to New York but Imelda was as healthy as a cow, so accompanied by dozens of suitcases, Imelda was escorted to New York City aboard Doris's plane to meet with federal officials.

When bond for Imelda was set at $5 million, a nearly hysterical Chandi begged Doris to pay the money because Imelda's fortune was frozen. Doris later told family members that she was dazed when she agreed to post $5.3 million in bonds for Imelda.

"I had just taken some of Chandi's health injections," she told family members later. "We were taking shots of all sorts of stuff."

"This was like Doris in one way and unlike her in another," said her cousin Angier Biddle Duke. "It was most unlike Doris to spend that kind of money but not unusual for her to support an unpopular friend."

Doris was revolted to see her name in headlines. She admitted later to being embarrassed about her involvement in the Marcos mess. "I did it for Chandi and for Ferdinand," she said. "I was never . . . I . . . I just didn't like Imelda." In the end, Doris estimated that Imelda managed to cost her about $10 million. (Doris was told that when Imelda was acquitted of all charges, one of the first things the former First Lady of Manila did was to try to have the $5.3 million in Duke bonds refunded . . . to Imelda Marcos.

North Carolina newspapers and gossips at Duke University were anxious to have a different slant on the publicity being generated by their richest expatriate daughter, Doris Duke. These rumors centered on the mysterious relationship between Doris and Chandi. The social and academic set of Durham bubbled with lesbian rumors. These lesbian rumors ultimately could cost Duke University hundreds of millions in potential dollars. When Doris was told that the lesbian stories had even made it to the pages of a local newspaper whose ownership had hated the Dukes since the days when Washington Duke had had the effrontery to be both rich and Republican, Doris exploded.

"I know exactly where this started," Doris roared. "This reeks of those boring ladies in their black dresses at Duke who resent me. They are just waiting for me to die because they think they have more of a right to my money than I do. I wish I could keep them from getting the money in Daddy's trusts."

In an elaborate series of trusts left by Buck Duke, there were hundreds of millions of dollars. Two-thirds of the income would go to Doris during her lifetime. This interest could be left to an heir, but if Doris died without an heir, the money would come under the complete control of a group of North Carolinians with the closest of ties to Duke University.

"I wish there were a way that they would never get a dime." Doris pondered.

As Doris would recall later, Chandi had a solution. Chandi had changed from a demeaning little mouse to an often screaming monster. She was arrogant to the servants and appeared uncomfortable in the presence of Doris's blue-blooded relatives and friends. Doris was lonely and she wanted that second chance to have her Arden, but Chandi was becoming a major irritation.

Sooner or later, if something irritated Doris Duke, that something was removed. This is when, Doris believed, Chandi decided she needed a better legal position on the Duke money than a potential palimony suit.

Chandi, with Imelda's advice, suggested that Doris legally adopt her reincarnated daughter and Chandi would punish those biddies at Duke University. The idea had some appeal to Doris because she did not believe that it would diminish her actual fortune, which had already been placed in several powerful foundations.

After a few more injections of Chandi's special "youth" treatments, the possibility of adoption seemed to have more merit. On November 10, shaky and vacant-eyed, Doris Duke and an excited Chandi Heffner arrived without announcement at the courthouse in Somerville, New Jersey, where preprepared adoption papers were signed.

Courthouse officials said Doris appeared to be confused. In less than ten minutes Chandi Heffner had become Chandi Duke Heffner. Later Doris was surprised to learn that Chandi had not dropped her former last name because Chandi had always professed to be estranged from her family, though she wasn't.

Chandi continued telling everyone that she was very rich and had no interest in the Duke money. She just wanted to be reunited with her previous life mother. She listed her assets at $3.5 million but did not mention that all of these assets had been gifted to her by Doris Duke.

When Ambassador Angier Biddle Duke read of the adoption in the following morning's newspapers, he was again agog at his cousin's actions. Ever the diplomat, he quickly penned a note welcoming Chandi to the family. Doris immediately called Angier.

"It was as if she were trying to explain why she had done it," the ambassador said. "I just listened. She was almost apologetic. She knew even then that this was a mistake." Meanwhile Ferdinand Marcos was dying.

As the dictator faded, Doris seemed to gain strength. She believed that she had a mystical power in her hands to heal the sick and she was determined to save Marcos. Every day she would go to the Honolulu hospital where she would massage his withered body and brush his hair, pouring her strength into his declining carcass. Here she would meet with Dr. Rolando L. Atiga, Marcos's personal physician, to discuss the benefits, if any, of her treatments.

"Doris became very protective of President Marcos," a family member said. "She had Irwin Bloom, that business manager that Chandi found, well, she had him transfer what we believed to be four tons of gold out of her Swiss banks when the Swiss government cooperated with the United States officials in locating Marcos's assets."

In spite of Doris's efforts, it was evident that Marcos was dying. While Imelda made dramatic public demonstrations of her great love for her husband, it was Doris who spent the most time with President Marcos. If fact, Imelda was often busy entertaining guests at Shangri-La with her protégé Chandi at her side. It was at this time that Imelda announced that Chandi was worth $900 million herself as an heir to Uniroyal. This was a blatant fabrication that Doris later speculated was a plot between Chandi and Imelda to improve Chandi's public image so that when Doris died, there would be less comment about the intentions of the adopted daughter. According to the Imelda version, the adoption had taken place expressly to mix the two great fortunes which would later be used for the benefit of animals.

"What unmitigated bullshit," Doris said years later when she was told of these statements by Imelda and Chandi. "That little bloodsucker never had a dime that I didn't give her or that she didn't steal from me."

President Marcos died on September 28, 1989. Chandi was dismayed to find that when the dictator was gone Doris was far less tolerant of having Imelda underfoot. So Chandi made new friends. Comedian Jim Nabors introduced her to Paul Reubens, better known as Pee-Wee Herman. Reubens and a male companion lived in a house rented from Nabors. Chandi became Reubens's female companion.

"Reubens was far sleazier than any of my sleazy Hollywood friends," Doris laughed to family members. In 1989 while Doris was back in the continental United States, Chandi transformed Shangri-La into a wedding chapel for Reubens to marry his male friend while Imelda and Jim Nabors bellowed out the music. Later when Reubens faced public humiliation after being arrested in a theater showing pornographic female films, Doris permitted him to hide in one of the guest houses at Duke Farms. But she was tiring of her daughter's antics.

When Chandi installed a very handsome pile of masculine beefcake by the name of James Burns as her personal bodyguard, it became evident that he was doing more with Chandi's body than guarding it from a theorized potential assassination plot by some previous Duke employees.

"I think either I or Imelda was supposed to be jealous," Doris told a family member. "I did not care for him. He reminded me of Jimmy Cromwell."

Chandi seemed to become more and more frantic. She was ruder to servants and business associates. She even called Imelda "a bitch" to her face.

But Chandi still found the time to attentively hand-prepare her special youth shots and potions for her new mother.

Doris was starting to deteriorate. She was pale under the layers of makeup. Her body was a skeleton. She was having problems walking. Her family and friends were finding that more often their calls to Doris were being intercepted by either Chandi or her loyal butler Bernard Lafferty.

But, much to Chandi's dismay, Bernard had his own agenda. Frantic and nearly hysterical, Bernard told Doris and several of her immediate associates that he believed that "Something awful is being done to Miss Duke."

Without telling Chandi, Doris boarded the 737 in February of 1991 and fled. When Chandi returned to Shangri-La a few hours later, she was turned away by the guards. The Age of Chandi was over.

According to a statement made in writing on December 11, 1991, by former Marcos physician Dr. Rolando Atiga, Doris Duke was being poisoned.

"I have known Miss Duke since late in 1986," Dr. Atiga wrote,

> and through the years have had numerous contacts with her. I have seen her on various occasions as a friend and have become intimately acquainted with her medical history, having had visits in her home both in Honolulu and in Los Angeles. During these years, I have been seeing her as a friend and unofficially as a Physician. On several occasions, by late 1989, and all of 1990, she would complain that she would feel quite weak each time 'she was given many medicines' by Chandi Heffner. On one occasion, Miss Duke had shown me several cartridges (some of these are in my possession) of what appeared to be Heparin which apparently, had been given by Ms. Heffner intramuscularly or subcutaneously at various sites to Miss Duke without doctor's orders. In addition, I have noticed scattered areas of ecchymoses on the arms, and all over Miss Duke's body. There apparently had been frank hemorrhages in the gastrointestinal tract. One of such episodes happened in Rhode Island, where Miss Duke fainted, appeared shocky and was rushed to a nearby

> hospital where she subsequently had multiple transfusions. Miss Duke also described Chandi giving her as much as 4–6 of the same 'heart-pills' medicine which appeared to be Digoxin (Lanoxin). Thus slowing her heart rate and had been dig. toxic. I have advised Miss Duke not to allow Chandi to give her any more of the shots and the medicines as well and immediately consult her Physician(s) in Honolulu. She likewise, told me she was being given as much as 3–4 doses of 'sleeping pills' at nite [*sic*] by Chandi. which made her quite lethargic and weak for two days after.

Doris told Dr. Atiga she had talked to her Hawaiian physicians.

"She was told by early 1991, by her Physicians," Dr. Atiga wrote, "in Honolulu to stay away from Chandi as she was being 'poisoned,' to get her inheritance sooner."

"I was being slowly murdered," a terrified Doris confided to a family member. "I should have her arrested but I don't want any more headlines. Those miserable reporters would just say I have faked this illness to get rid of my lesbian girlfriend without paying her off. But I promise you this. She will never get a dime of my money. She took my health. She is not going to get another damn thing from me."

# 21
# POISON

Doris's body continued to deteriorate.

Well into her seventies, Doris Duke was proud of her tight and carefully tended skin. She would swim laps daily in her pools or in the icy Atlantic Ocean at Rough Point to maintain her athletic body. She was often mistaken for a woman in her forties or fifties.

But all that started to change in the early nineties.

Doris seldom spoke of Chandi Heffner in the years following the exile of her adopted daughter. This entire situation was an embarrassment to her. She disliked meeting her family or old friends because she believed that they considered her to be a foolish old woman. Chandi Heffner had humiliated and, perhaps, even tried to poison her, or so Doris Duke deeply believed.

"I hate her," was all she would say.

Thus she found herself even more isolated in her mansions with her fussing butler and companion Lafferty adding to her self-imposed solitary confinement. She was frightened. Bernard Lafferty had warned the sickening woman that Chandi had always been after her money to give to the Hare Krishna movement. She feared that Chandi was a brainwashed disciple, ready to kill her new mother on orders from her religious organization. She was positive that orange-robed zombies would someday be living in her beautiful houses and spending her beautiful money. She feared that if Chandi could not kill her, some other glassy-eyed Hare Krishna would make it through her security systems and dispatch her to Nirvana.

All these factors made Doris even more reclusive and removed. Her life was hidden behind the heavy gates of her estates. Like the American royalty she was, Doris was constantly attended to by her maid Nuku Makasaile, her personal chef, Colin Shanley, and her butler, Bernard Lafferty.

Each of the houses had full-time staff. At Falcon's Lair in Beverly Hills, the housekeeper was Ann Bostich and the caretaker was Mariano De Velasco.

Chef Colin Shanley was first employed by Doris Duke in the fall of 1988 to operate the kitchen at Rough Point, the mammoth Newport cottage. Doris had an annual routine: the summer months were spent at Rough Point and Duke Farms (she would use her helicopter to fly between these estates), on about November 22 (her birthday) she would fly to Falcon's Lair in her big jet, and the rest of the winter she would be located at Shangri-La in Hawaii.

Colin Shanley had quit his job several times. "In October of 1989, I told Miss Duke that I could not work for her any longer because of difficulties I was having with Charlene Gail Heffner, who was disrupting my work," Shanley said in a sworn deposition. "After Heffner was gone," Shanley continued, "Miss Duke never even mentioned her name. Nor could anyone else mention her name. I was instructed by Miss Duke not to prepare any foods that were in any way reminiscent of Heffner, such as Krishna dishes or pizza."

In early 1991, after Chandi's banishment, Shanley was asked to resume his duties in the Duke kitchen.

"Before Miss Duke terminated her relationship with Heffner," Shanley continued, "Lafferty had a very limited role as the butler. Lafferty was responsible for polishing the silver (a task which he often passed off on other, elder employees), answering the door at the households (there were, however, very few visitors), and serving Miss Duke's food to her on a tray (each day while she was eating Lafferty would be required to wait—sometimes for hours—in the hall outside of her room until she rang her bell, at which time he would be allowed to come into the room to remove the tray)." This image of Bernard Lafferty is the one remembered by other Duke relatives who visited Doris during the last years of her life.

"He just sort of lurked quietly in the background," explained Pandy (Pandora) Biddle, who helped Doris redecorate the mansion at Duke Farms and was planning to redo the interior of the Duke jet when Doris died. "He was a strange little mouse and I got the feeling that Doris did not like him that much. She often spoke harshly to Lafferty because she thought he was somewhat stupid and slow."

Doris either made a joke of calling the butler "Rafferty" because "he has bats in his rafters" or, more probably, she did not even remember his real name. Bernard Lafferty always called her "Miss Duke" or "madam."

Until Doris Duke's health and mental faculties began to deteriorate, Bernard Lafferty was a servant and was expected to act like a servant.

"Miss Duke knew that Lafferty was a very simple, illiterate man. When she had possession of her faculties, she never asked him for any advice." Shanley added, "Indeed, she was almost intolerant of his illiteracy—his inability to verbalize or understand things. At times, for example, he barely understood jokes that she had made.

"When Miss Duke was well enough to be aware of her surroundings," the chef continued, "Lafferty was required to wear a formal butler's uniform, which included a white jacket, white shirt, bow tie, and black pants, all of which were adorned by many buttons. (When we were in Hawaii, Miss Duke made Lafferty wear Filipino-style butler's shirts.) Miss Duke devoted no attention to Lafferty's clothing because he was required to wear a uniform."

Shanley also refutes Lafferty's allegations that Doris frequently had him accompany her to social events as a close friend and adviser.

"I recall the one and only occasion when Lafferty went with Miss Duke to a social event," Shanley said. "He assisted Irwin Bloom in attending to her at an event that was held at the New York Club, Tatou."

Friends who saw Doris Duke at Tatou that night commented that this very proud woman brought two men to help her walk rather than use a cane.

"When Miss Duke was in good health, she had little patience for Lafferty," Shanley added. "It was obvious that she thought he was slow. She would get frustrated when he could not understand a simple instruction. She did not like it when he would 'hover' around her. On several occasions, I saw her brush him away; I often heard her say 'get away from me.'"

The servants saw a different side of Bernard Lafferty. To Doris he was a soft-spoken lapdog who appeared to idolize her. Behind the scenes, he was a loud, often drunken, bigot who mocked his employer and her treasures.

"For example," Colin Shanley said, "Miss Duke loved African-American culture and music. Lafferty couldn't stand music by James Brown or Aretha Franklin, or any other African-American artist. When Miss Duke played music by black artists, he would say 'she has those wailing niggers on again.'"

Bernard Lafferty did not approve of Doris Duke's taste in art, either.

"Lafferty also could not understand Miss Duke's interest in Islamic art. Miss Duke had a vast collection of Islamic art, including tapestries and plates. Lafferty would point to one cracked Islamic plate (which was in a case in the dining room in Honolulu) and say 'can you believe this piece of shit is worth millions of dollars?' Lafferty would say the Islamic art was made by 'sand niggers.'"

It might be mentioned at this point that one art expert from Christie's who was permitted to enter the Shangri-La palace was astounded at the quality of Islamic and Eastern treasures exhibited there. He later told family members that he was stunned to realize that treasures that had been missing for sixty years or more were casually displayed in the house. The art in the Honolulu house alone might be worth more than $1 billion when, or if, it is ever appraised. (A deposition taken from one of the other servants says that in 1994 lawyers for the Duke estate made a trip to Honolulu to empty the contents of the safe.)

Even Doris herself did not escape Lafferty's mocking, although he never would have dared to make a jest to her face.

"In the early years of my employment," Shanley stated, "Miss Duke would practice playing the piano and would sing. Her voice had become quite crackly. Lafferty would make fun of her behind her back."

After Chandi Heffner was gone, Bernard Lafferty began to make himself more and more indispensable in the life of his rich mistress.

"After Heffner left, Lafferty spent more time with Miss Duke. He began to enhance his role in the household outside of her presence and without her knowledge," Colin Shanley said. "Miss Duke still treated him as a butler (for example, she would never have meals with him as she would with a guest or Miss Heffner). Nonetheless, he was taking advantage of Miss Duke's depression which resulted from her concern that she had been deceived by Heffner. He would tell Miss Duke very bad things that Heffner had done to him and her in order to ingratiate himself to Miss Duke. He began to fill Miss Duke's head with all sorts of 'conspiracy' theories about Heffner and others. He tried to convince Miss Duke that she needed to implement elaborate security systems, such as bulletproof glass in the Newport mansion, in order to protect herself from Heffner."

In late 1991 and early 1992, Lafferty was becoming more powerful. He also became a barrier between Doris Duke and the outside world.

"If a telephone call came in, he would make false statements about Miss Duke's frame of mind, whereabouts, or activities, to either mislead the caller or to make the caller believe that they should check with Lafferty before speaking to Miss Duke," Shanley said. "He often refused to put calls through to her. As time went on, he effectively cut her off from the outside world."

Family members were offended and sometimes repulsed when they attempted to call Doris. More than once an apologetic Lafferty would give a family member a very flimsy excuse as to why Doris would not take a call. He left the impression that Doris Duke was snubbing the caller for some unknown reason.

"You cannot help but wonder how different things might have been had Doris been permitted to contact the caliber of lawyer that her family recommended and trusted," Pony Duke lamented. "She might be alive today."

Lafferty was controlling his mistress's life but, at that time, she did not realize it. It would have been inconceivable to her that the nearly illiterate and often drunken servant could have usurped so much of her power and control.

But the full story of that control would not become known until after her death, when the Surrogate Court appointed former District Attorney Richard Kuh to investigate. The Kuh Report that resulted from that probe is based on thousands of pages of deposition transcripts and sworn statements from employees and others detailing the last years of her decaying life, which was controlled by Bernard Lafferty and the hangers-on around him.

According to housekeeper Ann Bostich, Doris, in typical Doris Duke fashion, decided in April of 1992 to begin her life again by having Dr. Harry Glassman, the plastic surgeon husband of actress Victoria Principal, give her still another face-lift. Later, once he attained power of attorney, Bernard Lafferty would authorize a five-hundred-thousand-dollar payment to Dr. Glassman for his services, making this probably the most expensive face-lift in nip-and-tuck history. Two days after the surgery, Doris Duke fell and broke her hip.

The broken hip was Doris Duke's first experience with being an invalid and Bernard Lafferty was ready to help.

At this time Doris's physicians began to clash.

"In late 1991 and in 1992, Miss Duke was treated by a Dr. Rolando Atiga, who later received $1 million from Lafferty, who was acting under his power of attorney from Miss Duke," Shanley said. "I heard Lafferty telling Atiga that if everything 'went well,' the loan would be treated as 'a gift.' Dr. Atiga had been the personal physician to Ferdinand Marcos. Miss Duke had been convinced, by Lafferty and Bloom, that Heffner had poisoned her. Dr. Atiga apparently was engaged in a procedure which was referred to around the household as 'blood cleaning,' which supposedly was designed to remove poisons from the blood. He would come to the house and run her blood through a dialysis-like machine. These treatments appeared to have a devastating effect on Miss Duke's physical condition."

Dr. Glassman did not approve of Dr. Atiga. "Dr. Glassman made many comments that indicated that he did not approve of Dr. Atiga, in a purely social sense," Shanley said. "Dr. Glassman said that Dr. Atiga was 'gauche.' Dr. Glassman complained that Dr. Atiga drove a white Rolls-Royce and wore polyester suits, which according to Dr. Glassman (who drove a black Daimler and wore Versace and Armani) were signs that Dr. Atiga was 'yesterday's man.' Dr. Glassman said that Miss Duke should have a 'Beverly Hills' doctor."

Dr. Charles Kivowitz was most definitely a Beverly Hills doctor. "Dr. Kivowitz had an unusual relationship with Miss Duke," Colin Shanley continued. "He would see her quite a bit, but his visits appeared to be primarily social. His visits usually occurred in the afternoon, around 5 P.M. It appeared to me that Dr. Kivowitz was flirting with Miss Duke. When he would arrive at the house, Lafferty would announce with giggles that Miss Duke's 'gentleman caller' had arrived. When Miss Duke was at home, or in the hospital, Dr. Kivowitz often would sit in her room with her (as her physical condition declined, Lafferty began to join them). They would drink expensive champagne, although Dr. Kivowitz would drink very little. (I was purchasing cases of champagne at $1,000 each—Louis Roederer Cristal—approximately two times per month for these sessions.) Dr. Glassman and Dr. Braiker attended a number of these sessions."

Within months Doris would be dead.

The more Bernard Lafferty became involved in Doris Duke's life, the more her health deteriorated. By 1992, she was no longer swimming laps in her pools and was losing weight.

In April of 1992, Lafferty finally made it into the newest Doris Duke will. In a codicil, he was named co-executor with her half-nephew Walker. At that time, Doris Duke still was in control of enough of her faculties to insist that a family member remain in an important position of control of the future foundations.

"Later in 1992, however, Lafferty began to criticize Walker Inman and his new wife, Helena," Shanley remembers. "Lafferty would tell Miss Duke that Helena and Inman were 'double dealing' and that Helena was a 'gold-digger.' Lafferty began to refuse to put Inman's calls through to Miss Duke. He would tell Inman that Miss Duke wasn't feeling well, and then make up some message from Miss Duke to Inman." Soon Walker Inman would be removed as co-executor.

In January and February of 1993 Doris Duke went to her powerful cousin, Ambassador Angier Biddle Duke, on several occasions and asked his help in disposing of the crew of lawyers and others who had been guiding her. Ambassador Duke and his son, Pony, now believe that Doris was crying for their help to save her life.

By February of 1993, Lafferty had taken complete control of the Duke empire. Servants watched as he isolated Doris. When the phone would ring, he would rush to answer, put the caller on hold saying, "Let me talk to Miss Duke about this," and would wait a few minutes to return to the phone with instructions that were supposedly coming from Doris. Only he never told Doris Duke, who was now feeling that she was a very lonely and forgotten old woman.

She started to believe that the only friend she had was her faithful butler.

"By early 1993," Chef Shanley said, "Lafferty frequently told me that he had complete control over Miss Duke and her affairs. He said he could get her to do whatever he wanted her to do."

Housekeeper Ann Bostich recalled that Doris Duke was hospitalized after suffering a stroke in February of 1993. "After Miss Duke's February 1993 stroke, she had episodes of disorientation and confusion, during which she was not capable of understanding what was happening to her," Bostich said. "It is difficult for me to say how long these episodes lasted because I was not always in her presence."

In February of 1993, Dr. Barry Braiker performed surgery to replace both of Miss Duke's knee joints at the same time. Following that surgery, Doris had to be helped aboard her plane for a brief visit to Honolulu because the surgery had been a failure.

Doris Duke was hospitalized in a private suite at the Cedars-Sinai Medical Center on the edge of Beverly Hills from late February to the middle part of April.

But she was not ready to concede control of her life to the group of hangers-on who had attached themselves to her and her bank accounts.

One morning that March, Ambassador Duke received a call from Doris. "She sounded like her old self," he recalled. "She seemed to be very much in control and wanted a favor. She said she wanted new lawyers and wanted us to recommend someone who was honest and capable. She intended to fire everyone because she was not satisfied with their efforts."

Both Pony Duke and his father sifted through a pile of possible selections and finally narrowed the choices to a small and very carefully considered group for Doris's consideration.

On March 16, 1993, Ambassador Duke wrote to Doris:

> I have given further thought to the problem of a good lawyer for you. My man, Bob Littman, is not versatile enough, but I have recently had a good experience with Larry Croskin, whose Bio I attach. He is on his own, not a member of a big firm [Doris had said she no longer wanted any association with a large and manipulative law firm], but has been very effective on a Canadian-U.S. estate matter with which I am peripherally involved.
>
> I told him I had a "friend" who was interested and did not give your name. He is in my eyes, a younger man, probably less than 50, and has a good reputation. Should you wish to pursue this, let me know how we should proceed.

Then Ambassador Duke wrote the words that must have sent chills up the spines of anyone attempting to take control of Doris and her fortune: "I am planning to go to Japan in mid-April and if you are still there (Los Angeles or Hawaii) I could stop over en route. Hope all is well with you."

He signed the letter "Dearest Love . . ."

The lawyer's résumé was faxed to Doris as was this letter. Months later when Pony Duke and his father realized what a serious situation had been devouring their relative, they also understood what panic this fax must have caused in the minds of those who might be attempting to manipulate Doris Duke. Angier Duke was one of the earliest supporters of the OSS, which later became the CIA. If he were to get the slightest hint that anything were amiss with Doris, he had the power to launch an investigation on the highest levels of the government.

There was absolutely no response to the fax. "At the time, my father and I were offended in a way," Pony Duke said. "It was like Doris to ignore all the effort that we had expended to find her good legal representation."

Today Pony believes that Doris never saw the faxes. "It is upsetting to think that those faxes were probably hidden from Doris. She must have thought that we ignored her request for help."

This was the last time she would ask her family for anything.

It was around this time that her doctors and lawyers, along with Lafferty, had taken the groggy Doris to the hospital where she remained under their control until her death. When Ambassador Duke arrived in Los Angeles, he was not told that Doris was hospitalized so he continued to Japan without seeing her.

"We cannot help but wonder that Doris might have actually seen the fax," Ambassador Duke said after her death. "She might have told them that they were finished. This would be very much like my cousin. She was ready to move very fast when she spoke with me." This move could have killed her.

Ann Bostich was summoned to the hospital room where Doris was waiting in the company of Bernard Lafferty and her lawyer William Doyle.

"In March of 1993, I was asked to serve as a witness to a codicil that was being signed by Miss Duke," Ann Bostich recalled. "Lafferty told me that she had suffered a stroke, he said she was dying. When I arrived at Miss Duke's room, Makasiale and Alan Croll [another attorney] were waiting in the hallway. I entered the room, where Lafferty and William Doyle were waiting. Miss Duke's bed was raised so that she was in an upright position; she was not talking, moving, or even looking at anyone. Doyle asked Miss Duke some 'yes' or 'no' questions, but Miss Duke's voice quavered and strained and was difficult to understand due to the strokes."

Ann Bostich continued, "Doyle gave Miss Duke the document which he wanted her to sign. Miss Duke appeared to start to sign the document, but Doyle stopped her. Doyle said 'let me put my briefcase on your lap.' Doyle then did so. He slid his own hand under her wrist. He propped her hand up with his hand. Doyle then pushed her hand along the page, guiding the hand.

"After the codicil had been signed," Ann Bostich remembered, "I told Lafferty that I would never agree that Miss Duke was of sound mind when she signed it."

In the summer of 1993, Chicago attorney William Doyle told Lafferty to circulate a memorandum to all of Doris Duke's employees that stated that from that time on, Lafferty would be acting on behalf of Miss Duke.

Lafferty did an Irish jig in the kitchen of Falcon's Lair when one of the staff read the memo to him. He had already raised Dr. Kivowitz's fee to a thousand dollars a day and joked with Colin Shanley that Miss Duke "would never in her imagination think anybody on the planet earth worth a thousand dollars per day."

In the spring of 1993, the chef recalled, the former butler had offered to use his newfound power to help a member of Dr. Kivowitz's family. "Lafferty told me that Dr. Kivowitz had a daughter who wanted to attend Duke University. Lafferty told me that he had offered to communicate with the president of Duke University and had offered to pay for Dr. Kivowitz's daughter to tour the Duke campus." (Lafferty claimed that he could make arrangements with Duke University whereby any person he "sent" there would receive a free education because he would have the power to decide whether the university would receive money from Miss Duke's charitable foundations.)

While the servants and nurses were aware that Doris was deteriorating, the mistress of the Duke empire had reason to believe that she was actually improving. In July of 1993, she went to the UCLA Medical Center for new surgery to correct the bungled knee surgery performed months earlier.

"Lafferty told me," Shanley recalled, "that Dr. Kivowitz had informed Miss Duke that she would be 'strolling the streets of Paris' with him in the fall. Dr. Kivowitz had instructed me, at about the same time, to bring Miss Duke a menu from L'Orangerie, a Los Angeles French restaurant. He told her that she would have a remarkable recovery by the fall of 1993. He made these statements even though she was very sick, by then, she was incontinent and very confused."

This was about the same time that an occasionally lucid Doris Duke said that she wanted to be taken to the Duke Medical Center in North Carolina, one of the finest hospitals in the world. "You had better believe that if Doris had made it to the Duke Medical Center," one family member said with more than a touch of anger in his voice, "that everything that could have been done to save this woman would have been done for the daughter of the man whose name is over the door. No woman on earth could have gotten better care than Doris Duke could have received at the Duke Medical Center." But Doris Duke would never receive that kind of care. She never made it to Duke.

Her sedation was increased.

At about this time, a worried Walker Inman decided to visit his aunt in spite of Lafferty's warnings that she did not want to speak with him. As he tried to reach her, Bernard Lafferty told the guards to push Inman's car through the gates out into the street. Inman never saw his aunt.

He notified several members of the family as to what had happened but calls to Falcon's Lair were answered in an Irish voice that assured the Dukes that "madam is fine but unable to come to the phone."

It should be noted here that Walker Inman has remained very silent concerning the death of his aunt. Other family members believe that this is due to a clause that was inserted in the new will that ordered his considerable trust fund be dissolved should he contest any aspect of the will.

As Doris Duke's world became a hazy drugged blur, Bernard Lafferty now spent more time as the master of the Duke fortune and less time as the servant to Miss Duke. At one time, he used to squeal with joy as he would wash and brush Doris Duke's carefully tended hair. This was one task he had overlooked in the last days of her life.

"On one occasion two weeks before Miss Duke died," Ann Bostich testified, "I escorted the nurses to Miss Duke's room. The nurses asked me to watch Miss Duke while they prepared for their shift, and in particular, to observe whether Miss Duke would attempt to remove her 'trach tube.' As I stood by her bedside, Miss Duke, in what appeared to me to be a drug stupor, asked me where she was and who I was. I don't think she recognized me. She then asked me where her Joe Castro was [Castro was her boyfriend in the 1960s]. After I answered her questions, and she moved her hand away from the 'trach tube,' she began trying to scratch her head." For the first time in her pampered life, Doris Duke had filthy hair.

"When Miss Duke reached up to scratch her head," Ann Bostich added, "she could do so only with great difficulty. I asked her if she wanted me to scratch her head. She said 'yes.' I started to scratch her head. I discovered that her hair was a solid, filthy, greasy and knotted compact mass, like a rat's nest. This neglect of her hair care shocked and upset me because Miss Duke had always been very particular about her appearance and because Lafferty and the nurses had done nothing to care for her hair. Lafferty was responsible for caring for Miss Duke's hair." Ann Bostich decided to wash the hair herself.

"The next morning, I bought several bottles of hair detangler. I asked Joy Williams, one of the nurses, why Miss Duke's hair had been neglected. When Ms. Williams began to respond, Lafferty overheard the conversation. He grabbed the bottles out of my hand and said threateningly, 'Well, if Madam [Miss Duke] wants to give somebody a hard time this morning, I going to teach her.' He then rushed downstairs to Miss Duke's room. I went downstairs to Miss Duke's room about 45 minutes later to see how they were progressing with Miss Duke's hair. I stopped just outside the bedroom door, where I saw Miss Duke in a wheel chair. Ms. Williams was holding a plastic wash basin under Miss Duke's head. Lafferty was yanking Miss Duke's hair in such violent brutal strokes that he was tearing her hair out. Miss Duke's body was slumped in the wheel chair. She did not seem to be responding to Lafferty's actions. Lafferty and Williams later told me they had to cut the knots out."

One of the richest and most powerful women in the world was now a helpless and abused invalid. Ann Bostich was sickened. "I was so shocked by their actions I stopped in my footsteps," she said. "I was unable to go into the room. I felt paralyzed. I went to my room and cried. I broke down thereafter and was unable to leave my bed for the next few days, except to visit my physician."

In the period of a few months, Doris Duke had been reduced from a pampered woman of immense wealth to a withered carcass that was about to die.

# 22
# THE LAST DAYS

No member of the Duke family was able to contact their reclusive relative Doris Duke during the summer of 1993—the last summer of her life.

Doris was not following her usual schedule. Springs and summers were usually spent at Duke Farms and the austere-looking Rough Point mansion on the Atlantic Ocean at Newport. Winters were always at Shangri-La in Honolulu. The penthouse on Park Avenue was merely a comfortable roost above Manhattan for an overnight stay in the big city. Falcon's Lair, the Beverly Hills house, seemed to perform the same function as the penthouse, a stopover between the East Coast and Hawaii.

For decades Doris had followed the same pattern in her annual travels within the luxury confines of her kingdom. When she did not appear at her usual haunts at the usual times, relatives and friends started calling to check on her.

Every call was answered by Bernard Lafferty.

"Miss Duke is not available. I will tell her you have called," he would promise in his soft Irish lilt or "Miss Duke has been ill and is not able to talk but she is recovering nicely," or "Miss Duke is fine." But Miss Duke was not fine: she was just weeks away from the grave.

Attempts by old acquaintances and a few family members to go to the Beverly Hills house to check on Doris were met with actual rudeness. Most were refused entry at the gates.

Only a few people knew what was happening inside the Beverly Hills mansion. One of those people was Tammy Payette, a former navy nurse who had been honorably discharged in 1991. Since that time she had worked as a home nurse in the Southern California area.

Nurse Payette has impressive credentials. She spent two years at prestigious Boston University and graduated in 1989 from Husson College in Maine with a bachelor of nursing science degree with a concentration in psychology.

In a lengthy statement, Miss Payette stated, "I am coming forward voluntarily because of my knowledge of what happened to Miss Duke and because I have heard different things are being said in the case by other people. I want to tell what the truth is as I know it first-hand [*sic*], and which I believe is the right thing to do."

Slowly she told the story of what happened to Doris Duke between September and October of 1993, a period of time when many people had attempted to check on her condition and been told "She is fine and will call you back."

Evidently, Doris had been readmitted to Cedars-Sinai Medical Center in September after suffering a stroke. Miss Payette was hired on September 20, 1993, as one of six nurses assigned to her home medical care once when she was released from the hospital.

Dr. Charles Kivowitz was in charge of the mini-hospital that was set up in the master bedroom of Falcon's Lair. He was assisted by plastic surgeon Dr. Harry Glassman, who made daily visits to the house. Dr. Glassman frequently advised the nurses what to do and what prescriptions to administer.

Nurse Payette was assigned to travel with Doris Duke when she left her suite in the Cedars-Sinai Medical Center for the mansion high in Beverly Hills, which looked out over all of Los Angeles. Doris Duke was very lucid on the trip home.

Initially the plan of care for Miss Duke was to take her home and begin a rehabilitation program. Doris told Nurse Payette that she wanted to be rehabilitated so that she could return to Duke Farms in New Jersey.

"That sounds very much like Doris," a family member remarked when told of Doris Duke's intention of going back to the East Coast. "She considered Duke Farms to be her home and she felt safe there in the house her father built."

Doris had all the technicians and equipment needed for her rehabilitation, including a cardiac chair, a bedside commode, and other special rehabilitation therapy equipment. She had two nurses on a round-the-clock basis. There were also physical therapists and respiratory therapists. Doris Duke cooperated with the nurses.

"This is also very much like Doris," the family member continued. "When it came to her face and her body, she would have state-of-the-art services and she would have done whatever she had to to become well and whole again."

In other words, Doris Duke was behaving like Doris Duke. She had a plan for her recovery and she had marshaled her troops to facilitate that recovery. She did not expect to die.

"At the time Miss Duke left the hospital and first arrived home," Miss Payette said, "Dr. Kivowitz told me that we were to have physical therapy for Miss Duke and we were to work on her swallowing, which would eventually lead to the removal of her tracheostomy tube and gastrostomy tube. Miss Duke wanted these removed very much. Dr. Kivowitz told Miss Duke she was going to get better very soon, and that she would be able to go to New Jersey soon." Doris Duke was evidently well on her way to a recovery when she was released from Cedars-Sinai Medical Center.

"When Miss Duke arrived home from the hospital," Nurse Payette continued, "she was in a good stable condition and alert. There was total potential for her to become rehabilitated to some form of independence with continued nursing care. At this time based on my observations and past experiences with patients and general nursing knowledge, Miss Duke's life expectancy was, at least, five years, if she had been kept on the rehabilitation plan." No one thought that Doris Duke was in a life-threatening situation.

"Miss Duke was not, and Dr. Kivowitz never said that Miss Duke was, in a hospice situation or in critical or terminal condition," Miss Payette said, "until October 26, 1993."

Nurse Payette kept detailed records of medication and doctors' treatments of Doris Duke during the weeks of her employment. "To my knowledge," she continued, "Dr. Kivowitz never told Miss Duke that she was in critical or terminal condition."

But before there was time for the therapy to begin bringing results, the program was abruptly changed. "Within a short period of time after she arrived home, Miss Duke's physical therapy was cut off and she was placed on a massive sedation regime by Dr. Kivowitz," Nurse Payette stated in a sworn deposition to the Surrogate Court of Manhattan, "at the request of Bernard Lafferty, Miss Duke's butler."

Doris Duke started to deteriorate.

"Dr. Kivowitz told the nurses, including me, not to worry about over medication or too much sedation," Miss Payette remembered. "Miss Duke's drugs were being administered by gastrostomy tube and she was not aware of the drugs that were being given."

As Doris Duke drifted deeper into the drug-induced state, Bernard Lafferty gave orders to the nurses not to tell her what drugs she was being given. This action surprised Nurse Payette.

"Immediately after her return home from the hospital, Miss Duke's medical condition was stable and she expressed interest in and expectation to continue rehabilitation in order to improve her quality of life. Miss Duke frequently said she wanted to get out of bed, to go out, and to be independent, as much as possible. No one ever told me that Miss Duke was in critical or terminal condition," Miss Payette reiterated.

Each day, Dr. Kivowitz reviewed the extensive daily log and notes that the nurses kept on the condition, the treatments, the medications, and the progress of Doris Duke.

Before she was sedated, Doris Duke was starting to behave in her normal fashion, according to the surviving records that were kept by Miss Payette and the other nurses.

"Miss Duke was a very wealthy person and she seemed to me to have a habit of having things her own way," the nurse continued. "She was eighty years old and she was used to giving orders to her employees and expected her wishes to be carried out. She could be difficult and demanding, but she always treated me fairly. Miss Duke appreciated the efforts of the nursing staff very much."

It must have been a shock to Doris Duke when her requests to begin plans for the trip back to Duke Farms were never acted on. "It was probably the first time in her life when she gave an order like that and it was ignored," a family member said. "Such action would have been inconceivable to her."

"During the time period, September 20 to October 28, Miss Duke was not in any serious pain," the nurse explained. "She constantly said she was not generally in pain. Miss Duke did have localized discomfort around her tracheostomy tube and some stiffness from being in bed. Her general denial of pain is documented many, many times in the nursing notes, written by me and the other five nurses."

The nurses relieved the trachea discomfort by a simple application of a topical ointment and the administration of Tylenol.

The doctor's logs and records show that while Doris Duke was trying to cooperate with the nurses and therapists to hasten her recovery, Dr. Kivowitz was prescribing Haldol, Ativan, and Valium with orders that they be administered daily for Miss Duke's "anxiety." Later, Dr. Kivowitz directed that Doris Duke be sedated if she became "combative" or difficult.

Nurse Payette further stated that during the entire period of her care of Doris Duke, her vital signs were stable, her pulse was strong, and she had little, if any, respiratory discomfort. "She was not anxious or combative," Miss Payette said, "except as would be expected from a person who was impatient to get better and get out of bed."

The strong Duke constitution enabled Doris to pull herself out of the drug-induced confusion and question what was happening to her. She called Bernard Lafferty to her bedside and told him that she thought that things were not being done right. Bernard made some changes.

"Bernard often asked me to increase Miss Duke's sedation and to keep her quiet," Miss Payette remembered. "Dr. Kivowitz instructed me and Pearl Rosenstein to give Miss Duke sedatives on the instruction of Bernard, to give her whatever Bernard wanted." They nicknamed these doses "Pearl's cocktails."

Pearl Rosenstein later stated that she believed that there was nothing unusual about the drug doses prescribed by Dr. Kivowitz. She has also retained a criminal defense attorney. This attorney is being financed by the Duke estate.

But Bernard Lafferty had other plans for the Valium that arrived in an endless supply at the gates of Falcon's Lair and was rushed to his open hands by the security guards. "Bernard also took Miss Duke's Valium for himself," Miss Payette recalled.

Even with the massive doses of drugs, Doris Duke managed to talk. She could still see and recognized her nurses as they arrived on duty each day. As always throughout her life, she particularly wanted to maintain her appearance. Doris Duke might have wanted the nurses' help in applying her makeup and doing her hair had she been allowed to talk to her friends or relatives who phoned or came to the house.

"Miss Duke was not permitted to have any phone calls except those screened by Bernard," the nurse explained, "and Bernard only permitted visitors approved by him. The lawyers from Mr. Doyle's office [the Chicago attorney who drew up the controversial last will] and a plastic surgeon, Dr. Glassman, were often in Miss Duke's house, outside her presence."

Finally Doris, in what was to be her last attempt to retake control of her life, became enraged and made her last demands.

"About two weeks after Miss Duke left the hospital, she became very agitated and said she wanted to return to Cedars-Sinai or go to the Duke Medical Center." Miss Payette remembered the trauma in the elderly woman's tone. "Bernard heard these statements and called Dr. Kivowitz. These events in summary are noted in the nurses' notes."

This desire to be taken to the Duke Medical Center indicates to many people who knew Doris Duke that she was making a desperate attempt to save her own life. She knew that she would be safe at Duke University. Everything that could be done by modern medical science to save the life of Doris Duke would be done if she could somehow find a way to go to the safety of the Duke Medical Center. This threat to leave Falcon's Lair concerned Lafferty.

"At this time, Dr. Kivowitz ordered that Miss Duke be given injections of Demerol, although Miss Duke was not in pain," Miss Payette continued in her deposition filed with the Surrogate Court. "The injections of Demerol were increased, until eventually Miss Duke was put on a Demerol drip intravenously. Miss Duke began to have body spasms, and Dr. Kivowitz said those were due to the high doses of Demerol."

During this period, Doris Duke's vital signs remained good. Her pulse and breathing rate were strong. Her lungs were clear and required only the minimum suctioning through the trach tube. Occasionally she even regained consciousness but most of the time she remained in the drug-induced stupor.

Despite the massive doses of Demerol, Miss Duke began to "break through" and recover consciousness on October 27. The possibility of her awakening resulted in the doctors and Bernard Lafferty calling a long meeting with lawyer Doyle. "I was not present in the room but they were all in the house," Miss Payette said. "They all came into Miss Duke's bedroom and Dr. Kivowitz told me and Pearl Rosenstein that it was time for Miss Duke to go." At that time her vital signs were stable.

"Dr. Kivowitz then directed me to prepare an intravenous bag and under the instruction of Dr. Kivowitz, morphine was placed in the solution. He directed that Miss Duke should receive 15 mg per hour. Bernard asked Dr. Kivowitz how long it was [*sic*] take for Miss Duke to die. After he injected her, Dr. Kivowitz answered, 'less than an hour.'"

Dr. Kivowitz left the house and instructed that his associate Dr. Trabulus should be called when Doris Duke expired. It was Dr. Trabulus who would later sign the death certificate. It would have been questionable if Dr. Kivowitz had signed the death certificate since his had been the first signature to witness Doris Duke's last will.

Still, the old woman was not ready to die. An anxious Bernard Lafferty, just hours away from gaining control of one of the world's greatest fortunes, and lawyer Doyle waited throughout the night for Doris Duke to finally take her last breath. Doris Duke made them wait.

Miss Payette said the nurses' records proved that her respiration was stable before the morphine was administered. Her breathing slowed down as a result of the morphine drip. Still, despite the massive doses of Demerol and morphine, Doris Duke clung to life.

"Later in the evening, Bernard became very excited and impatient because Miss Duke was lingering," Miss Payette testified, "and called Dr. Kivowitz explaining that Miss Duke had not expired."

Dr. Kivowitz again returned to the mansion. He injected a needle into the IV tube and began to "push" morphine. This increased the rate of the flow of the potent drug and further slowed down Doris Duke's respiration. The doctor kept increasing the morphine and Doris was taking fewer and fewer breaths. Finally her kidneys began to fail, her lungs filled with fluid, and her circulation began to deteriorate. Morphine is a very powerful respiratory depressant and rapid injection increases its effect.

While one of the causes of death was attributed to pulmonary edema, Nurse Payette has stated that the records prove that Doris Duke did not have a pulmonary edema and no doctor had ever diagnosed pulmonary edema.

Even with these massive doses of drugs shutting down her bodily systems, it still took several more hours for her to die at 5:30 A.M.

Bernard Lafferty, no longer a butler, no longer a servant but an instant millionaire, went to the phone and called several Duke relatives. (More than a year later when the Los Angeles police opened the murder investigation they were amazed to learn that Doris Duke did, indeed, have some powerful living relatives.

They had been told by people at Falcon's Lair that Doris had no living relatives. No member of the family was ever asked whether Doris should be euthanized.)

Nurse Payette was upset with what she had witnessed.

"Miss Duke did not die of natural causes and was not in danger of dying until the large doses of morphine were given to her," she swore under oath. "She was asleep, medicated with a large amount of Demerol and certainly was not in pain when the morphine was administered. Miss Duke did not ask that a lethal dose of morphine be given and she was not aware that this was being done."

However, Miss Payette's credibility was severely damaged when she was later arrested for grand larceny and admitted stealing twenty thousand dollars' worth of ivory from another wealthy client. When confronted by Los Angeles police, who were rumored to have been tipped off about the thefts by investigators for the Duke estate, Miss Payette immediately admitted the theft. She said that she had been under pressure following the publicity that resulted from being involved in the possible murder of Doris Duke, which had hindered her ability to obtain work, and she needed the money.

She remains adamant that she is telling the truth about the death of Doris Duke and is confident that the records kept by her and the other nurses will prove that she had been truthful.

Dr. Kivowitz, in his own deposition, has stated emphatically that he only provided the morphine to make Doris Duke's last hours more comfortable and the drug only hastened the death by hours. California law permits the removal of life support at the request of the family or guardian but the hastening of death through the use of strong drugs is a very different matter. Many physicians consider this form of euthanasia to be immoral, unethical, and possibly illegal.

After eight decades of a life that had everything that money could buy, Doris Duke was dead.

But there was still action to be taken.

In spite of the fact that Doris had left explicit orders that her body was to be buried at sea and was not to be cremated, within two hours of her death her corpse was reduced to a pile of sterilized ashes. There would never be the opportunity for a through autopsy that might reveal signs of wrongdoing. The hasty death certificate indicated to the coroner's office that this was just a simple case of an eighty-year-old woman dying of natural causes. No one mentioned to the coroner that this woman was also one of the richest women in the world.

"The cremation of Doris is the most alarming part of this whole mess," one close friend confided. "She had told everyone who knew her for years that she wanted to be buried at sea in some sort of Hawaiian tradition."

"I want to be eaten by sharks," Doris Duke often said. She would continue to explain that she believed that she would be reunited with her tiny dead daughter, Arden, if she were buried at sea as Arden was.

Doris had also stated in the will that she wanted her eyes donated to the New York Eye Bank but that instruction was ignored in the rush to the incinerator.

The Chicago attorney William Doyle was also busy in the hours following the death of the heiress. He gathered the original nurses' notes which had been kept in Doris Duke's bedroom and started to remove them from the house.

"I asked him not to remove these records," remembers Nurse Payette, who was at Doris Duke's side when she died. "Mr. Doyle told me he would take these records, make a photo copy and give me the original back."

The nurse never saw the original notes again but she was given copies of some of the records that were taken from Falcon's Lair the morning Doris Duke died. However, she does not know where the nurses' records of the last days and the death of Doris Duke have gone.

# 23
# THE JUDGE

She is so tiny and fragile that she resembles one of the delicate figurines that line the walls of her Park Avenue apartment, but anyone who has dealt with Judge Marie Lambert knows that she is a New York City street fighter. She is positive that Doris Duke was murdered.

"Doris Duke was poisoned," the almost grandmotherly septuagenarian said while eating a plate of highly seasoned spare ribs at one of the East Side's more trendy Chinese restaurants.

Marie Lambert is an expert on probate cases in the State of New York. For several decades, she served as a judge of the Surrogate Court of New York City. Always outspoken, she has been criticized for her flamboyant shoot-from-the-lip judicial statements, the most outrageous of which have been her recent comments on the Doris Duke estate.

Judge Lambert, who is now in private practice, was representing former will executor Irwin Bloom in his attempt to have the final will overturned.

"Doris Duke never had a chance," the former legal terror said clearly in a voice that was a cross between Dr. Ruth and Clarence Darrow. "There were a lot of people involved."

Judge Lambert's scenario follows the path of careful manipulation of the billionairess by the barefoot butler Bernard Lafferty, who, with the shrewd advice of personal physicians and lawyers recommended by aging actress Elizabeth Taylor, has successfully taken control of $2.2 billion dollars.

The announced estimates of the estate have ranged from $1.2 billion to $1.4 billion but the diminutive Judge Lambert is firm that more than $1 billion has already disappeared.

"It was $2.2 billion," she said quietly but very firmly as she reached for the hot mustard.

Lambert believes that Doris Duke's mania for privacy and fear that her closest associates were after her money was the psychological basis for the Svengali-like plot to take control of one of the world's great fortunes.

But if Bernard Lafferty is a Svengali . . . he is an unlikely Svengali. An Irishman with a love of twelve-hundred-dollar brandy, Lafferty was considered a charity case when Chandi Heffner brought him into the Doris Duke circle. Those servants and retainers in the inner circle who liked the charming Lafferty would lament that he suffered from the typical Irish love of booze. Those who were less fond of the butler who did Miss Duke's hair said he was little more than a sloppy reeling drunk.

But Bernard Lafferty was more like a cunning Irish wolfhound who silently stalks its prey until all the other animals are off the scent and it alone is there for the final kill. After Chandi's exile, Lafferty's next step in the plan to capture the Duke billions (according to Judge Lambert) was to isolate Doris from anyone else whom she might have trusted. Her accountant and business adviser Irwin Bloom (also a Chandi family retainer) was pitched after Doris was told that he was profiting to the tune of several million dollars by manipulating her vast portfolio of stocks and bonds. Then her doctor of many years Harry Demopoulos was also told to pack his bags of vitamins and antitoxins and go.

Members of the family did not realize that Bernard Lafferty had become the Rasputin of the court of Doris Duke by 1991. That summer was the last hurrah of Doris Duke. She danced. She parried verbally (in her Jackie and Marilyn calculated whisper of a voice) with the likes of Sophia Loren, Imelda, and the ever-so-gay occasional movie producer Franco Rossellini. She insulted photographers and seemed to be having a marvelous time. Lafferty was always at her side.

The summer of 1992 was very different. She seemed fragile to the family and the cavernous rooms of Rough Point were too cold for her system even in the heat of a Newport July.

The elaborate upholstered and predictable life of Doris Duke changed suddenly that year. In the past, Doris had summered in the echoing grandeur of Rough Point, watched fall color the gardens at Duke Farms, spent the early winter running between her beloved farm and the grand Park Avenue penthouse, and finally would avoid the coldest months behind the gates and hibiscus of the Diamond Head estate. Oh yes, there was Falcon's Lair, the Beverly Hills house, but that was more of a place to pause between the East Coast and Hawaii. For decades this routine had been followed without variance.

Until 1993.

In 1993, Lafferty, deciding that Hawaii was too close to Chandi, kept the western-bound entourage in Beverly Hills for the winter. Bernard liked the flamboyance of the Hollywood crowd. It was here that he could sample the delights of the Santa Monica Boulevard openly gay world of the Los Angeles entertainment community. Since he sat at the right hand of Doris the financial almighty, many of the plastic surgery perfect crowd of the Hollywood Hills gravitated toward Bernard. They laughed at his jokes and Lafferty suddenly found that he was far more charming and devastatingly witty than he had ever been in his life. He was adored by the famous and the powerful.

Even Elizabeth Taylor thought Bernard Lafferty was the best thing to come from Ireland since Brendan Behan. He was amazed and flattered that Liz ("Call me Liz") focused on him at dinner and twittered (Elizabeth Taylor does twitter) at his Irish stories.

A union was formed between Taylor and Lafferty, Judge Lambert explains; a union that was based on an extreme interest in the very wealthy Doris Duke.

Within months the following occurred:

First, Elizabeth Taylor's friend and physician Charles Kivowitz and his associates assumed all medical responsibility for the treatment of the billionairess Doris Duke.

Then, Chicago attorney William M. Doyle, who according to Judge Lambert frequently finds himself representing Dr. Kivowitz's more affluent patients, was brought into the inner circle and Doris's longtime New York law firms were dismissed.

Next, Miss Taylor's public relations firm replaced the New York firm that had worked for Doris Duke for years.

"Doris Duke was being isolated," Judge Lambert contends. "She might as well have been a prisoner."

In the winter and spring of 1993, friends and family members were suddenly unable to contact Cousin Doris. Even calls to Doris on the super-secret private lines were always answered by Bernard Lafferty, even if those calls were placed in the middle of the night. "We began to wonder whether he was sleeping in her room in case one of us called," one Duke family member said. "It was eerie."

"Miss Duke is doing well," Lafferty would say. "She is getting better."

According to Judge Lambert's version of the last days of Doris Duke in April of 1993, Doris was taken to the Cedars-Sinai Medical Center in Los Angeles where she was isolated in one of the suites reserved for movie stars and billionaires. It was at this time, Judge Lambert asserts, that Dr. Kivowitz summoned attorney Doyle to create a new will, a will that would give Bernard Lafferty incredible power over the administration of the foundations that would disperse the Duke billions.

As noted, on April 5, 1993, in her bed at the hospital, Doris Duke signed the new will in a hand so shaky and childlike that it bore only the faintest resemblance to her signature.

The main witness to the signing was Dr. Charles Kivowitz. Dr. Kivowitz was most happy to be the witness but the second signatory on the will, Dr. Jerald Federman, later lamented his involvement. "I want everyone to realize that I was not in any way taking care of her," Federman said in a telephone interview. "I was just walking down the hall and I was dragged into this. I didn't know any of the people except Charlie. I was just asked to sign the will by Charlie. I have made that clear to everyone." The remaining witnesses were Ann Bostich and employees of either the hospital or Dr. Kivowitz himself.

"Somewhere in all this," Judge Lambert continued, "Elizabeth Taylor was given a check for either $1 million or $2 million . . . for her AIDS work. I have demanded an accounting of what happened to this money and I have been ignored by Taylor." Family records show that Doris Duke did give a check for $2 million to the Duke Medical Center in Durham with the stipulation that the money be used for AIDS research.

Originally singer Michael Jackson was scheduled to receive a couple of million dollars for his "good work with children" foundations but this plan was dropped after he was accused of child molestation. Butler Lafferty desperately wanted to cultivate a relationship between Doris and Jackson and even charged a pair of puppies to Doris which were presented to her as a gift from the "gloved one."

Doris Duke survived the April hospital stay and Bernard Lafferty took her back to the splendor of Falcon's Lair. The massive iron gates slammed shut on the last days of Doris Duke. No family member would be permitted to see Doris Duke.

But lots of people saw Bernard Lafferty, particularly the staffs of the exclusive men's clothing stores, most especially Georgio Armani, and the jewelry stores of Rodeo Drive, dubbed the most expensive shopping street in the world. Judge Lambert unearthed records showing that Lafferty used his nearly comatose benefactor's Platinum American Express credit card to purchase sixty thousand dollars' worth of Georgio Armani clothes and luxuries. He said in a later deposition that the shopping spree had been ordered by Miss Duke so that he would look the part of her representative.

He also took the infamous fuel-guzzling jet, loaded it with his friends, and filed a flight plan for London where they partied for the weekend.

In a memorandum filed in New York's Surrogate Court, Judge Lambert writes:

> Discovery has thus far revealed that while Doris Duke apparently lay dying, Lafferty was flitting about on Rodeo Drive engaging in a massive shopping spree. Lafferty who professes loyalty to Doris Duke obviously was not so concerned with her health and welfare: otherwise, he would have been at her bedside, rather than running around spending thousands of dollars of her money apparently outfitting himself with trendy attire and other personal accouterments. This behavior also calls into serious question Lafferty's motives and veracity with respect to the procurement of Miss Duke's will proffered by him for probate of which he was named executor and a substantial beneficiary.

The will gave Lafferty $5 million up front and complete discretion in how the rest of the money is spent. He could use many millions for his own agenda.

The statement continues:

> Lafferty's conduct reveals not only his lack of concern for his employer; it also reveals his willingness to take advantage of her at a time when she apparently no longer was able to protect her own interests. Lafferty spent $60,000 of Doris Duke's money on lavish clothing, jewelry and other items. He ran up these charges on her credit card within the last few weeks of her life. His conduct simply shocks the conscience of those who have heard it.

Lafferty later admitted in a written response to these charges that at least some of the purchases that he made were for his own benefit but he also explained that some of the purchases were made at the explicit request of the bedridden Doris Duke.

Lafferty also admitted that at the time of Doris Duke's death, he "had virtually no funds."

What is even more disturbing to Judge Lambert are the actions of the United States Trust Corporation, the corporate co-executor of the Duke fortune, a bank that is supposed to strictly oversee the money.

"When U.S. Trust learned that the butler had taken the credit cards on a spending spree," Judge Lambert continued, "they ordered him to repay the funds. But he has already admitted that he was penniless, so they loaned him the money to replace the funds. How many banks do you know who would loan a 'penniless' man $60,000? Not only is this unethical, it is probably illegal."

Why would a respected trust group leave themselves open to such criticism? Under the terms of the new will, Bernard Lafferty can replace the trust. This would cost the bank tens of millions of dollars in fees and services costs over the next few decades.

"When the butler tells them to jump," Judge Lambert added, "they jump or else."

While these charges are serious, it is the judge's accusations of poisoning that have most concerned the family and business associates of Doris Duke.

"I dislike even considering the possibility that my cousin might have been murdered," one close relative said while playing with a plate of stewed breakfast prunes in the dining room of the River Club. "I hope it is not true. But I also find it intolerable that any member of the Duke family might have been murdered and think that everything should be done to find the truth, whatever the truth might be."

Judge Marie Lambert feels she has the evidence. While Dr. Kivowitz has thus far avoided giving Judge Lambert the records of Doris Duke's last year of medical treatment, Bernard Lafferty did send a huge box of copies of all of the heiress's bills for the last months of care.

"He goofed and didn't realize it," Judge Lambert added. "There were bills for prescriptions given by both Dr. Kivowitz and his associates and I had some experts looks at these prescriptions. While no prescriptions alone could kill her, combinations of the various drugs could have killed her. Did not these doctors who were supposedly working together to save her, ever consider what the other was prescribing? I think they did!"

"Just to make sure," Judge Lambert continued, "Bernard Lafferty has admitted that he provided her with daily doses of Valium and champagne. That would poison her," Judge Lambert said. "That would kill her."

During the months after the death of Doris Duke, Bernard Lafferty, at first, ignored calls or letters from the Duke family. While it would seem logical that family members who are the only persons aware of the details of the intricate business network of the Duke assets would be asked for advice, no such advice or counsel has been sought.

But late in 1994, Bernard Lafferty became astute in winning over the Duke family. He announced plans to give a seven-figure sum to Boys Harbor, the life's work charity of Tony Duke. He then petitioned the court to withhold his $5 million inheritance and $500,000 annual salary if the courts would only permit the dispersal of some of the moneys to charity.

"The family liked that a lot," a family member commented.

"It is as if Bernard Lafferty has become Doris Duke," one family member said. "We have had people tell us that Lafferty believes that he is the living incarnation of Doris. That she has returned through him."

According to family members, the often erratic Lafferty might have believed that Doris Duke had returned from the dead and was literally occupying his body. During frequent bouts with booze, Lafferty would appear wearing Doris's clothing and jewelry. He had his hair dyed and cut in the color and style that was a Doris Duke trademark. He ordered Doris's personal maid to apply the exact same makeup that was used by the now-dead mistress. He even started speaking in the trademark husky Doris Duke whisper voice.

"We are beginning to believe that Bernard really cared about Doris," the family member continued in the first days after the will had been read (long before the accusations of manipulation and murder surfaced). "We are on the verge of being four-square behind Bernard."

Except for one disturbing fact. The family also believes that if Doris Duke could return, she would be very angry about what was done with her body in the hours after her death. Throughout her life, Doris Duke had a religious aversion to cremation. It was common knowledge in the family that Doris was terrified of fire. She was vain and would not have burned her face. She wanted her body buried at sea and fed to the sharks in some kind of pact she had established between herself and Duke Kahanamoku, just as she had done with the body of her day-old daughter some five decades earlier. But Lafferty ordered that the body be cremated.

"I know that would have been completely against Doris's wishes," Ambassador Duke said. "Of course, I am sure that it is against the law to take a body out to sea and feed it to the sharks, even if that is what she requested, but she would not have wanted to be cremated. It was against all of her beliefs. It might have been the only thing that Bernard could do legally."

"It is called destroying the evidence," Judge Lambert snapped.

She became even more vocal in a hallway outside the surrogate courtroom in Manhattan when she screamed at Lafferty's lawyer, William Doyle, Jr., "You're a cremator!" This is the same lawyer who drew the final will giving the empire to the butler.

In the days following the death and cremation of Doris Duke, Bernard Lafferty, now the world's most powerful butler, wasted little time in assuming a firm control of the estate. His barefoot and sweatered attire was replaced by carefully tailored suits and his small diamond earring was eclipsed by a thirty-five carat rock that covers most of his ear. One family member noted that while Doris was not overly fond of jewelry (except for some of the world's most exquisite emeralds) she had collected bags of high-quality gems as an investment. It was wondered if the $1 million perfect rock stuffed into Lafferty's ear might be part of that stash as the now elegant Lafferty is still ostensibly a poor man until the contested will is finally probated.

Longtime employees of Doris Duke who affronted Lafferty by still considering him a butler instead of the incarnation of Miss Duke, were axed. The whispered joke around the various Duke mansions was "The queen is dead . . . long live the queen." In a strong comparison to Doris, Bernard demands complete loyalty and any indiscretion means immediate unemployment.

But the barbarians were at the gates.

Chandi Duke Heffner, the adopted child who loved only animals and nature and cared nothing for money or material trappings, hired a New Jersey law firm and demanded that she get every dime of the estate. Other relatives were being offered sherry at various white shoe law firms in Manhattan as they discussed their possible claims against the estate. Bloom was suing and screaming bloody murder. As was Dr. Demopoulos.

Newspaper headlines and television investigative reporters hinted that Lafferty and lawyer Doyle had conspired to destroy evidence by incinerating the heiress before her body was barely cold. The most aristocratic members of the Duke and Biddle families were appalled at the sordid headlines and miserable publicity that was reflecting on them and their family memorial, Duke University.

Insiders at the estate said that Lafferty, who had nurtured the image that he was securely on the wagon, was so concerned with the possibility of grand jury and murder investigations, that he had again started making trips to the Duke wine cellar with its racks of the world's finest brandy. Lafferty needed help.

He got Elizabeth Taylor and her sophisticated public relations team. The concept was to appoint a board to administer the Doris Duke Charitable Foundation that would be so respected and so powerful that any district attorney who might be considering a grand jury investigation would be hit with a case of political blindness.

Appointment Number One: Christine Todd Whitman, the governor of New Jersey, who would cow most of the municipal rabble leaning toward a more thorough investigation. Governor Whitman would be protecting the position of the State of New Jersey where the 2,700 manicured acres of the Duke estate are expected to become a major tourist attraction and state asset. And, as one very high-profile lawyer pointed out, should the last will be thrown out, there is a good chance that Doris Duke would be deemed to have died without a will and the whole estate would be taxed instead of sheltered by the foundations. This could mean $500 million or more for the State of New Jersey.

Appointment Number Two: Marion Oates "Oatsie" Charles, the only authentic blue blood on the board who was a close friend of Doris. Oatsie was shocked, make that horrified, that she had been drafted onto the board and immediately wanted to resign but family interests have implored her to remain as the only authentic insider selected. (It is also thought that in the rush to have Doris sign the new will, the lawyers overlooked dumping Oatsie, who was named in previous wills as a co-executor junior grade to the all-powerful Lafferty.)

Appointment Number Three: J. Carter Brown, the shrewd former director of the National Gallery in Washington and a director of the Newport Restoration Society. He is extremely well connected on the federal government level.

Appointment Number Four: Nannerl O. Keohane, the president of Duke University, where some officials were unimpressed with the mere $10 million left to the family namesake institution by the will and hope the presence of their chief officer on the board will ensure more money in the future.

Appointment Number Five: Actress Elizabeth Taylor, who has infinite connections in Los Angeles (remember she flew Michael Jackson away from pending child abuse charges in her jet with nary a raised eyebrow from state and federal officials). While it would be logical that any future police investigation or potential indictments should take place in Los Angeles, the presence of THE LIZ on the board gives Lafferty the same high-powered clout that saved Michael Jackson. With Liz's political and public relations power and the hundreds of millions in the Duke estate, the image of Bernard Lafferty can be polished until he would be transformed from unusual butler into beneficent master of the billions.

No member of the Duke family was appointed to the board, which is most unusual because only family members would understand the elaborate maze of finances that formed the foundation of the various Duke trusts and business of the last hundred years. Only family members know about items such as small paintings worth millions that rest in innocuous oblivion on eighteenth-century tables worth hundreds of thousands of dollars. Or the existence of bags of diamonds large enough to hide a man's ear.

But there may be problems on the billion-dollar board.

Already Governor Whitman is utilizing a more political and reserved tone when referring to her purpose on the board. At one of those social evenings where politicians shake hands and make small talk with each other, Governor Whitman and Ambassador Duke exchanged these comments.

"All of us in the family are delighted to hear that you have joined the Doris Duke Charitable Foundation," the ambassador told the governor.

"Well yes." Governor Whitman seemed to be calculating her words. "There is a lot of money there and I want to be sure that New Jersey gets its share."

She paused and continued, "I look forward to it, but you know I will be serving in an ex-officio capacity."

"I did not know that," Ambassador Duke answered. "I understand that there are some legal hurdles yet to overcome."

Governor Whitman smiled and Ambassador Duke passed down the receiving line. The ramrod erect ambassador paused, ran a fingernail across the smooth finish of his silk tie, and felt a tightening in his stomach. He had hoped that this vast fortune would be used to do so much good. While his controversial cousin Doris had supported some unusual and occasionally useless schemes during her lifetime, she had carefully outlined what she wanted done after her death. And now, people such as the graceful governor of New Jersey were starting to distance themselves from the foundations. A sense of distaste enveloped the ambassador.

There was also a pang of guilt. Too many times, Ambassador Duke, who had dedicated his life to the service of the people of the United States and, in turn, written a new page of accomplishment in the Duke history that until his contribution had been mostly devoted to empire building, had found himself and the Duke name embarrassed by the antics of cousin Doris. Her extravagance. Her husbands. The death at the gates of Rough Point. The adoption and, oh God yes, the support of Imelda

Marcos and Pee-Wee Herman. Those headlines that splotched gallons of tabloid ink across the reputation of the Duke family had made him distance himself from Doris. All too late, he realized that he should have made more of an effort to protect this seemingly strong woman who always appeared so capable of forcing her own destiny. But she was a Duke and Dukes protect Dukes. That was the tradition set by Washington and Ben and Buck. This should never have happened to cousin Doris.

Doris Duke loved a good scandal, the ambassador thought as his outward countenance greeted dignitary after luminary in the receiving line, but she would not have wanted this. Indeed, in a horrific way, Doris Duke was getting her last wish:

Her remains are being eaten by the sharks after all.

# 24

# THE BILLION-DOLLAR CAPER

"Whatever really happened to my cousin," Ambassador Angier Biddle Duke began, "the time has come to look toward the future and the good that can be done with this money. Maybe Doris can accomplish in death what she could not in life."

Ambassador Duke and his son, one of the authors of this book, blame the adopted daughter Chandi for starting the chain of events that are now culminating in the courts and newspaper headlines.

Charlene Heffner's humble Hawaiian lifestyle could not have been anymore opposite the luxurious world that revolved around the aged Doris Duke and her growing fortune. At least, that is what Chandi said.

In reality, she was the daughter of a prosperous family and the product of private schools. Her calculated flower child disdain of material pleasures was an act.

And Chandi did a good job of convincing Doris that she "cared nothing about the money or the material things." In previous decades, the canny Doris would not have bought this line for even a millisecond. She had been the target of every possible scam and con artist since the day she was born.

But Doris believed that Chandi was the incarnation of Arden. She believed—really believed—that Chandi was the reincarnation of her dead daughter, a child who died under mysterious circumstances.

To Chandi's credit, she did not openly pretend to be Arden. "Doris might believe that I am Arden," she told friends, "but I don't," Chandi said frequently.

Still, there are worse things to have happen to you than to be thought to be the reincarnated daughter of a very rich and very lonely woman in her final years. A woman who wanted the one thing she could not buy, the return of a dead daughter.

When the newly adopted Chandi Duke Heffner was physically and legally ensconced in the affairs of Doris Duke, Chandi seemed to forget what she had repeatedly said before the adoption: "I did not consent to be adopted because of any financial consideration whatsoever!"

Yet, for someone who had no interest in money and power, Chandi immediately started replacing longtime Duke employees with people loyal to her, like Bernard Lafferty and Irwin Bloom.

Both were recommended by Chandi's sister, Mrs. Nelson Peltz. Both were previously employees of the Nelson Peltzes. Lafferty's purpose was to control the household and Bloom's purpose was to manage the financial empire.

In the reams of legal garble filed and counterfiled between Bloom and the lawyers for Lafferty and the estate, a statement made in behalf of Lafferty's position is very revealing about the extent of Bloom's influence after the ouster of Chandi.

"Contrary to his fantasies, Bloom was not, as he contends, Miss Duke's principal advisor for over seven years. Rather, he was an accountant who assisted with various accounting functions in connection with her personal, business and charitable affairs. Although his responsibilities included acting on behalf of Miss Duke with respect to a variety of legal, banking, investment and other business matters, Miss Duke began to increasingly distrust Bloom's motives. By at least early 1993, Miss Duke believed Bloom was trying to control her affairs, as if he, not Miss Duke, was running them."

For a brief time, Bloom was running them.

No lawyer, no business manager, and very few friends during Doris Duke's last three decades would last more than a few years. She wisely mistrusted lawyers and would replace prestigious law firm with prestigious law firm on a regular basis.

"Lawyers tend to become greedy if you keep them around too long," Doris Duke would say to explain her rotation of barristers. "They start to believe that they are better at running your business than you are."

Members of the family realize all too well that should Doris have lived a few more years, the final cast of characters, the lawyers and doctors and latest devoted friends, would have been replaced by another group of Duke groupies.

"Doris collected people," Pony Duke, one of the authors of this book, said, "and then she threw them away. She would keep a fine rug or old master painting forever but think little of disposing of a friend."

Doctors, too, were often replaced but for different reasons. As she grew older and more desperate, Doris became susceptible to any physician who might promise to make her aging body feel better. She even briefly hoped that some near quacks could return her youth with a mixture of vitamins and herbs or injections of some exotic serum.

The attending doctor who signed her death certificate had only been a part of the Duke entourage for less than two years. On the death certificate, Dr. Joshua Trabulus of Beverly Hills (a close associate of Dr. Kivowitz) stated that he had been attending Doris Duke since April 19, 1992.

The "immediate cause of death" was septicemia-urosepsis, which is a poisonous infection in the blood and urine that had been present in her system for "days."

According to Dr. Trabulus, these infections were "due to a multiple cerebrovascular accident," which is a stroke that affected the brain, a problem that Dr. Trabulus says had been present in Doris Duke for "months."

This means Doris had suffered a brain-damaging stroke sometime in the last twelve months of her life. It was in April of 1993 when she signed that final will. (A note here: The signature on the will was very much like that signature on Irwin Bloom's letter of dismissal but that letter was signed by Bernard Lafferty using his power-of-attorney to sign for Doris Duke. Bloom was later to say, "I do not think that Miss Duke even knew that I had been fired.")

But there were more causes of death.

The physician's statement on the death certificate further admits that he had known that Doris Duke suffered from hypertension (high blood pressure) and arterial fibrillation (a heart problem) for "years." "Other significant contributions to death" included: anemia, a tracheostomy (a breathing tube in her throat) and a castrostomy [*sic*] (a tube in the stomach). In the weeks prior to her death, the only occasionally conscious Doris remained in her Beverly Hills bedroom connected to state-of-the-art life support apparatus. Since she was immediately cremated, no further tests or autopsies were conducted.

In spite of her protestations that she had no interest in the money, Chandi Duke Heffner filed a number of legal suits. In the end, Chandi Duke Heffner, who has now dropped the Duke from her name, was willing to accept $65 million as a final court-ordered settlement from the estate.

"Doris knew that Chandi was a fortune hunter or worse," Pony Duke explained. "Some of the family felt that Lafferty should offer her a settlement to end the media circus but the rest of us didn't want that little con artist to get a dime. If Doris had a last wish, it was to have Chandi out of her life."

Approval of Lafferty waned when he agreed to the $65 million payoff in an effort to lessen the cast of characters who were filing court challenges to his position.

When Chandi was out, Bloom stayed.

One statement in the endless legal statements filed by Irwin Bloom was of particular interest to some members of the Duke family; that was a statement that gave a twinge of truth to the legend of Buck Duke's secret horde of gold bullion.

"I have stored away a few tons of gold in Switzerland," Buck had told many of his friends and associates. "It's a little emergency fund in case things should go bad someday."

Over the decades, everyone who had heard that story from Buck's lips had died and people began to question whether the story was true or just another exaggerated tale of the fabulous Duke fortunes. Bloom states that there was a "large" amount of gold in foreign accounts, some of which he helped to sell on behalf of Doris in the last few years. It is not known whether there were tons of gold as Buck said so many times to members of the family, but Bloom stated that the amount was "significant." He provided no details as to what was done with the proceeds.

One ton of gold would be worth $20 million today. There might be hundreds of tons hidden somewhere in Switzerland. These billions might be lost forever unless some member of the family or Bernard Lafferty know how to access these accounts.

"We do know that there was gold in Switzerland," Pony Duke commented. "I do not know if any member of the family can locate the accounts but I do know that I don't have the numbers."

Why would Doris Duke want to exchange bullion that had been safely hidden away from the tax men for nearly seven decades for cash that would be hugely depreciated by capital gains taxes should she ever try to return it to the United States? She was immensely wealthy. She never had a debt, unlike other lesser billionaires such as Donald Trump. Doris Duke never had to borrow a dime.

Still, Irwin Bloom admits that there were large gold transactions and that he was the man who Doris Duke trusted to oversee these megabuck transfers.

But Bloom was fired by Bernard Lafferty on behalf of his employer, Doris Duke. And in the end, Bernard Lafferty was the one person in the world who was at the side of the dying Doris as she lay unconscious with breath gurgling through a tube in her throat while other tubes pumped poisoned urine and bile out of her stomach.

Since her death, three servants at the Beverly Hills mansion where Doris Duke gasped her last breath have filed lawsuits alleging they were forced to sign papers certifying Duke was competent when she was not of sound mind. They also said that Doris was subjected to unnecessary medical procedures and that the dates of some of her medical records were altered to correspond with documents she had signed, including the controversial final will.

Her chef, Colin Shanley, her housekeeper, Ann Bostich, and Bostich's handyman husband Mariano De Velasco have said they had been given promises including lifetime employment, huge pensions, and new houses if they remained silent and supported Lafferty's position. In effect, they have said that Lafferty bribed them not to tell the police and authorities what they knew and then welched on his promises.

If Bernard Lafferty survives the lawsuits and the accusations of foul play, and some of the people closest to Doris feel that he might, he will control one of the most powerful philanthropies in the world. He has immense discretion as to how the assets of this estate can be spent.

Since the death of Doris Duke, Bernard Lafferty had been hospitalized several times in unsuccessful attempts to control his alcoholism. Family members wonder whether his latest bout of excessive drinking is part of his grieving over the death of Doris or a celebration of his control of the Duke fortune.

There is little doubt that this drinking is hurting Lafferty.

In February of 1994, former chef Colin Shanley was with Lafferty when Lafferty suffered a particularly violent drinking bout at the exclusive Breakers Hotel in Palm Beach. According to Shanley, Dr. Glassman raced to Lafferty's side when his heart started acting abnormally.

"Oh, thank God I got to him just in time," Shanley remembered Dr. Glassman's words. Dr. Glassman said that Lafferty's heart rate "was disappearing" and that "we almost lost him."

This is when Lafferty supposedly authorized a five-hundred-thousand-dollar check to Dr. Glassman.

"On or about May of 1994, I confronted Doyle regarding this issue," Shanley stated under oath. "I told him I was concerned about the $500,000 check. Doyle said 'it is none of your concern' and that I 'should keep the focus on Bernard and keep him out of trouble.'"

Attorney Doyle is finding that keeping the image of Bernard

Lafferty pristine enough to convince the New York Surrogate Court that he is competent to handle the vast estate is a vexing problem even for a high-powered two-hundred-lawyer firm.

Housekeeper Ann Bostich remembers one argument between the attorney and the world's most powerful butler early in 1994. Lafferty had been on a spending spree and had just ordered another fifty thousand dollars' worth of interior design for Falcon's Lair, which he now considers along with the Park Avenue penthouse to be his principal residence.

"At one point in early 1994," Bostich said in a sworn statement, "Doyle and Lafferty had a disagreement over a $9,000 bill for living room curtains. I was in the room when Lafferty responded to Doyle's call. In a conversation that lasted about one hour, Doyle told Lafferty that he could not spend money making improvements on the house. Lafferty responded with what only can be compared to a child's temper tantrum. He screamed at Doyle. That conversation took place just as Lafferty was leaving for a Patti LaBelle concert. He was wearing a black Armani outfit. Makasiale [*sic*] (Doris Duke's former personal maid) had applied makeup and lipstick to Lafferty. By the time Lafferty was done screaming at Doyle—and crying—the makeup had run down his face, streaking it. He was screaming that Miss Duke left him her houses and her money to do with as he pleased."

"Whenever Doyle or someone from the Bank tried to rein in Lafferty's spending," Ann Bostich continued, "he would tell them, 'well, I always can find another law firm. I can always find another bank.'"

The Duke family was surprised that neither Lafferty nor United States Trust selected any family member to be on the foundation board. Only other family members would know the complete extent of the financial empire. They also had a massive collective memory of the art treasures that filled the houses.

"We knew the estate was undervalued at $1.2 billion," a family member commented. "Then we learned that was only the liquid assets such as stocks and bonds and cash and that the art treasures were only superficially examined by Christie's. There could be several billion dollars just in art and antiques."

But Bernard Lafferty distanced himself from members of the Duke family and their lifetimes of memories of the Doris Duke treasure.

While he was not the family's first choice for executor, Lafferty was once again gaining some support. "I was starting to believe that Lafferty was, indeed, Doris's last real friend," Pony Duke explained. "Certainly, he has done some things that are questionable but he seemed to be sincere about his dedication to Doris. He acted as if he wanted to honor the terms of her last requests. I hope so."

There is a pragmatic side to Pony Duke's support of Lafferty. Should Lafferty be ousted as executor, he might be replaced by previous administrators, including an accountant whose ethics have been questioned, a physician who has been called a quack, or Chandi Heffner.

"I would prefer Mr. Lafferty to any of that crowd," Pony Duke added.

"Since we can see no way that Chandi can be unadopted," Pony Duke explained, "she will probably get the income from the $90 million share of Doris Duke Trust in North Carolina designated for Doris. Under the terms of Buck Duke's will, Chandi and the rest of us who receive income from that trust will be given our share of the principal when the last relative who was alive at the time of Buck's death passes away. That is a family trust and, while I dislike it, Chandi Heffner was adopted into our family. This was Doris's worst mistake."

Duke attorneys have posed an even more drastic fate for the Doris Duke billions should the last will be thrown out of court. Pony Duke has been told that the possibility exists that all the previous wills could be declared invalid and his godmother would die intestate—without a will. Then instead of going to the foundations, much of the money would be divided among the federal tax people and the state taxing authorities involved, with the remainder thrown to the relatives.

"That would be a feeding frenzy that I do not want," Pony Duke said.

In a letter to his son, Pony, Ambassador Duke wrote what might be considered the final eulogy of Doris Duke:

> She was self-centered, selfish and willful," he wrote, "and yet, very unsure of herself. Her apparent coldness of manner was probably a protective shield to conceal her lack of self-confidence. What I am trying to get at, here, is an explanation for the evolution of her thinking as reflected in the central themes of the Will: protection of animals, particularly wildlife; protection of children; improving the environment including farmlands; and of certain cultural interests including Islamic and Asian art, historic preservation, music and dance.
>
> She never was successful in projecting these interests and bringing them into being while she lived, mainly because she was a loner who mistrusted people and could not maintain a sustained relationship with anyone. In the eyes of some, the main achievement of Doris Duke's life was the management of her money and the continued amassing of it. There must be some point to all this—a point that is outlined in her last will and testament. What must have been a largely wasted and empty life can become transformed at her death. She tried for self-fulfillment in many ways: mysticism, gospel religion, sex, adoption, probably drugs, art, music and dance. In the end, her real achievement should be the Doris Duke Charitable Foundations.

"I think it can be said," Ambassador Duke continued, "that she can find fulfillment in the knowledge that her fortune which she had guarded, nourished and increased during her lifetime would, at the last, be the instrument for great social good."

"If there is one real legacy that Doris Duke left her family," Pony Duke responded, "it is that her death has served to reunite and stimulate the family. Nothing stimulates Dukes more than a billion dollars or more. Long ago Buck and Ben Duke acted in loving unison . . . as brothers . . . as family . . . and some of that spirit has brought many of us together today. This immense charitable trust has the potential to do great good. The family's abiding interest is that Duke University will be served by this money in the same spirit that my great-great-grandfather, Washington Duke, felt when he first moved Trinity College to Durham. This was the spirit that motivated Ben Duke to keep alive the family interest in the school. And this was the spirit that led Buck Duke to bring it all to a reality when he endowed the school so that it could become Duke University, one of the world's great institutions. Every member is talking about the potential to continue this tradition. We are a family again.

"With luck the will can be probated," Pony Duke continued, "and Doris will be able to do more good in death than she ever was able to complete in life. Death has brought Doris Duke her chance at greatness!"

It looked at the end of 1994 as if former butler Bernard Lafferty was going to survive all the challenges to become the living incarnation of Doris Duke.

But that was about to change.

# 25
# CRACKS IN THE PERFECT PLAN

In January of 1995, Bernard Lafferty was the undisputed master of the manor. He had moved into Doris Duke's private quarters in the New York City penthouse, Duke Farms, and Falcon's Lair, where his employer and benefactor had died. His shirts were silk and his booze was the very best.

But there was a small hairy problem: a tiny bundle of fur named Rodeo, the small pet dog that had been willed one hundred thousand dollars by his owner, Doris Duke. Bernard Lafferty hated the dog and the yapping little creature seemed to despise the former butler. While Doris had made explicit arrangements for the well-being of the animal, Lafferty wanted to be rid of the tiny dog that roamed the halls of the placid Beverly Hills mansion in search of his dead mistress.

Other servants tried to rescue the irate and barking Rodeo from the potential wrath of Lafferty but the dog was angry at the Irishman who would kick and swear at the relentless animal. Lafferty started throwing Rodeo out of the house.

But the lawns of Falcon's Lair were not a safe place for a tiny animal weighing less than fifteen pounds. The massive guard dogs that traveled the property in a snarling and protective pack thought the elegant little dog was nothing more than another creature that could be dispatched to doggie heaven in a few clamps of heavily toothed jaws. Repeatedly the tiny dog was evicted but watchful servants would rescue Rodeo before he became a chew toy. One night the big dogs got to Rodeo.

Instead of joining his beloved mistress in the hereafter, the brutally mauled dog managed to survive though very badly injured. The Beverly Hills servants who loved the dog were outraged. They later said that they had been made promises by Bernard Lafferty, immediately following the death of Miss Duke, that included lifetime employment contracts, new houses, and fat retirement funds. None of the promises were being kept and the attack on the dog was the final frustration. The servants hired a lawyer.

But Rodeo was not the only one of Doris Duke's treasured animals to suffer from Bernard Lafferty's actions. Her beloved camels paid the ultimate price for not satisfying the wants of their new master. "Lafferty had little patience with Miss Duke's beloved animals," chef Colin Shanley said. "For example, he neglected her camels. Miss Duke had spent more than a hundred and thirty thousand dollars to buy a horse trailer to move the camels between New Jersey and Newport. She would move them to Newport in the summer, because the white-tailed deer at the Somerville estate carried certain fleas which would have caused a disease fatal to the camels. I understand that after Miss Duke's death, Lafferty (knowing the danger to the camels) nonetheless wanted to show them off in New Jersey in the summer. This caused the death of one of the camels."

Doris had told family members about this problem with the deer fleas and ticks. Since she would not permit animals to be harmed on her property, canny deer migrated to the safety of Duke Farms during the hunting season (much to the disgust of hunters, who could only stare at the grazing deer over the walls). The result was that the estate was covered with deer droppings and infested with deer fleas and ticks, which were a problem for the dogs, cattle, and horses but could be fatal for exotic animals such as the camels.

While Lafferty might have been cruel to the animals and his once fellow servants, he was anxious to cater to those who were the social and business equals of his former mistress. Lafferty was busy cementing his position with everyone who needed to be coddled by promising them millions. Duke family members had been promised money for all their favorite charities and the officials of Duke University were salivating over a proposed $20 million donation to establish the Doris Duke School of Environmental Studies. The family had also been told that he had offered Chandi Heffner "something less" than $50 million plus an heir's interest in a North Carolina trust fund that would provide her a few millions more as an annual income with a someday balloon payment in excess of another $80 million. She was reportedly ready to snatch the money and run after signing a pile of legal documents sometime around January 20, 1995. Bernard was passing out the gold and all the chosen few had to do to get their shares was to shut up and agree that he was, indeed, the second coming of Doris Duke.

Then Tammy Payette started talking to lawyers.

The nurse who attended to Doris during the last few weeks of the billionairess's life decided to tell what she had seen and been a part of during those final days.

Nurse Payette's testimony has been clouded by her arrest for theft of some very valuable ivory statues from another rich client. Payette, who had made a highly believable impression on many members of the press who questioned her, almost immediately admitted her guilt in the twenty-thousand-dollar theft. She said that stress from being associated with the possible murder of Doris Duke had caused her to steal the costly ivory and she quickly repented and confessed. She was later accused of stealing four hundred thousand dollars' worth of property from her clients, including Doris Duke. Much of the evidence against Miss Payette was given to the Los Angeles police by detectives hired by Bernard Lafferty. A distraught Payette once again admitted that she had taken from her employers. She pointed out that her income had suffered when she was branded a nurse who had been involved in the death of Doris Duke. Bernard Lafferty hopes that this will diminish the credibility of her future testimony but her detailed records could still be damaging. The fact that she could not live with herself following the theft of the ivory and had to tell the truth could be used to prove that she is basically an honest person.

Nurse Payette also told police that she feared for her own safety. Former military nurse Payette was afraid that she, too, might soon be murdered and went to a young New York lawyer, Raymond Dowd.

"Nobody took this Dowd person seriously," a Duke family member commented. "He was all alone against all the estate's massive law firms. It was like David and Goliath only, in this case, no one gave Dowd a chance against the power and resources of the lawyers for the estate and Lafferty."

Not only was Payette afraid that Lafferty, who has reportedly made strong threats against many people involved in the case, would use the Duke billions to try to quiet the talkative nurse but she was concerned that, should she remain silent, someday she could be charged as an accessory to a possible murder.

Finally the Los Angeles District Attorney's office decided to open an investigation into Doris's death and ordered the Homicide-Robbery Department of the Los Angeles Police Department to start scrutinizing the facts.

There were those who thought Los Angeles authorities would never open the case because of the power that Lafferty's friend and foundation board member Elizabeth Taylor wields in the city of the stars.

It is interesting to note that Elizabeth Taylor was said to be a close friend of Eddie Tirella, the charming and handsome Hollywood set designer who was crushed to death at the gates of Rough Point. Tirella was also a very dear friend and former employee of singer Peggy Lee, who later provided a reference when Bernard Lafferty applied for the butler's position at the Duke estates. It is not known whether Tirella and Lafferty had been friends.

Private detectives who were employed to explore the background of Bernard Lafferty know that he was born out of wedlock in Ireland and grew up very close to his mother. But the facts about much of his life remain a secret. His history seems to end sometime in his early teens and surfaces later in the 1970s with his employment by Peggy Lee and as a headwaiter in various hotels and expensive restaurants.

As Lafferty and the physicians found themselves in the newspaper headlines, the accusations of possible murder caused the man who is now the world's most powerful butler to become nervous, causing him to return to his addictions to drugs and alcohol.

Soon everyone involved in the case found themselves hiring criminal attorneys. Lafferty started negotiations with famous appeals lawyer Alan Dershowitz, and was worried about how to pay a million-dollar fee should United States Trust or the Surrogate Court decide to cease the flow of cash from the estate. Lafferty was always represented by celebrity lawyer Howard Weitzman, who had briefly been O. J. Simpson's lawyer before his relationship with the former football star and accused double murderer abruptly ended. Weitzman also represented Michael Jackson against charges of child molestation.

Dr. Charles Kivowitz, the Beverly Hills physician to the rich who has been accused of administering the fatal morphine dose, found himself hiring a Beverly Hills criminal lawyer.

Pearl Rosenstein, a nurse and close associate of Dr. Kivowitz, who was known to have administered the complex doses of sedatives known as "Pearl's cocktails" (a mixture of Valium and meprobamate) to Doris Duke, employed her own criminal defense counsel, who is being financed by the Duke estate.

Dr. Kivowitz has stated that he only authorized the final drugging of Doris Duke to ease her pain in the last hours of death. In a deposition when he was asked if he increased the dosage so that she would die, Dr. Kivowitz responded, "The answer is that I increased the morphine so that she would not linger, that she would not suffer, and ultimately that she would die perhaps shortly or sooner than she would have otherwise died from her medical conditions, which I judged within a 48-hour period were of a terminal nature."

"Good God," one close friend of Doris Duke commented when hearing that statement, "Doris would not even permit one of her dogs to be put down like that. She believed that life was sacred and no one had the right to put any animal or any person out of its misery."

Dr. Kivowitz said that Doris Duke was considering suicide. "In substance I remember very clearly a statement that she made that she was desperate that she couldn't go on living the way she was living at the time, that she was despondent and that she was considering suicide," Dr. Kivowitz said.

"That does not sound like the Doris Duke I have known all my life," a family member commented.

Doris Duke, who would refuse to euthanize a sick animal, was, in effect, euthanized herself. Dr. Kivowitz has admitted in sworn statements that he hastened her death to prevent her suffering. This kind of action sends shudders through other medical experts who point out that it is one thing to take a terminally ill person off all life support and quite another to pour drugs into a helpless eighty-year-old woman to hasten her death.

Bernard Lafferty, who admitted he has a drug and alcohol problem (one of the depositions said he helped himself to the Valium that had been prescribed for Doris Duke), was starting to unravel as details of his background and actions were revealed. A diary he kept was barely literate and it was soon revealed that he had only a fifth-grade education, which brought into question his ability to manage the complex and sophisticated series of trusts.

An example of Bernard Lafferty's lack of responsibility occurred on June 2, 1994, when he crashed his new, fifty-four-thousand-dollar Cadillac (bought with Doris Duke Charitable Foundation money) over the tops of three cars on Sunset Boulevard and smashed through the front windows of Whiskey A Go-Go, the landmark Los Angeles nightclub. He didn't even have a driver's license.

"I don't have a driver's license because I have always had a chauffeur," said Lafferty, who only a few months earlier had given depositions in which he stated he "was virtually penniless." Suddenly he sounded very much like a billionaire, or rather, a nouveau-billionaire.

"My chauffeur, Ann Bostich, was driving us home," Lafferty told the amazed West Hollywood police. "I was arguing with my housekeeper [Nuku Makasaile, who was a longtime personal maid to Doris]." He went on to tell police that Bostich (who is now suing the estate) jumped out of his car and left it stranded in the street. Lafferty took the wheel and ventured onto busy Sunset Boulevard and was progressing at about fifty miles per hour (in a thirty-five-mile-an-hour zone) when he lost control, hit a curb, became airborne, struck three cars (including a late model Saab), and came to rest embedded in the front of the nightclub. Both Lafferty and Makasaile were taken to the hospital for minor injuries.

The driver of the Saab convertible, who was in the car when the airborne Cadillac passed overhead, said, "The guy who was driving the Cadillac, He was airborne over my convertible. To be airborne in West Hollywood—the traffic is so heavy—you have to be out of your mind."

Perhaps the most humorous aspect of the reports of the accident was that Lafferty listed his age as thirty-nine. While his exact age remains vague, he has been reported to be as old as fifty-five.

There is no record of any charges being filed.

Ann Bostich and Lafferty had been battling almost from the minute Doris died. According to Bostich, no sooner was the body on the way to the crematorium than Lafferty was arranging to remodel the Beverly Hills house in a manner that was more in accord with his personal taste. Doris had taken great pains in the careful planning of the designs of each of her mansions and intended that the art and antiques in these houses be a part of her legacy.

"Doris would have wanted nothing changed," a family member said.

In a particularly bitter moment of disagreement between Bostich and Lafferty, the former housekeeper said that he "threatened to cut my tits off."

His diary, which was saved from the shredder by a Duke employee following Doris's death, sometimes is incoherent but one particular excerpt is very revealing: "I was nver refuse . . . Dr. Glassman [Harry Glassman, a famous Beverly Hills plastic surgeon, is the husband of actress Victoria Principal, the former star of *Dallas,* who now has her own children's foundation, which is looking for funding from the Duke fortune. He also prescribed many drugs for Doris Duke.] made sure of that . . . I have lost alot & I have for very little in return. No bodey but me underst Doris Duke and now I know whie. My mothe & I wear poor. But I was brough up very well no thers is to many people involved."

The diary contained threats. In his own handwriting he listed people who "has to be destroyed . . . the time has come to figh & nothin is gowin to stope it. I will goo to no ends."

Lafferty had one very powerful enemy. Cindy Adams, the *New York Post* columnist, was intent on exposing the butler as a possible murderer. She was the first member of the press to go after Lafferty, who at the time had been reshaped by a cunning public relations expert, and demand action from authorities who were reluctant to challenge an estate with unlimited funding for legal battles.

Adams revealed that Lafferty wanted to hire someone to slash the face of ex-employee Thomas Rybak, who was the first member of the Duke staff to expose Lafferty's drunkenness. Depositions state that he was hospitalized at least three times as a "chronic alcoholic." He has allegedly been taken to the hospital in a drunken coma at least once.

Lafferty had also tried "to find someone to kill Chandi Heffner." He was also ready to dispose of lawyer Irwin Bloom, "that balding Jew bastard."

He had threatened to cut the breasts "off" a maid should she ever reveal any of his lavish spending sprees.

But most of Lafferty's animosity was saved for Colin Shanley, the chef in the Beverly Hills mansion, who was ordered to drive Lafferty to gay bathhouses, gay bars, and pornography shops in the West Hollywood area while Doris lay in an induced coma a few miles away behind the gates of Falcon's Lair.

Chef Shanley has stated that a star-struck Lafferty spent ten thousand dollars a week on flowers, with one-third of them going to Elizabeth Taylor; that he bought himself long gowns with long trains; that he ordered a gilt throne and dais when he was appointed head of the trusts and installed this apparition in Doris Duke's former bedroom; and that he has spent more than two thousand dollars having his hair dyed blond and styled to resemble Doris Duke's classic cut.

The butler's excesses ranged from flowers for his male lover to pony- and snakeskin boots, a $3,300 gold "snake" bracelet with ruby eyes, and a $676 leather baseball jacket.

But it was Shanley's sworn statement as to what happened the day before the death of the heiress that helped to force the authorities to take a thorough look into the death of Doris Duke.

Shanley said that he was in the kitchen of Falcon's Lair with Lafferty the afternoon before the death when a package was delivered to the back gate and brought to the kitchen by one of the security guards.

"I received the parcel and read aloud to Lafferty the sender and the addressee information," Shanley stated in his sworn statement to the Surrogate Court. "Upon hearing the information, Lafferty leapt across the kitchen, grabbed the parcel out of my hand and stated that 'Miss Duke is going to die tonight.'"

Shanley continued that this comment came as no surprise because Lafferty had been telling the staff that Miss Duke was close to death from incurable leukemia (records show she never had this disease).

"A short time later when one of the afternoon shift nurses came up to the kitchen to use the phone," Shanley continued, "I heard her telling the night shift nurses that they 'wouldn't be needed.' Then I began to suspect that Lafferty's statement might be true."

The package contained a massive quantity of Demerol, a painkiller.

A few hours later, Doris Duke was dead.

But according to one member of the Duke family who spoke to Lafferty immediately following the death, the now powerful head of one of the world's richest foundations did not feel that Doris Duke was gone.

"He told me he was the living incarnate of Doris Duke," the

relative explained with a twinge of incredulity in his voice. "He said he was Doris Duke."

Lafferty's lawyers are complaining about the thoroughness of the investigation ordered by New York City Surrogate judge Eve Preminger. She appointed former Manhattan District Attorney Richard Kuh, the man who investigated the elegant Claus von Bulow in the attempted murder of his rich wife, Sunny, to examine the case. Kuh searched every residence, took statements from servants, and in what was most upsetting to Lafferty's lawyers, started questioning whether Doris Duke was competent when she signed the will that placed Lafferty in control of the billions.

It is thought that Judge Preminger might have hopes of salvaging the essence of the will while disposing of Bernard Lafferty. If she is unable to do this and the Surrogate Court should overturn the will, Doris Duke would have died intestate. Instead of being spent on the charitable foundations that had been consistently outlined in every will during the last few decades, much of the money would go to the federal government in estate taxes.

This is probably the reason Judge Preminger released the $10.5 million that was designated as a first donation to Duke University. No one could question the fact that Doris would have wanted some of her money to go to Duke University. This releasing of money in accordance with the terms of the will in effect activates the terms of the will. It now will be more difficult to set aside other terms.

"I believe that it will be difficult to prove that Lafferty and Kivowitz killed Doris," said one family member. "It looks as if the judge would like to have Lafferty resign but I am sure he wants a big settlement." Lafferty has become used to big settlements.

Chandi Heffner was completely silent as required by the terms of her secret settlement that would make her a millionairess. Throughout all the publicity, she did not once raise her voice to demand an investigation into the possible murder of her adopted mother.

All Chandi Heffner requested was money.

And she will get it.

# AFTERTHOUGHT

A billionaire seldom dies.

In the last few decades only names like Sam Walton of Wal-Mart and John D. Rockefeller III come to mind in the category of the very rich and the very dead. The extremely rich do not die like the rest of us. Seldom do we hear great scandals about their deaths. This is because they have multitudes of attorneys to draw up wills that will not cause controversy. The Doris Duke will is not one of those wills.

This could be caused, as many believe, by a pack of legal and social jackals who are pulling at the well-fleshed bones of an estate that is worth billions of dollars.

People who never gave Doris Duke any attention during her life are fighting over the vast treasure she left. Other people who tried to scam Doris in life are now scamming her in death.

The players' positions are clear.

Most members of her family were rich enough or proud enough that they did not need or would not ask for any help from a relative who was apt to respond with a curt insult.

It seems that Cousin Mary Semens is again stepping into Doris Duke's role as she always has. It was Mary Semens, the second-richest member of the Duke family, who moved into the position in the $1.4 billion Duke Trust in North Carolina and the seat on the board of Duke University that would have gone to Doris had she shown any interest. Now Mary Semens has had meetings with the instant millionaire butler Bernard Lafferty in the elegant dining room of the four-star Washington Duke Inn in Durham to discuss what should be done with the $1.3 billion (at least) that remained in Doris Duke's estate at her death. If Mary Semens includes her own personal fortune, she is positioning herself to control more than $3 billion.

"If anything ever actually brings Doris back from the dead," one family member said with a snicker, "it will be because Mary might gain control of all of the Buck Duke money. Mary has done wonderful things at Duke University but Doris was always touchy about Mary usurping what should have been Doris's position. This was in reality more Doris's fault for neglecting her heritage at the university. Mary is a driven and ambitious woman who saw an opportunity to gain power and help Duke University even though it was at Doris's expense. All Doris ever would have had to do was pick up the phone and she could have taken control of the trust and the board of directors, but she never did. She would complain that Mary was building her reputation with Buck Duke's money but Doris did not have the attention span necessary to successfully oversee the future of Duke University. Maybe Mary will be the living incarnation of Doris Duke."

The butler is rumored to have slept in Doris Duke's bed and to have arisen for breakfast wearing some of his mistress's most expensive silk and satin flowing robes and night clothes. Lafferty even told one family member in a whisper that is eerily reminiscent of Doris Duke's delicate whisper, "I am the living incarnation of Doris Duke. She has come back."

But Bernard Lafferty is now gone.

The probate court ordered that Lafferty and United States Trust be removed from any positions of responsibility for the poorly administered estate. Temporary executors have been appointed while the dozens of court cases are advanced. Bernard, once the richest butler in the world, is hoping he still gets his $5 million (much of which will be needed to pay his massive debt to United States Trust) as well as the annual income of $500,000. He is also hoping that he will not be indicted.

"Bernard," one family member said, "is threatening to kill himself and since he no longer controls the estate, nobody really cares whether he does or not."

Just as Doris used so many people for her personal pleasure and amusement in life, there are still people, ranging from lawyers to long-forgotten quacks who once were part of the Doris Duke menagerie, who are fighting for the opportunity to use this woman one last time in death.

Her husbands and lovers all used her for her money, just as she used them to acquire freedom or great sex.

Her friends came and went. To some, such as Pee-Wee Herman, she gave shelter, and to others, such as Imelda Marcos, she offered her money.

She gave millions to phony hustlers like Chandi Heffner, her "devoted" adopted daughter, who first convinced Doris Duke that she too was a poor little rich girl who had been victimized by the curse of too much money, and then said all she wanted was a mother to love her, that money meant nothing.

"Doris's worst mistake in life was marrying Jimmy Cromwell," one member of the family said, "and the worst mistake she made in death will be Chandi Heffner."

"I absolutely hate that Chandi Heffner." Doris Duke hissed out the words as if they had been soaked in venom. "The two worst people in my life were Chandi Heffner and Jimmy Cromwell. I hope they both burn together in hell if there is a hell." Doris Duke's religious theories did not include the concepts of heaven and hell but for those two people from her past, she was willing to rethink her convictions.

"I now understand what it is to hate with a deep and burning passion," Doris Duke said. "That is how I feel about Miss Heffner. It is the strongest emotion I have ever felt."

Chandi Heffner and Jimmy Cromwell had much in common.

Doris Duke's money.

Chandi Heffner sued for every dime she could get. As a member of the family exclaimed, "We will know whether Bernard Lafferty is really trying to do what Doris wanted when we see how he handles that little fortune hunter. Doris would have spent whatever had to be spent and done whatever had to be done to see to it that Chandi never got another dime. If he pays her off, then he is merely trying to protect his own position because such an extortion would not be tolerated by Doris."

Lafferty was eager to pay off Heffner.

Lafferty reportedly offered Chandi the $65 million and the interest in a trust fund that would ultimately be worth more than $80 to $100 million, all hers if she would shut up and go back to her ranch in Hawaii.

In the end, it appears that Chandi will get the millions of dollars she had always told Doris she did not want and would not accept. Doris would be furious at the size of the settlement and if she could come back from the dead, she would fire Bernard Lafferty herself for again defying her wishes.

"Lafferty was a most fortunate man," a family member commented. "Doris rewrote wills and changed executors as often as she remodeled one of the rooms of her houses. It was her hobby. If Doris had not died when she did, she would most probably have replaced Lafferty with someone new who was in her favor at the moment.

"She died at the perfect time for Bernard," the family member added.

It seemed unlikely that the uneducated and alcoholic Lafferty could have survived long as the head of this vast and eccentric trust. And he didn't! Bets had been made by friends of Doris as to which one of the gaggle of law firms would swoop down on the fortune and the endless fees it generates when Lafferty self-destructed.

The law firm had billed some $13 million in services to the estate until the probate court ordered a halt to that expense.

The doctors, the lawyers, the charity men, and the thieves have filed lawsuits for their portions of the estate. Even her servants who feel slighted because one former butler seems to have gotten the golden ring have sued as if to cry, "Where's my billion?"

But does anybody really miss Doris Duke?

It is said that Rodeo, the shaggy little dog that was left one hundred thousand dollars in the will, cried at the door of Doris's Beverly Hills bedroom after her death. The dog now dines on regular dog food instead of his favorite boiled chicken in the kitchen of a mobile home far away from any Duke mansion.

One movie producer who is considering filming Doris Duke's life as a television mini-series commented, "Her life was sort of a combination of *Sunset Boulevard* meets *Whatever Happened to Baby Jane?* with a large dash of *Citizen Kane* and more than a trace of *The Servant.*"

One very wealthy friend of Doris remarked, "This film would most probably be an employment training and hiring film for people of means. After what happened to Doris, I can tell you that people from Newport to Beverly Hills are taking second looks at their servants and lawyers. And the doctors, good God, after learning about Doris's doctors I have decided to become a Christian Scientist."

Doris Duke would have secretly enjoyed the thought of her life being made into a glitzy and glamorous mini-series. Doris always considered her life to be a soap opera. She was the poor little rich girl, selfish but sometimes generous, cruel but often kind, and private but overtly exhibitionistic.

Most of the good she ever did in her life was done in absolute secrecy because she was a woman who was equally uncomfortable whether she was thanked or not thanked. She was the founder of the American orchid industry. She gave scholarships. She bailed friends out of business disasters. She donated pipe organs to hundreds of black churches. She will not be remembered for any of that.

In her will she had set up foundations to support art, artists, and the environment and nature. Her money formed a perfect world of art and nature with which she sheltered herself from anything that displeased her. Now her money can make the environment so much more enjoyable for so many people.

Maybe she will be remembered and missed by those who, at this time, do not know Doris Duke because of the good that can be done by her foundations. Maybe someday someone will hear the name of Doris Duke and give thanks for the kindness she brought to the world.

Doris wanted much of her wealth to be spent to prevent child abuse. This was so important to her. She was a loved child and she was a rich child but she was an abused child. Doris Duke spent her life looking for just a few people to love her and found only her father.

Her mother didn't love or even like her. Her husbands sometimes made love to her but never actually loved her. Friends might have loved her but she usually exiled them after the first sign of imperfection, never giving them a chance to develop relationships. Her family was sometimes embarrassed by her actions and other times repulsed by her self-centeredness. She found lasting love only from her dogs and deer and horses and cattle.

She trusted her animals. She knew their affection was not prompted by her bank account but by the reality of her hidden caring nature that would be shown only to creatures other than humans.

In the end there was Bernard Lafferty. Was this former failure who briefly and flamboyantly controlled the imperial purse an innocent like her animals who awakened the same kind of trust in an old lady who had given up trusting or was he an opportunist who just happened to survive longer than the rest of the vultures?

"I don't care whether he snuffed the old girl or not," one member of the family said after being promised anonymity. "She was a selfish, self-centered old bitch who never did anything for anyone. If Bernard Lafferty can use some of her money to do some good in the Duke name, I don't care if he fed the old girl champagne and Valium and pills until her stomach exploded."

Of course, that relative was not in the will.

# INDEX